AF647209

PHILOSOPHICAL HUMANISM
AND
CONTEMPORARY INDIA

By the Same Author

1. Indian Political Thought, Vol. I :—*Studies in Hindu Political Thought and its Metaphysical Foundations* (Revised 3rd edition, Motilal Banarsidass, Delhi, Patna).
2. Indian Political Thought, Vol. II: —*Modern Indian Political Thought* (4th edition, Laxmi Narayan Agrawal, Agra, 1971).
3. *Vaidika Rajanitisastra.* (Hindi Grantha Academy Patna,).
4. *Early Buddhism and its Origins* (Munshiram Manoharlal, Delhi).
5. *The Life and Philosophy of Lokamanya Tilak* (Laxmi Narayan Agrawal, Agra, 1978).
6. *Political Philosophy of Mahatma Gandhi and Sarvodaya* (Laxmi Narayan Agrawal, Agra, 3rd edition, 1972).
7. *The Political Philosophy of Sri Aurobindo* (Motilal Banarsidass, Delhi, 1974).
8. *Bhartiya Darshana* (Laxmi Narayan Agrawal, Agra).
9. *Paschatya Rajanitika Vicharadhara Ka Itihasa* : In Hindi. (Hindi Committee of the U.P. Government, Lucknow, 1964).
10. *Visvarajaniti.* In Hindi. (Gyanpitha, Patna, 1960).
11. *Political Philosophy.* (Laxmi Narayan Agrawal, Agra).
12. *Rajaniti Aur Darshana.* In Hindi. (Bihar Rashtrabhasha Parishad, Patna, 1956).
13. *Philosophy of Public Administration* (Minerva Associates, Calcutta, 1972).
14. *Report on Fourth General Elections in Bihar* : (Part I, pp. 100, P.U.).
15. *Report on the Mid-Term Elections* (1969) *in Bihar*. (Part I, pp. 144, P.U.).
16. *Report on Parliamentary Elections in Bihar*, 1971 (Government of Bihar Project).
17. *Nirvachana Aur Rananiti.* (Hindi Grantha Academy, Patna).
18. *Adhunika Bharatiya Rajanitika Chintana* (Laxmi Narayan Agrawal, Agra).

PHILOSOPHICAL HUMANISM AND CONTEMPORARY INDIA

VISHWANATH PRASAD VARMA

MOTILAL BANARSIDASS
Delhi :: Varanasi :: Patna

© MOTILAL BANARSIDASS

Indological Publishers and Booksellers
Head Office: BUNGALOW ROAD, JAWAHAR NAGAR, DELHI-7
Branches : 1. CHOWK, VARANASI-1 (U.P.)
2. ASHOK RAJPATH, PATNA-4 (BIHAR)

ISBN 0-89684-054-9

First Edition: *Delhi*, 1979

Printed in India

BY SHANTILAL JAIN, AT SHRI JAINENDRA PRESS, A-45, PHASE-I, INDUSTRIAL AREA, NARAINA, NEW DELHI-28 AND PUBLISHED BY NARENDRA PRAKASH JAIN, FOR MOTILAL BANARSIDASS, BUNGALOW ROAD, JAWAHAR NAGAR, DELHI-7

PREFACE

In 1949, when I was a research scholar for the Ph.D. Degree at the University of Chicago, I met the late Prof. Harold Laski who had gone to the United States to deliver a series of lectures on Trade Unions. He asked me to write a thesis on how India should be governed. But I could not address myself to that task in view of my other preoccupations and assignments. In 1956, my book *Rajaniti Aur Darshana* was published. The main assumption there is the recognition of man as a moral and spiritual subject. The historical, sociological and philosophical modes of enquiry have been substantiated there. A similar plea for the validity of a comprehensive approach was also made in my presidential address to the Bombay session of the All India Political Science Conference.

In this book the basic theme of man as a moral and spiritual subject has been re-asserted in the light of newer advancements in knowledge. On the basis of this philosophical assumption an attempt has been made to prepare a manifesto for the political, administrative, social and economic reconstruction of the country. It is hoped the work will be useful both for the theoreticians and the practitioners.

Rajendra Nagar, Patna
March 4, 1978

VISHWANATH PRASAD VARMA

CONTENTS

PREFACE v

CHAPTER

I The Theoretical Foundations of Spiritual Humanism 1-62
- Introduction 1
- The Meaning of Humanism 6
- Ontology 12
- The Epistemological Problems of Humanism 18
- Time, Space and Causality 25
- Monotheism and Spiritual Humanism 27
- Humanism and Religion 29
- Humanism, Science and History 33
- Evolution and Humanism 35
- Humanism and Dialectic 37
- Humanism and Existentialism 40
- Humanism and the Behavioural Sciences 45
- Humanism as a Philosophy of Life 50
- Critique of Economic Determinism 55
- Humanism as Ontopolitics : Man as a Moral and Spiritual Subject 57

II Ethical Absolutism and Humanist Values 63-80
- The Scientific Methodology and Ethical Absolutism 63
- Sources of Idealist Humanist Ethics 71
- Humanism and Values 75
- Humanism and Non-Violence 78
- Conclusion 79

III The Methodology and Concepts of Idealist Humanism 81-119
- The Multi-dimensional Man and the Multi-disciplinary Approach to Political Philosophy 81

	Ontopolitics and Empirical Political Analysis	91
	Ontopolitics and Historical Materialism	97
	Spiritual Humanism, Political Obligation and Satyagraha	102
	Spiritual Humanism, Sovereignty and Natural Right	104
	Justice	109
	Theory of Punishment	110
	Humanism and Conservatism	112
	Humanism and Internationalism	113
	Conclusion	117
IV	Humanism and the Indian Political System	120-141
	The Indian Cultural Immanence	120
	The Crisis in the Indian Political System	123
	Nation-Building and Political Development in Modern India	125
V	Idealist Humanism and Public Administration	142-155
VI	The Social Philosophy of Idealist Humanism	156-166
VII	The Economics of Philosophical Humanism	167-188
	The Capitalist Model of Development	167
	The Marxist Model of Development	168
	The Revision of Gandhian Economics	170
	A Manifesto for Indian Economic Development	174
VIII	Generalized Conclusions, Reflections and Suggestions	189-198
INDEX		199-203
CORRECTIONS		204

CHAPTER I

THE THEORETICAL FOUNDATIONS OF SPIRITUAL HUMANISM

Introduction

The civilization of the West is of the uppermost political category in the modern world. It has several theoretical roots. The Jews contributed to the genesis of this civilization the notion of a stern monotheism, uncompromising in exalting the majesty of a jealous Jehova. They also stressed the concept of the eventual vindication of justice under the governance of God. Christianity stood for the moralization of individual and political life. The primacy of moral considerations and the notion of the sanctity of obligation to God was stressed by Christ, Paul, St Augustine, Thomas Aquinas and Luther. The materialistic-technological foundations of the modern Western civilization are rooted in science. Although Euclid, Archimedes and Ptolemy had laid the foundations, the edifice of the natural sciences has been built only since the Renaissance due to the painstaking researches of eminent figures like Copernicus, Leonardo, Galileo, Newton, Lavosier, Lagrange, Planck, Einstein and others.

At the sociological, economic and political levels, the western civilization is expressing itself in two forms. On one side is the West-European-American tradition of liberal, constitutional, polyarchical representative democracy with its stress on individual freedom. The Magna Carta, The Petition of Right (1628), Becun's *Novum Organon*, Milton's *Areopagitica*, Locke's *Civil*

Government, Rousseau's *Social Contract*, The American Declaration of Independence, Ricardo's *Political* economy and Mill's *On Liberty* are some of the dominant expressions of this libertarian tradition. In the realm of academic political theory, teachers like Barker, Cole, Laski, Merriam, MacIver, and Morgenthau have reinforced the Lincolnian quest for a government of the people by the people for the people.

The other dominant tradition of modern times is the East-European-Soviet philosophy of dialectical and historical materialism. Rooted in the materialism of Democritus, Epicurus, Diderot and Feuerbach, in the dialectic of Kant, Fichte and Hegel, the evolutionism of Darwin, in the economics of Ricardo, in the anthropology of Morgan and in the socialism of Moses, Hess and others, in its total form, Marxism has appeared as a militant gospel of atheism, violence for the expropriation of the capitalist expropriators, armed proletarian dictatorship and a classless society conceived as an association of free producers. Maoism is an application of some of the basic notions of Marx and Engels to the predominantly agrarian conditions of China, just as Leninism was the application of Marxism to the Russian agrarian society in the era of finance capitalism and imperialism. Armed with the latest annihilationist weaponry of the super-powers both American pragmatism, systems analysis, behavioural research and empirical democracy on the one side, and Russian communism with its quest for the immanent apodictic laws of objective dialectic like self-movement of matter, evolutionary leap and the modal line of measurements in external nature and in human history on the other are clamouring for supremacy.

The earlier triumphs of the British, French, Spanish and Czarist imperialism and the contemporary political, economic and Military triumphs of the two great powers have necessarily added immense prestige to the ideologies, emanating from Europe, Russia and America. Lockean empiricism, Humean scepticism, Darwinian evolutionism, dialectical idealism and historical materialism, the Nietzschean cult of the mighty Teutonic superman, Freudian pansexualism and Einsteinean relativity are generally the ideological supports of the world-views emanating from the west in recent times. These explosive doctrines have shattering effect on the traditional Christian cosmology and the trinitarian formula. Their alienation-generating impact has been felt also on the Eastern lands. The existentialism of Kierkegaard, Herdegger and Jaspers has proved itself ineffective in stemming the tide of dialectical penetration of opposites and the march of the material tentacles of objective power. Hence several thinkers hold that today there is present an either-or intellectual dichotomy. One has to be either an empirical democratic behaviouralist or a dialectical materialist.

Indealistic philosophical humanism, to the contrary, holds that there is a third vital alternative for India and also to a certain extent, for the world. The perennial Indian culture nurtured in the Himalayan glaciers, in the land of the Sapta-Sindhu, and in the territory watered by the Ganga and the Jamuna, Narmada and Cavery, has given birth to a philosophy of nature and history which can still be a nourishing, vital force for civilizational sustenance. This culture has been poly-dimensional but always been committed to the enshrinement of man as a moral and spiritual subject. The Rigveda, the principal Upanishads, Badarayana Vyasa, Samkara, Ramanuja, Dayananda, Vivekananda and Ramatirtha have proclaimed the eternal supremacy of a primordial cosmic-transcendent Absolute Real Existence which is Gnosis (*chit*) itself. Mahavira, Gautama Buddha, the Bhagavadgita, Patanjali's *Yoga-Sutra*, the *Bhagavata Purana* and Gandhi proclaim the sanctity of moral values. The concept of political freedom for the realization of the human spiritual and moral potentialities has been the latent gospel of several prime exponents of ancient and medieval Indian political philosophy. In modern times eloquent testimonies to the profundity of the spiritual and moral quest of India have been paid by Schopenhauer who found immense consolation in the Upanishads, by Frederick Schlegel who regarded the wisdom of India as highly essential for re-fertilizing the parched land of Judea, Athens and Rome, by Max Müller who considered the Vedanta as a sustaining source of inner ethical virtues, by Deussen who found kinship in the idealism of Plato, Samkara and Kant, and by other Indologists and historians. Emerson, Thoreau, Humboldt, Beauatski and Besant were also influenced by the Vedanta and the Bhagavadgita. The Buddhist stream of Indian culture influenced not only the developments in western Asia but also cast deep transforming influence on Ceylon, Tibet, Mongolia, China and Japan. Even in modern times Indian creativism has monumental achievements to its credit in the fields of natural sciences, philosophy, literature, aesthetics and art. Hence there is the need of the re-assertion of the immanent spiritual and moral humanism of India as a vital gospel that can provide the *elan* to face the contemporary challenges and provide strength, puissance and vigour in an era infected with agonies, predicaments, psychic maladies, terrible alienations, social and economic contradictions, anxieties and incongruities. The Yajurveda has proclaimed the vital message of a fullness of living for a hundred years. Buddhism teaches the renunciation of sovereignty for the realization of the evanascence of worldly lust and enjoyments and the Mahabharata unequivocally proclaims the certitude of the victory of the eternal moral principles. In India, at the intellectual level, were cherished gospels of world-affirmation, enlightened moral authority, functional specialization leading to the enhancement of skills and competence, and the reverence for the lives not only of human beings but of the total living creatures. Idealistic integral humanism is committed to the preservation and enrichment of this spiritual and moral heritage. But integral idealistic humanism is not a philosophy of revivalism. It does not believe in going back to the old scriptures. The modern world is too complex and gigantic to make any scholastic revival possible even if one wanted to do so. Idealistic humanism is committed to one basic theme — the preservation of the vitality and sanctity of the human body and spirit against the devastating ravages of the forces of dissonance and destruction. It is opposed to the spirit of the magnification of power and the penalization of the weak and the forlorn. Knowledge gives power but the advance of learning is to be used for the promotion of common good, nay, the good of all living creatures. A materialistic scientific society based on the canons of the superior reasons of the state and the exploitation of agricultural and industrial labourers results in megapolitanism and commercialism. A collectivism and a communism solely inspired by feelings of jealousy against the holders of wealth degenerate into proletarian virulence, armed authoritarianism, democratic centralism and party elitism. Hence a philosophy proclaiming the superiority of moral values for spiritual uplift and committed to the vindication of truth, goodness, justice, generosity, magnanimity and freedom has a permanent relevance to thinking philosophers.

Protagoras is regarded as the founder of Greek humanism because he proclaimed that man is the measure of all things. Erasmus and the other leading figures of the humanist European Renaissance like Petrarch, Boccaccio, Paracelsus and Montaigue, proclaimed the richness of human cognitive powers against its submergence by revelatory knowledge. The essence of the humanist quest is to exalt the dignity of man because he can question the validity of all belief systems, intuitions and hypotheses and, through knowledge, extend his control over nature. Idealistic humanism does not aim to sever its connection with the dominant spiritual and moral heritage of the land. The essence of Indian humanism is the proclamation — *Ayamatma brahma* — the human self is big or great or cosmic. To exalt the psychic self to the heights of the cosmic and even the transcendent self is a great intellectual endeavour. According to several schools of Indian thought the Atman or the Purusha is infinite. Sometimes it is regarded as knowledge itself. These philosophical notions may have to be recast in the light of the advances of natural science and analytical metaphysics.

But idealistic humanism is deeply conscious of the historical stark fact that at the operative level of role-performance, social mobilisation, political accommodation and national integration, the stream of Indian national life became partially stagnant and hence the healthy progress of nation was arrested. The moral values became confined only to the external and intellectual layers of adherence but were not transformed into concrete policy-decisions for creating a structure based on inter-connected subsystemic and systemic unity for meeting external and internal challenges to national life. However during the freedom struggle a mighty attempt was made by patriarchs and stalwarts like Dayananda, Tilak, Gokhale, Gandhi, Shraddhananda, Aurobindo, Malaviya, Savarkara, Hedgewar and others to build a political *elan* on the immanent cultural roots which have nurtured amidst all tribulations, depressions and calamities the notion that man is not a subservient instrumental means for being exploited by the dominant elite but is a self-legislating autonomous person and belongs to a spiritual and moral kingdom of Rita, Dharma and Shila.

The Meaning of Humanism

Humanism (from the Latin *humanitas*) implying ontological individualism and the quest for the perfection of the human spirit through the consummation of man's inherent potentialities is subjectivistic and optimistic in its orientation.[1] The worship of a cold indeterminate abstract, immobile, impersonal, substance or the fission of the molecules, atoms and particles of physics and chemistry, or the marvels of the big structures of a bourgeois metropolitan civilization do not absorb its total attention. It also finds meaning and significance in the leaves of grass (Darbha), in the beauty of the lotus and the daffodils, in the chirping of the goose and the cuckoo,[2] in Rama's grief for Jatayu, in the pathos of Gautama Buddha for a stricken dear, in the nursing of a diseased patient, in the perspiring stone-breaking widow in the midday sun and in the laments of an aggrieved Gandhari for her sons dead in the Mahabharata war. In other words, it looks to the convincing character of deep inward authentic experiences.[3] Specificity and depth of sensitivity characterize the humanist's experience. Humanism holds that

1. Condorcet, *Esquisse d'un Tableau Historique des Progres de l' Espirit Humain* (1793). J. S. Mackenzie, *Lectures on Humanism* (London, 1907); F. C. S. Schiller, *Humanism : Philosophical Essays* (London, 1912); F.C.S. Schiller, *Studies in Humanism*; Viscount Haldane, *Philosophy of Humanism* (London, 1922).

2. Humanism has more in common with romanticism than with symbolism and the classical quest for geometrical proportion.

3. Cf.

"Once read thine own heart aright
And thou hast done with fears
Man gets no other light
Search he a thousand years.
Sink in thyself ! There ask what ails thee at that shrine."

(Matthew Arnold, Empedocles On Etna).

through interactions with explorations into and encounter with response-generating objects personality is built and solidified. In place of over-stressing formal disquisitions it is more inspired by the depth of authentic inner experience. Experience, according to the humanist, is not confined to collective euphoria, the revolutionary upsurge of enraged emotions and etherealisation in the sanctuary of the mystic or the ascetic anchorite. The philosopher systematizing his experiences of life in the context of their transcendental background, the historian critically evaluating the experiences of the nation and analysing the causes of historical pseudomorphosis and decline, the poet contemplating in solitude and the behavioural scientist studying the attitude-constellations of his interview-schedule respondents through factor analysis, are equally concerned with the genuineness of primary as well as reflective experience.[1] The categories of Aristotle or the twelve categories of understanding formulated by Kant or even the sixteen categories of Gautama and Vatsyayana are only formal and rational modes of systematizing logical and metaphysical experiences. In the quest of experiences, the Freudian or the existentialist tends to exalt his own feelings, ideals, failings, weaknesses and aspirations. Even his agonies and anxieties are deemed of a vital significance for him. But to the humanist, the novelty of concrete experience is to be attained along with the pursuit of the rationalist epistemology of the Navya Nyaya and the probabilistic models of the symbolic logicians.

Humanism is opposed to credel denominationalism and theological orthodoxy or ecclesiastical fanaticism. The external ritualism of religions leaves it cold. It craves for personal piety and simple modes of deference-offering. To it, no caste or race or nation has the monopoly of reason and wisdom. In their protest against the ritualist mathematics of the sacrificers the sages of the Upanishads, Mahavira, Makkhali Gosala

1. Cf. F. H. Bradley, *Appearance and Reality*, p. 465 : "The self is one of the results gained by transcending the first imperfect form of experience. But experience and Reality are each the same thing when taken at full, and they cannot be transcended." H. Bergson : *Introductian to Metaphysics* : "Metaphysics can therefore be defined as integral experience."

and Buddha marked a humanist protest. Against the Puranic cosmogonies and conflicts of the gods, the leaders of the Nirguna Bhakti school like Kabir and Nanak heralded a humanist protest in the name of the weaker and despised sections of the contemporary society. In the face of the sanction of social cruelties and illogical state ments by the narrow-minded legists like Parasara, Kamalakara and Raghunandana, the exponents of the renascent Indian spirit like Ram Mohan, Dayananda, Ramakrishna, Vivekananda, Shraddhananda, Rama Tirtha, Narayana Swami and others marked a quest for deep tolerance, comprehensive universality and inclusive brotherhood. It is not the creed or the code but the fullness of qualitative development of the emotional and cogitative potencies of the empirical human *Jiva*, that is the object of quest of the humanist.

Dante who flourished at the junction of the European Middle Ages and the fifteenth century Renaissance[1] has showed through his personality and writings that the humanist must be a man of wide learning and comprehensive orientation to the problems of the cosmos. Even in fields where his competence is limited, he should have the capacity to appreciate their achievements. The Renaissance had sponsored the ideal of some kind of a semi-encyclopaedism (*enkyklios paideia, enkyklios*=comprehensive) for the cultured man. The eighteenth century Enlightenment headed by Voltaire, Diderot and the other encyclopaedists had also heralded a similar point of view. Patanjali, Nagarjuna, Hemacandra and Kshemendra have also strengthened a similar point of view through their literary achievements and personality. It is true that with the unprecedented and enormous advance in the specialized fields of the various sciences, the mere mention of whose names and titles can stagger the imagination, it is not possible to be a cognitive encyclopaedist. However, to encourage boundless curiosity and to train the mind and heart to appreciate, in howsoever limited a way it be, the achievements in the diverse departments of the arts and sciences is not an impossible task.

1. The word *hominis* occurs in some of the books written during the period of the Italian Renaissance. G. Manetti, *De dignitate et excellentia hominis* (1452), G. Mirandola, *Oratio de hominis dignitate* (1486).

The humanist must rise above petty jealousies, vain-glory, envy, pride, hatred, passions and narrow parochial allegiances. Nothing human should be alien to him. Sloth, mental heaviness, schizophrenia and irreverence should yield to activity, dexterity and the cultivation of the balanced intellect. If he does not have the patience to hear the glory of people belonging to different nations and races he cannot be a writer of permanent worth. He must not use vulgar and rustic words and his sentences must breathe a message of goodness and welfare.[1] He cannot afford to inculcate vengefulness, religious intolerance, perfidy, treachery, deceit, trickery, wrath, unnecessary pugnacity, rancour, malice.

There is one fundamental difference between Greek humanism and Indian moral spiritual humanism. The Greek sophists challenged some of the existing conventions and norms. But they were committed to the acceptance of the dominant significance of the *polis* or the city-state. But Indian idealistic humanism has asserted the supremacy of the person who embodies in himself knowledge and character. The Bhikshu, the Sannyasin or the Acharya has always had deference paid to him. Ajatashatru acknowledged the superiority of Buddha. Dasaratha and Rama bowed before Vasistha. Thus at the institutional level, Indian idealistic humanism does not acknowledge the supremacy of the organized political collectivity to some extent as the Greek and German idealistic traditions do. Hence it may be said that moral personalism and ontological individualism is the essence of Indian idealism. *Abhayam* is the necessary moral and spiritual attribute of the humanist. Abhayam is a more comprehensive concept than liberty which, generally, signifies freedom both from external imperialism and from the internal pretensions of the sovereign imperator. Liberty has, generally, a limited civic and political connotation although now there is a demand for extending its sphere to cover industrial self-government also. But *abhayam* is a profound concept and signifies a spirit of total fearlessness. It includes the transcendence of *abhinivesha* or the

1. In the words of the Buddhist Tripitakas (*D. N.* III, 192 and the *Theragatha*) it can be said that "liberality, courtesy, benevolence, unselfishness under all circumstances" and "concord of fraternity" mark the life of the humanist.

fear of death. *Abhayam* is founded on a philosophic awareness of cosmic truth and the realisation of the vanity of all worldly pleasures and utility. It posits a sense of identity with all creatures because a humanist who manifests *abhayam* is not afraid of a mad elephant, like Buddha, or of a tiger, like Rama Tirtha. *Abhayam* demands a transcendence of the fear of objectivity or the 'other'. Only a person of supreme spiritual and moral consciousness can manifest *abhayam*. *Abhayam*, thus, is a more comprehensive and profounder notion than liberty or freedom as generally understood in the western social sciences. The realisation of *abhayam* is a distinguishing attribute of the moral and spiritual humanist. The attitude of such a person towards the acquisition and retention of political power is—*atmarthe prithivim tyajet*—for the sake of the Atman one should renounce even the earth. This notion contains the essence of the political philosophy of humanism. It is the culmination of reverence for the dignity of man. It is the supreme affirmation of the creative dynamic spontaneity of man attained by encountering reality with heroic courage and realistic spirit. Plato's *Republic*, Hobbes's *Leviathan* and Hegel's *Philosophy of Right* do not contain any concept that can be equated with the Vedic concept of *abhayam*. *Abhayam* enshrines a higher ideal for realisation than the concept of liberty cherished by John Stuart Mill, Green and Laski. Idealist humanism upholds *abhayam* as its fundamental value and supports on metaphysical foundations.

The anti-humanist, tends to debase and degrade the human spirit by perpetuating alienation, exploitation and tension-generating social maladies. He may do it in the name of a vengeful God who wants the sacrifice of the non-believer; he may do it in the name of a complete closed, militant, gospel contained in a divinely revealed book; he may do it for exalting the glory of the expanding imperialist nation seeking profits from the underdeveloped lands of Asia and Africa, he may do it in the name of bolstering the privileges of a priestly caste or he may be the apologist of the merciless landlord and the exploiting capitalist. Humanism, to the contrary, wants to redeem the most degraded, exploited, depressed, backward and condemned 'last' man and the 'lost' individual.

The concept 'integral'[1] was popularized by the exponents of integral calculus. Leibniz and Newton were the founders of integral and differential calculus.[2] Spencer formulated the twin methods of evolutionary progression in the shape of differentiation and integration.[3] Aurobindo claims to have advocated a synthesis of Karmayoga, (leading to *sadharmya mukti*) Jnanayoga (leading to *sayujya mukti*) and Bhaktiyoga (leading to *samipya* or *salokya mukti* or *bhukti*) in his Integral Yoga. This integral yoga is the technic of collective liberation, perfection and total transformation.[4] Sorokin is regarded as an advocate of integralist sociology because he wanted a genuine fusion of the sensate, the idealistic and the ideational modes of cognition in an (integral) total truth. Only thus, he felt, the crisis of the age consequent upon the resplendence of the sensate age could be transcended. Humanist idealism claims to be a total philosophy because on the foundations of cosmological

1. The Latin word *Integer* means untouched or undivided or whole. 'Integral' is derived from the Latin *integralis.* It signifies something different from the differentials and fragments and derivatives.

2. "The differential and integral calculus *was* invented independently by Newton and Leibniz." B. Russell, *H. W. P.*, p. 536.

"The infinitesimal calculus was developed in different forms by Newton and Leibniz..." Dampier, *History of Science.* p. 174.

Integral calculus deals with the methods of ascertaining indefinite integrals and applying them to the solution of differential equations and the determining of areas, volumes and lengths. In Mathematics terms like integral curve, integral domain, integral equation and integral test are used.

3. According to Leopold Von Wiese there are two categories of social processes : (1) Differentiating and (2) Integrating.

The *differentiating processes* are :—

(i) the genesis of disparities;
(ii) domination and submission;
(iii) gradation, stratification and selection;
(iv) individuation, separation and estrangement.

The *integrating* processes are :—

(i) uniformation;
(ii) ordination, superordination and subordination.
(iii) socialization.

4. Spencer formulated a hierarchy of sciences like Physics, Chemistry and Biology and culminating in Sociology. But in Aurobindo the highest science is supramental gnosis based on Yogic realisation.

speculations based both on metaphysics and the natural sciences, it builds a political philosophy and propounds sociological and economic notions. Spiritual humanism postulates a comprehensive multi-disciplinary approach to the discovery and proof of knowledge. Obviously, while its philosophical and political-theoretical notions are universalistic in orientation, its sociological and economic generalizations are relevant, mainly, to the Indian context but some of the concrete suggestions may have relevance to the socio-economic set up in the other developing nations.

The integral man aims at a comprehensive perfection of potencies. Like Rama, Krishna, Bhishma and Drona, he tries to combine the enlightening forces of spiritual and moral liberation with the developmental forces of the earth for the building up of a utility-gratifying, wealth-sharing solidarist society. He aspires to conquer discord, diremption and disparity by the transforming power of spiritual integrity, moral uprightness, rectitude and rational enlightenment. He is not against civilization but only condemns its crude technics of the exploitation of man. He is for the cultivation of simplicity and health but is not a primitivist. He wants to universalize the foundational ethical and spiritual principles of Indian culture for the redemption of humanity.

Ontology

Philosophical humanism is rooted in a metaphysical idealism and the rationalist epistemology. The Vedantic concept of *Brahman* or *Bhuma*[1] is a conceptualization of the infinite, eternal continuum which has inexhaustible possibilities of manifestation. The infinite solar systems,[2] constellations and

1. The absolute Reality can also be conceptuated as Chiti which is a Vedic word signifying a ritualist process in space. In the *Vajasaneyi Samhita*, Chiti (feminine) connotes understanding. In the *Samkshepa-Sariraka* also, it (feminine) signifies conscious self-resplendence and luminosity. In the *Devimahatmya* (V. 36), Chiti is used as masculine and implies the thinking mind or intellect. In the *Devi-Bhagavata Purana* (43 or 45) it is used in the sense of the female Goddess.

2. R. H. Baker & L. W. Frederick, *An Introduction to Astronomy* (New York, 1968), p. 343 : "... we should be prepared to conclude that the universe is much older than the current estimate of 10 billion years. Perhaps it is 30 billion or even 50 billion years old."

comets, the solid and gaseous spheres, — all are the modes and reflections of the subtle proto-atomic energy-moments of this vast cosmic-transcendent Absolute. Idealistic humanism starts with the notion of a spiritual Existent, or an absolute indeterminate — determinate substantial subject. Existence is common to the different existing particulars. The existence within space and time implies a spaceless and timeless *Being* because there can be no specific terminal point beyond which it can be stated that there is nothing.[1] This vast eternal Reality is the great foundational concrete universal but without any internal differences. It is the highest being, the not-non-being. Its particular modes or determinations do not modify it. This pure *Being* is the essence of both the finite subjects and objects. It is the thought of thought and hence its fullness cannot be categorized in conceptual mode. But it refuses to accept the notion of the universe as phenomenal or illusory or as characterized by illegitimate transposition (*Adhyasa*). To conceive of Reality as one and organic is a cardinal Vedic and Vedantic notion. Prajapati or Brahmanaspati, or Prana, or Skambha, or *Tad Ekam*, or *Sarvakarma*, *Sarvakama Sarvarasa* Ishvara, or the mighty Godhead or Siva who can be cognised through concentration, meditation and absorption or through mystical illumination or dialectical *noesis*, is an absolute organic being. But it is not the original creator of the universe in the same sense as the potter is the maker of the jar. It is a pathetic desire of the human self to impose a total immanent hominocentric teleology on the whole universe as if the millions and millions of astronomical bodies were operative to act merely according to the dictates of the human mind. The universe is not unitary and mechanical but organic. There is no temporal creation of the universe nor its utter dissolution. Both the moments of knowledge and the electrons, protons, neutrons and other particles of matter (or atom) are integral moments of the Absolute Spirit or Sempiternal Idea which is manifesting its eternal realistic-symbolic creativity from the electrons to

1. Parmenides accepted the 'One' reality on the basis of the logical argument as to the impossibility of not-being and not on mystical or religious grounds. — B. Russell, *Our Knowledge of the External World*, p. 171.

the igneous rocks, from the molecules to the stellar spheres and from the protozoa to the primates. Hence the universe is not the self-alienation or the eternal negativity of the Absolute but a permanent mode of it. *Brahman* or *Bhuma* being an infinite consciousness cannot be said to have Inconscience or Nescience inherent in it. The universe and the *Jivas* are essentially consubstantial with the Bhuma but are modes of it. The organic universe has been partly cognised by the human mind and therein consists the latter's greatness. The human mind, of course, is not a dominant ethereal entity but its functional essence is a permanent part of the universe.

Whatever else one may negate, one cannot negate the fact of knowledge. I exist because I can cogitate, feel and imagine. Every act of experiencing is a creative endeavour. There are innumerable moments and cognitive predication of knowledge as experience. Even atheism, agnosticism and scepticism are indirect modes of the acceptance of the knowing *I* because they are the conceptual formations of a subject. There can be thus no retreat from the acknowledgement of the reality of knowing. Even the so-called external, hard, dense, rigid matter is also a cluster of points or electronic charges whose existence is testified to by the functioning of our awareness. Humanism starts from the fact of knowing because being is fundamentally related to being perceived. The process of cognition and the universality of existence are beyond question and ultimately they are one as modes of the Absolute.

Humanism recognises the human self as the knowing subject which attempts to cognise both itself and the external world. At an ultimate level the constituents of which the individual human being is made is qualitatively of the same kind as the other existing entities in universe. Hence it may be possible to say that there is an infinite Absolute Good or perfect spirit or Totality of cognising selves of which the empirical selves are modes or aspects.[1] This mighty Absolute with its organic

1. Cf. F. H. Bradley, *Appearance and Reality*, pp. 228-29 : "The Reality certainly must appear within my psychical experience, but it is quite another thing to limit its whole nature to that field. ... My self is certainly not the Absolute, but, without it, the Absolute would not be itself."

components of cognising selves is an eternal[1] vast consciousness. Through cognitive awareness, critical self-introspection and deep absorption it is possible for the human mind to know itself, the spirit, and the other external objects or non-selves. The human mind can know the external entities also as a part of the vast illimitable Self. The Upanishadic conception of the unknowability of the supreme knower (Vijnata) and the Kantian concept of the unknowability and unknownness of the things-in-themselves cannot be accepted as valid in the era of the vast advancement of the frontiers of knowledge specially in metaphysics, physics, chemistry, geology, physiology and psychology. Hence we can rest content with the satisfaction that, progressively, knowledge will expand and the margin of ignorance which was magnified in the days of limited comprehension when some of the impressive metaphysical books were written, will be reduced. Empirical perceptual plurality and the multiplicity of sense-data and scientific objects are amenable to investigation by science and it is not a correct mode of predication to decry scientific knowledge as *apara Vidya.* Both *para* (supreme spiritual ontology) and *apara* (cosmic-terrestrial and scientific) Vidya constitute one total mass of luminous awareness. It became a fashion in some mystical schools to decry the empirical and logical gnosis of the external world. But that was only a reflection of the gnoseological limitations of those days when the instruments of obtaining knowledge were crude and hence it was a quick recipe to dismiss bookish and scholastic knowledge. Humanism in the contemporary world will never sponsor and glorify that limited perspective. If the intuitionally elated mystic shows his contempt for the advancements in scientific researches, he is only betraying his limited knowledge. If Samadhi requires prolonged effort and mobilisation of will power, so does the creative advancement in all sectors of knowledge. Great books

1. In some schools of Western thought sometimes humanism is regarded as an intermediate position between naturalism and absolutism and sometimes between naturalism and transnaturalism. Cf. Willystine Goodsell, *The Conflict of Naturalism and Humanism* (New York, 1910); C. J. Keysen, *Humanism and Science*, (New York, 1931).

like Newton's *Principia*, Pareto's *Mind and Society,* Spengler's *The Decline of the West*, Sorokin's *Social and Cultural Dynamics*, Dasgupta's *A History of Indian Philosophy* or Toynbee's *A Study of History* have not required less expenditure of mental and volitional energy for their completion than the poems of Suradasa and Rumi. In unravelling the unending story of the advance of cognitive creativism, we are not to be guided by the eulogies of the devotees and the committed. Humanism is trenchantly opposed to the artificial separation between *para* (transcendent) and *apara* vidya. All modes of knowing are integral and necessary parts of the vast infinite Consciousness which is cognisable by the rational and spiritual endeavours of a creative, exploring being.

The Absolute Real as pure, perfect, eternal[1] duration and infinite expansion is Consciousness. It is the unity of knowledge and pure perfect activity. Its eternal flow, results in the manifestation of what appears evolved as matter, life and mind. Instinct or drive, intuition and overmind and rational intelligence are means of human comprehending and experiencing responses to the Real. The philosophy of idealistic humanism accepts the possibility of the development of the powers of man to know at least partly the Absolute Real. What appear differentiated as life, spontaneity, pure activity (*prana*) and philosophical meditative contemplation and absorption on the one side and matter, mass, motion, energy, colloids, elements and particles on the other, are all phases or modes of the Real.[2] They are not essentially differentiated double movements but appear to be so due to the evolutionary constraints on the cognising powers of the human mind. The Absolute may be considered as both the constituent and the integrating principle

1. Cf. F. H. Bradley, *Appearance and Reality*, p. 442 : "The Absolute has no history of its own, though it contains histories without number."

2. Cf. F. H. Bradley, *Appearance and Reality*, p. 114 : "And reality, set on one side and apart from all appearance, would assuredly be nothing." *Ibid.*, p. 129 : "... the Absolute is one system, and that its contents are nothing but sentient experience." *Ibid.*, p. 460 : "Reality is one. It must be single, because plurality, *taken* as real, contradicts itself. Plurality implies relations, and, through its relations, it unwillingly asserts always a superior unity."

of the universe. Moral dualities like good and evil or merit and demerit have no ultimate place in the perfect subjective substantiality and timeless duration of the eternal Consciousness.[1] Redemption is not a gift from a whimsical omnipotent God or the consequence of persuasion by and intercession of some favourite relation of God or his prophet but is the realisation of the enormous vastness and comprehensiveness of the Real through scientific (*apara*) and philosophical (*para*) knowledge. Ours is the day of specialization. The acquisition of an encyclopaedic knowledge of the various empirical sciences and the other branches of cognition is certainly a very difficult enterprise, if not completely impossible. In such a context, the Jaina theory of consciousness as the dominant essence of the soul and its view that every soul can manifest the omniscience and infinite power and infinite bliss which is inherent in it can be a source of great optimism, if metaphorically interpreted. Scientific researches, however, do not corroborate the view that in the state of ultimate (paramarthika) immediate knowledge, the consciousness of the soul is related to temporal entities without the transposition of the sense-organs.

Materialism, whether of the hylozoistic or mechanical or anthropological or dialectical variety is faced with the task of interpreting the phenomenon of consciousness. To conceive of thought as the aggregate cluster of sensations which are the functions of the motions in the brain or of neurological circuitry does not appeal to the moralist and the spiritualist because apprehendedness has the character of luminosity. The universe appears to be an infinite, vast, extension,— beginningless and endless. But the notions of infiniteness, beginninglessness or super-temporality, modality and quantitative and qualitative substantiality receive their conceptual characterizations from the human mind itself. It is possible that the quantity, quality, relation, modality, inherence, substantiality, activity, universality,

1. "Cf. F. H. Bradley, *Appearance and Reality*, pp. 380-81 : "... since in that Absolute no appearance is lost, the good is a main and essential factor in the universe . . . whether anything is better or worse, does without any doubt make a difference to the Absolute. And certainly the better anything is, the less totally in the end is its being overruled."

particularity and singularity, aspects in the light of which we regard the universe as material or electro-magnetic, are our own conceptual constructions. Matter as conceived in physics is a cluster of images. Historical or mathematical is only the subjective form of apperception to the acceptance of which we have been culturally conditioned. The Real as it is in itself or the supreme Noumenal Existent is not fully known and hence to call it material is only a limited mode of finite conceptualization. The notions of conservation of energy, persistence of force and indestructibility of matter are also limited modes of testifying to the reality of Absolute Reason and Truth. Matter is only a phenomenal localization of Reality.

Furthermore, there is no sanction for the notions of occasionalism and of psycho-physical parallelism according to philosophical humanism. To interpret each event as an occasion for Providential dispensation perhaps may satisfy our emotional and cultural quest but there is no public scrutinizable evidence for this. Nor do mind and matter or Purusha and Prakriti run in a parallel process of motion and locomotion.

Thus spiritual humanism is a philosophy of realistic absolutism. It does not consider the universe as unreal from the standpoint of the Absolute. The phenomenal universe is an organic component of the Absolute. But the Absolute is not in agony so as to seek perfection through manifestation in the universe. The endless appearances in the universe do not constitute the total staff of which only the Absolute consists. The Absolute has infinite modes and our earth and its really petty but poetically glamourized world-historical heroes and prophets and incarnations do not 'represent' the Absolute. Their appearance and exit makes no vital difference to the Absolute. They are also like the waves on a vast ocean surface.

The Epistemological Problems of Humanism

All knowledge is true. The modes of apprehension and comprehension developed in the scientific, historical, behavioural and philosophical ways of experiencing are true. Error is only limited unsynthesized knowledge. Poetic effusions and rhetorical statements are exaggerated modes of creative expression and may be true or false according to the scientific canons of verification. Even contrary statements, perversions, antitheses, contradictions and distortions of the laws of identity and excluded middle may, generally, be reconciled with the evolution of higher inclusive comprehending consciousness. The limited will be gradually perfected in the eternal vastness of the Real. What we regard as indescribable or incommunicable or as not capable of being etymologically derived (Anirvachaniya) is only the expression of the inadequacy of human knowledge. The confession about the unknowability of the Real Noumenon is a way of saying that it is unknown at the present moment to the predicating subject. But to put a permanent ban on the powers of the human mind is not acceptable to humanism.[1] The growing powers of the human mind will progressively expand the frontiers of both positive, cumulative scientific knowledge and concrete philosophical synthesis. Sometimes the illusory object may be constructed by human predilection or prejudice and sometimes the research investigator may mistake one real element for another. But the powers of cognition will be ever spurred to exercise themselves due to the demands of the evolutionary process and the natural quest of the creative human mind itself. Humanism, however, is not so sanguine as to assert that there will be no error and illusion at all with the perfection of cognitive powers in the future. The exploring human mind is ever on the march for the reconciliation of universality, particularity and singularity, of unity and diverse multiplicity and of permanent substantiality and quantitative-qualitative flux. The one important contribution of Jainism to idealist humanist philosophy is its notion of Anekantavada or multi-terminal reality. This position is grounded upon the acceptance of the possibility of multiple standpoints in the realm of philosophy.[2] Reality assumes infinite characters in

1. Contrast S. Radhakrishnan, *An Idealist View of Life*, p. 261 : "Even the greatest extension of physiological knowledge will not help us to infer mental activity from brain structure."

2. According to the Jainas the inherent qualities (Gunas) of the substances are permanent, but the accidental and contingent modifications (Paryayas) go on changing. Jainism, thus, unlike the dialectical materialist and the ontological idealist is opposed to considering either mere flux or total immobility as the character of the empirical reality.

the course of its manifestation which appear as temporal transformations. It is not possible to assert that the external object is a product of fancy or a mere construction of the percipient mind. Nor can it be said that there are no innate cognising powers in the human brain. Limited assertions and predications are being revised in the light of fresh researches and they certainly indicate the innate existence of human cognitive powers. But all existing predications cannot be said to be true unless they have been exposed to critical searching scrutiny and verification. In this way the acceptance and non-acceptance of what is true or false is a constantly growing and ongoing scientific and synthetic process. The miscombination of moments of experience due to the misapplication of scientific instruments of investigation and uncorrected serendipity are bound to result in the formulation of erroneous hypotheses which need to be further tested. But humanism is committed to the exercise of the powers of observation, determinate perception and logical analysis, experimentations both in the field and in the laboratories, and measurement and quantification. These stages pertain to the domain of science or *apara-vidya*. The domain of *para vidya* or metatheory is to synthesize the abstractions and verified generalizations of science into a cosmic-transcendent frame of reference for the evolution of an ever-expanding philosophy of the Real. There is no unbridgeable hiatus in knowledge. Every encounter with Reality is a moment of advance in the chain of reflective *noesis* culminating in the *Alayavijnana.* But the error of holding that every moment of knowledge fully and entirely involves the Absolute Idea or Indeterminate-determinate Substance is apparent because specific and limited moments of knowledge find their evolving consummation in the Real. The explorations of knowledge constitute arenas of the juxtaposition and interaction of the external object of perception and the investigating mind. In this way moments of knowledge are getting synthesised in the eternal constitution of the Absolute Consciousness. But the Buddhist concept of the mere momentariness will make impossible the rational explanation of memory and recognition. If all substances are momentary, then moral autonomy would have no significance.

Philosophical humanism starts with the fact of interaction between the external objects of nature and the appercipien cognising human mind. This interaction provides the basic data or information-points. There is no transmission or goingt away of the powers of the sense-organs to the external objects, on the other hand, the latter cast their impressions on the sense-organs. There must be some fundamental point of unity between the external entities and the human cognizing agencies to make such a process possible because two absolutely disparate objects cannot cast mutual influences. Otherwise there can be no rational or teleological explanation for such a conjuncture. But apart from the ontological question of the essential nature of the two agencies in the process of interaction, the epistemological process based on cognitive transactions has to be visualised. There is the casting of impressions on the afferent or auditory, olfactory, visual (optic); tactile and gustatory senses or receptive faculties. These latter are transmitted to the cerebral organism through the nerves. These are organized into connected pieces through their incorporation into the items of categories of reason which are, ultimately, the systematizations of accumulated cultural experiences. Thus the physiological data of perception are transformed into logically recognisable pieces of knowledge.

It is also possible for the cognising apparatus of man to engage in the process of the concrete consciousness of the self. Through the concentration of thinking powers, man tries to find the answer to the permanent problem — who am I ? What is my value and final destiny ? Through critical awareness there can be self-consciousness apart from object-consciousness.

The synthesis of the generalized conclusions derived from the operations of externally-oriented consciousness and the inner-directed self-consciousness is found in the integration of *apara* and *para* vidya. Knowledge attains its fullness when not only the powers of scientific and philosophical cognition become dynamically operative but are also enriched with whatever insights[1] can be received from poetic feelings, romantic

1. Karl Mannheim, *The Diagnosis of Our Time*, p. 159 also accepts the necessity of the mastery of the art of social isolation, contemplation, spiritualization, sublimation and religious ecstasy.

imaginations, symbolical representations and mystic overmental intuitions. Reality as Infinite Consciousness being a manifold complex, we cannot ignore any faculty of man that has been developed in the course of evolution. Judgment, hence, should be based on adequate evidence. The integration and totalization of knowledge by freeing it from exclusive limiting particularity is essential for the full realization of human potencies. The only imperative point is that nothing should be objectively claimed as a matter of special prophetic revelation and esoteric experience. Whatever has been claimed to be derived from these sources must also be subjected to the searchlight of critical enquiry and dispassionate public investigation.[1] Dream experiences, hysterical visions, megalomaniac fantasies, secret inspirations, supramental experiences, poetic and aesthetic feelings, — all must be capable of bearing rational scrutiny. The validity of systematic inductive judgment is guaranteed by the ascertainable reality of the external object and by the logical coherence of the judgments themselves. Extra-sensory perception has no physiological basis. Humanism is not esoteric. It is firmly committed to the view that reason is the sole final criterion of the verification and validation of knowledge. With the accumulation of further congruent or contrary pieces of information, a conclusion can be confirmed or revised. There is nothing like eternally perfect and complete human knowledge and hence omniscience and prophetic revelations are only poetic aspirations.

There can be only one valid cosmology for mankind because science is universalist. Metaphysics which is a higher level synthesis of the abstractions of the sciences, both natural and behavioural-historical, can only claim to be relatively universalist because the mode of synthesizing the scientific inductions

1. Anupalabdhi (non-apprehension) is not an independent source of valid knowledge because to say that is a vacant space an infinite number of entities like book, pen and so on *ad infinitum* are not perceived creates only semantic confusion and does not add to the cumulative stock of information. Similarly to regard *abhava* (absence) as a positive entity for cognition only creates confusion.

will be, to some extent, subjectively governed. Any metaphysics which is narrow and segmented in its method of approach cannot attempt the formulation of the fullness of reality. Hence the philosophical notions that were formulated by Vyasa Kapila, Saṁkara, Ramanuja, Plato, Aristotle, Kant and Hegel have to be re-tested in the light of advancements in the field of cosmogonic and cosmological knowledge. Even when a system of metaphysics is transcendental, esoteric and eschatological it does have an empirical foundation in the existing body of positive, scientific and historical cognition and situation. Hence only an integral approach which ever seeks to formulate propositions on the bases of positive advancements can be satisfactory to the seeker after truth. The contemporary man, is also an explorer just as the ancient Indian Rishis and Greek thinkers were. Hence a mode of apprehension and cognition has to be evolved which will be ever appreciative of the conclusions of the sciences. Hence the recent conclusions of physics, chemistry, zoology and physiology cannot be ignored by the seeker after truth. The latter will maintain a sceptical attitude towards propositions which seek to establish their reliability and validity on the basis of their intuitional, supramental, prophetic subliminal or inspirational roots. He will not ignore the latter but will try to reflect upon them through the exercise of his phenomenological and dialectical powers. An acceptance on mere trust and ideational faith is not the humanist mode of investigation. Thus at the level of universalist knowlegde, the method of enquiry can only be a resort to comprehensive and synthetic or integral rational understanding. All cosmological propositions wheresoever asserted — in the religious scriptures, in philosophical classics, in historical tomes, in prophetic and poetic inspirations and in text-books of astronomy, physics, and chemistry, would be carefully collected, compared, tested and re-tested and thus a network of reliable, interlocking propositions built. This is the essence of humanist methodology regarding cosmology and metaphysics. Thus the Buddhist concept of *pratitya-samutpada* or dependent origination may have to be re-stated in the light of recent advancements in physics and physiology, fully recognising that it was a monumental achievement at the time that it was first stated. Similarly the *Nama-rupa-skandha* of older Buddhism may need re-statement. The Vaisheshika and Jaina concepts of atomism should be re-formulated in the light of modern chemistry. This is the way to retain the constant freshness of the older formulations, otherwise they will only be appealing either to the devotees or to the historians of old thought. Thus the epistemology and methodology of humanism are inclusive. Imagination, sympathetic understanding, poetic apprehension, critical investigation, and experimentation are to be resorted to in accordance with their relevance to the subject matter under investigation.

Metaphysical and scientific knowledge is relatively or absolutely universalist. But at the level of sociological and political investigations, historical and religious traditions also play a part in gnoseological enquiries. There is considerable difference in the patterns of cultural configuration and evolution in the world. Hence the role of cultural determination of the contents of socio-political-economic knowledge has to be acknowledged. Thus there cannot be only two models of social and economic development. The heritage of Indian culture is much more ancient than that of the developed countries of today. The moral depth that permeates the Vedic-Buddhistic-Vaishnava tradition has profoundly affected the Indian mind. The tolerance of antithetical standpoints has been inherent in the Indian philosophical approach. A synthetic cultural apperception, nonetheless, makes it imperative that political, social and economic enquiries be also rooted in a full empirical and factual understanding of the immediately pressing problems and challenges. This awareness will add realistic dimensions to epistemology.

The epistemology of humanism is global, total universal and integral. It is opposed to the exaltation of any one sector or method of knowing at the cost of another without reference to the context. The different layers of neurological functioning on which humanist epistemology is based can be thus systematized.

(i) The most primitive mode of apprehension is instinctive. This results in illusion (*maya* and *adhyasa*) and *viparyaya* (misconception) the perception of shadows, and phantasmagoria and the magical displays of powers appertain to this realm.

(ii) The second realm is that of *indriya* and *prana*. It is the arena of indeterminate and determinate perception based on unstructured as well as controlled observation.

(iii) The third field is that of aesthetic intuitions and imagination and also of symbolical representation. Poetic inspirations, sympathetic projections, memory and recollection of past experiences and the vague attempts to gain knowledge by identification are also stages on the way to the acquisition of integral knowledge. The intimations of the inner voice, so long as they have not been tested and verified, belong to this realm.

(iv) The realm of *manas* and *chitta* is the field of understanding. It is the province of higher mental and overmental knowledge. Experiment-based hypotheses, inferences, comparative assessments and evaluation, implications and subsumptions, belong to this field which may be considered the arena of the exercise of negative dialectic and discursive reason. Plato includes mathematical propositions also in the field.

(v) Integral knowledge based on speculative reason marks the culmination of conceptual *noesis*. This is the stage of ultimate gnosis called *ritambhara prajna*. It includes the synthesised insights gained by *para* and *apara* vidya. It is the stage of *nididhyasana*. The intuitional and supramental synthesis gained by *samprajnata* and *asamprajnata samadhi* (or *nirvikalpa* samadhi or the stage of *samjna-vedayita nirodha*) provides comprehensive illumination and revelation of absolute truth. It is the province of *vyavasayatmika buddhi* or the totality of creative *dhih* and *ida* or intellectually tested and verified intuitions.

Time, Space and Causality

According to most of the Jaina philosophers and to Newton, time and space are real entities. But in the light of the advancements made by relativity physics, which substitutes events, in a relation of intente, for particles, however, this view regarding space and time has to be re-formulated.[1] Time is unreal and

1. There is an element of irreversibility in time. But at the operative level it is possible to move to and fro in space. Samuel Alexander and Eddington have only introduced confusion by positing a Space-Time.

only a subjective construct abstracted from social experiences of succession because if it were ontologically real in itself then it will have to be imparted a reality of its own, along with that of the Absolute Real.[1] The objectivity of space, on the other hand, appears to be less difficult of realisation because space both in the sense of directions (*dik*) and empty extension is something real and cognisable[2] although the older notion of space as the vehicle of word-transmission has been repudiated by the modern physical conception of the transmission of words by air.

At the metaphysical level, causality may be a super-physical notion based on custom operating on the imagination. But at the elementary and sociological levels, an antecedent classes of events causing a consequent classes of events is something which can be demonstrated. The repudiation of causality on the ground of the indeterminate or uncertain behaviour of the electron will only cause confusion. At concrete perceptual levels, the Newtonian notion that action generates counter-action appears meaningful. The entire theory of medical diagnosis, prognosis and treatment is based on the causal concept of etiology. The practice of medicine will become impossible if the causal investigation of diseases were given up for the sake of the vague notion of correlation and association. At the ethical level also, it is within experience that honest thinking culminates in moral action and the accumulated impressions and effects of moral actions lead to the transformation of

1. According to the Sarvastivadins time is not a Dharma. There is no duration because the past is past, the future is future, and the present does not exist separately from the thing existing at that. Cf. F. H. Bradley, *Appearance and Reality*, p. 185 : "Time is an appearance which contradicts itself. ..." "The Absolute is timeless, but it possesses time as an isolated aspect, an aspect which, in ceasing to be isolated, loses its special character." *Ibid.*, p. 185.

2. The Vaisheshika distinction between Akasha (extension or ether) as the material cause of sound and *dik* as space is somewhat confusing. There is no objective basis for positing (*The Life Divine*, Vol. II, pp. 80-81): (i) a purely physical space, (ii) a subjective space-extension (space in which the mind moves) and (iii) a pure spiritual space. According to John Dewey, *The Quest for Certainty*, p. 153, mathematical space is not different from physical and empirical space.

character. Thus at the empirical level of action, an invariable antecedent factor leading to an inevitable consequent emergent entity appears meaningful. Mere correlation cannot make possible will-directed and motivated action. Hence the humanist philosophy of integral social change on rational lines proceeds on the assumption of causal relationship among diverse social facts. Hence it takes the problem of historical causal explanation seriously and does not indifferently treat causality as mere sequentiality.

Monotheism and Spiritual Humanism

The infinite universe is not like a pitcher needing a primordial demiurgus for its creation. Hence the concept of God, the form of form, as the unmoved first mover appears unconvincing. Nor is the human notion of a perfect Existence enough to guarantee the real existence of a supreme Godhead. Of course there is evident a purpose in nature, but ours is not the best of all possible worlds. There is a lot of waste, irrationality and proposed issues in the world. Hence there is no valid sanction for recognising a God as the upholder of a universal teleology. Hence we cannot logically identify the Platonic Idea of Good with a God. If we hold along with the Bhaktas that God primordial providence is a postulate of moral and devotional life, there is not enough capacity in such a being to attract our credence because it is known to be a postulate at best. If God is only a regulative idea of reason and a principle of rational theology, he cannot demand an autonomous real, eternal existence. Hence it is best from the logical point to assert that the Absolute itself is God. If God is not Absolute he is not a full God. To see and know God on a mountain, or in the Asian desert, or in a temple is not the elitist privilege of a prophet or a priest but the birth right of a human being.

The doctrine of monotheism of the stern Semitic variety propounds the concept of an omnipotent God removed from the den of drudgery and struggles of man. A jealous and potent Jehova is much removed from the affairs of man. There is an almost insurmountable gulf between the great God and the cringing obeisant allegiant man. Man, in such a context, cannot be expected to assert himself. He can only crave for divine help in times of personal disaster, national predicaments and civilizational climacteries.

But a philosophy inculcating the motion of a transcendent-immanent God whose mode or integral portion is reflected in the form of human spirit is more in consonance with humanism because thereby man is exalted to a lofty position by being hailed as being divine in his inmost essence. This conception also leads to the attainment of strength and autonomy (*svarajya*) and the empirical self can make efforts to attain both scientific knowledge and supramental gnosis.

Hence the normative antithesis between the theocentric conception of the Western Middle Ages with its emphasis on the ontological argument for theism and the Renaissance world-view[1] of anthropocentrism sanctioning creative efforts on earth for the display of artistic excellence is not applicable in the Indian cultural context. Ram Mohan, Tagore, Gandhi and Rama Tirtha who were firm believers in Sachchidananda or Parameshvara were also great votaries of human uplift and emancipation. They loved and served men because they accepted the reality of a True Super-Spirit.

1. The following lines from Pope illustrate the spirit of anthropological this-worldly humanism :

"Know then thyself, presume not God to scan,
The proper study of mankind is man.
Placed on this isthmus of a middle state,
A being darkly wise, and rudely great :
With too much knowledge for the sceptic side,
With too much weakness for the stoic's pride,
He hangs between; in doubt to act, or rest."

(A. Pope, *Essay on Man*, II, lines 1-7).

Goethe's *Faust* also represents the ceaseless striving of the proud wanderer:

"Thus here, by dangers girt, shall glide away
Of childhood, manhood, age, the vigorous day :
* * * * *
Then dared I hail the Moment fleeing :
"Ah still delay—thou art so fair"
The traces cannot, of my earthly being,
In aeons perish,—they are there—
In proud fore-feeling of such lofty bliss,
I now enjoy the highest Moment,—this."

(*Faust*, Act V)

Humanism and Religion

There are different theories of the origin of religion.[1] Some would trace the origin of religious notions to magic. Several anthropologists would regard ancestor-worship and ghost-fear as the root of religious notions. According to Hobbes, religion has its genesis in fear. Marxism considers religion as the reflex of the relations of production Vivekananda found the root of religion in the superconsciousness of Samadhi. Western idealists have stressed an impulse towards the Transcendent and dependence on the Holy as the root of religion. The prophetic Semitic religions regard revelation from God[2] through super-human intermediaries as the source of religious maxims. The Homeric gods were highly anthropomorphic with enough of human feelings of jealousy and vanity. The Middle Ages were the epochs of the dominance of Christianity and Papalism in the West. With the rise of the Renaissance spirit and physical science, there has been a progressive decline of the cognitive influence of Christianity over intellectuals and different kinds of ideologies and philosophical world views have tried to fill the vacuum. Among these are the humanitarianism of the eighteenth century, the positivism of Auguste Comte, neo-Kantianism and ethical socialism. In the nineteenth century there was the growth of the theanthropic notions of religion of humanity wherein the bordering between the immortal and the mortal is attenuated. Eduard Bernstein, Herman Cohen and Adler propounded that Marxism should be supplemented with Kantian ethics.

In the ancient world, in several countries, the victory in battles was regarded as a gift of the gods. Marduk in Babylone, Jehova in the Old Testament and Indra in the Ṛgveda were the gods of victorian battles. The movement to separate religion and

1. F. H. Bradley, *Appearance and Reality*, pp. 388-38n : "Religion appears to have two roots, fear and admiration or approval. ... Wonder or curiosity seems not to be religious, unless it is in the service of these other feelings. ... Hence any object, in regard to which we feel a supreme fear or approval, will engage our attention, and be for us a Deity."

2. Sri Aurobindo, *The Isha Upanishad*, p. 54, regards as "vulgar" the idea of a Personal God as a magnified individual like man in his nature but greater and more powerful.

politics arose against theocratic notions and institutions with their implications of Cassaro-papalism. The Hebrew political system, the Islamic Caliphate and Tibetan Lamaism were examples of theocracy. The Leninist militant atheism and the propaganda of Godlessness was conceived in the framework of the activities of the Russian Orthodox Church for the support of Czarism. But in modern India, Tilak who supported Karma-yoga for the acquisition of political rights was an exponent of monistic Vedanta. Gandhi who claimed that he had taken to political work for spiritual emancipation (*moksha*) was a Vaishnava and also a Vedantist. Aurobindo was a prophet of political Vedantism, a supramental idealist and a Yogic mystic. The advance of modern Indian nationalism was helped by the political implications of morally-oriented religious teachings. This phenomenon shows that religion can be a creative and dynamic force for utilitarian concrescence.

Dharma in its highest philosophical sense is the eternal law governing nature and man. At the ontological level, it is the primordial immanent law controlling the universe and its phenomena. At the moral level, it means the normative injunction or code for the altruistic regulation of human conduct, both individual and intersubjective. There is also a sociological side of Dharma which becomes evident when it is equated with precepts, maxims, rituals and practices for social harmony and collective amelioration and integration. Jaimini uses Dharma in the sense of a categorical ritualistic command. Manu's ten categories of Dharma are basically moral in character and include terms signifying psychological regeneration and social coordination. Kanada uses Dharma in the sense of those principles which lead to worldly prosperity and development as well as to the attainment of transcendent bliss. The writers of the Dharmashastras, the Mahabharata and the Puranas include in the category of Dharma moral axioms and social precepts for the maintenance of Varnashrama. The concept of Raja-dharma popularized by them is sometimes equated with Arthashastra. It also comprehends the list of duties for the efficient and faithful role-performance and action-engineering by the holders of political authority. A peculiar ontological meaning of Dharma may be found in Vasubandhu's *Abhidharma-*

kosha wherein he has categorized seventy-five Dharmas[1] constituting total reality. The Vedic Rita with which Dharma became identified later on has also an ontological character. But, by and large, Dharma as used in the Smritis and the philosophical works has a moral and sociological relevance. To the extent that Dharma includes categories of universal moral significance, it can be regarded as the foundational "Grund-norm", and no political system can ignore it. But if it is equated with specific social and political norms, for the regulation of group behaviour, then for its inclusion among the code of governing political rules, regulations, constitutions and laws, its validity will have to be critically tested. A modern democratic egalitarian polity cannot sanction social suppression, crude vulgarity. socially deviant behaviour, political patronage, slavery, and the exploitation of women in the name of any religious text or prophet or incarnation. Liturgical and sectarian religious considerations and political considerations have to be separate. In this sense secularism is a prized objective, But in the name of religious autonomy no group or congregation can be allowed to practice institutional behaviour which run counter to the rational sense.

For the reconstruction of humanity, some of the moral insights of Dharma as true religion are needed. True religion postulates the cultivation of the integralist approach of reconciliation, universalism and harmony. There can be no consensus hence, on Toynbee's Christological interpretation of history.[2] Nor can

1. 75 Dharmas

Samskrita (=72)
1-11. *Rupa-skandha*
1 *Vedana-skandha*
1 *Samjna-skandha*
58 *Samskara-skandha* (including 46 *Caitta dharma*)
1 *Vijnana-skandha*
= 72

Asamskrita (=3)
Pratisamkhyanirodha
Apratisamkhyanirodha
Akasa or Space

2. According to Arnold Toynbee there is the transition from (i) underman and under-civilization to (ii) man and civilization and finally to (iii) superman and transfigured ethereal super-civilization of the kingdom of God. ... P. A. Sorokin *Social Philosophies of an Age of Crisis*, p. 120.

we afford to return to the New Middle Ages in the quest of "the new theocracy", after the end of the humanist-secular phase of western culture in the nineteenth century as Berdyaev holds. A plea for the revival of the gnostic spirit pervading western humanity before the Reformation as made by Voegelin is also not practicable. Any attachment to one particular revealed book will make that dispensation narrow and unacceptable to the non-believers in them. The concept of Dharma in the Buddhist *Dhammapadam*, the Kantian conception of the categorical imperative, and the interpretation put upon the Vedanta by Rama Tirtha are more universalist and can appeal to a wider audience than the countrymen of the philosophers concerned. Tagore's *Gitanjali* and *The Religion of Man* are also universalist in their orientation. It is evident that, in the modern rational world, a moral code, to be appealing, is not to be opposed to the conclusions of, if not rooted in, science. Hence Christian sociology and sophiology[1] cannot have much appeal today.

All true religions advocate the incorporation of moral principles in the political system. They want to infuse the structure of power with the canons of reason, equity and justice which provide higher legitimacy to the governing mechanism. They do not aim to glorify any established church as the city of God. Devarajya (the city of God) did not exist only in the mythical Golden Age or before Paradise was lost. It can re-exist provided the political cities cease to be the theatres of lust, cupidity, perversity and barbarity. The city of God did not come to an end with the fall of Jerusalem, Rome or Somnath. It can be founded upon the quest for peace and justice for all human beings. Some orthodox religions might have dreamt of an eschatological city of God to be attained after death but idealist humanism hopes that the city of God or Dharmarajya based upon the sovereignty of reason and committed to the unrestrained legitimacy of a compassionate view towards all existence is the sole antidote to nuclear global annihilation.

1. For Florensky's Sophiology see W. Berdyaev, *Dream and Reality*, pp. 166-67.

Humanism, Science and History

Humanism has been represented as an emancipation from the theological encumberings of the Middle Ages. The authenticity of manifold personal experiences, the vividity of human encounter with the diverse challenges of nature, the moral and aesthetic dimensions, rational creativity and man's achievements in the domain of art, literature and ethics are sought to be glorified by it. In place of obeisance to and faith in a personal God, being overwhelmed with the consciousness of sin, the western Renaissance humanism inculcated a sense of stupendous political power and dignity. It wanted to replace theocentrism by anthropocentrism and theocracy by the creed of individual omnipotence. In place of adherence to the antiquated cosmologies of the scriptures, humanism is committed to the acceptance of scientific cosmogonies and the notion of geological eras and the validity of cytological and hystological researches.

In the light of astronomical and geological history it will be potent untruth to maintain that the empirical world has no past, present or future. Thus the *ajatavada* (Non-creation) of Gaudapada is potently opposed to the evidences of science. Nor can the world be considered a solipsitic projection of the limited human self. It is the height of vanity for a death-governed empirical ego to arrogate to itself the potency of projecting the vast world and its spatio-temporal location. The objective, extra-mental character of the world studied by astronomy and physics is too vital, potent and deterministic to be repudiated. The only point of philosophical humanism is that it does not think that the objectivity of the external world detracts from the plenary existence of the Absolute. The external world is only a mode of the Absolute and does not exhaust its limitless possibilities of manifestation.

Humanism appreciates the enormous achievement of science[1] and the scientific methodology. But it refuses to accord to science the status of being the sole source of knowledge. Reality being multi-faced and multi-dimensional, it is not possible to

1. There is no evidence, however, for the optimism of bionomics that machines can be perfected to perform biological functions.

hold that quantification and measurement are the sole modes of apprehending the Real. Even Einstein has accepted that physical science is not the sole path to knowledge. Hence in places of a zealous adherence to scientism, positivism and experimentalism it is more useful for the advance of knowledge to adhere to a multi-method approach and relativistic logic. Galileo, Newton, Einstein, Aryabhata and Bhaskara are needed for the advancement of knowledge. But that recognition does not mean the acceptance of the irrelevance of Kalidasa, Sankara, Shakespeare and Milton to human knowledge. The teaching of Zoroaster, Buddha, Mahavira and Christ may contain some elements that sound incongruous with the conclusions of natural sciences but that does not negate their worthwhile place in a total philosophy based on the creative endeavours in the advance of human civilization. According to humanism, knowledge is not sealed in the religious scriptures nor is the totality of knowledge relevant to common good and collective emancipation contained entirely in the books of the astronomical and physical sciences. Ethical intuitions, moral values, cultural standards, historical precepts and socially-oriented traditions, maxims and prescriptions have also played their legitimate part in building the edifice of human civilization. In the contemporary world we have to use the criterion of reason for judging their congruence with the methodological and substantive need and demands of social liberation and political development.

Humanism does not consider the present era of scientific technology as an epoch of total decadence, distemper or decline. If there is dissonance and disruption, it has faith in the creative mobilisation of planned human energies for getting over them. It does not uphold that paradise was lost with the end of the Satyayuga, Treta and Dvapara. It is oriented to the realisation of futurist utopias based on the fullness of communication and information-transmission and the operation of corrective feedbacks. History is an ongoing continuous process governed by the interfusion of environmental factors and the dynamism of creative human will, reason and moral conscience. History is neither completely cyclical nor straightlinear in its forward march. There may be periods of decline and depression following an era of creative resplendence and prosperity. It is sheer fatalism to conceive that we are monotonously repeating what has occurred exactly similarly in the past. There are endless fluctuations in history. There is no exactly spiral or rectilinear progression in history. Nor are there inexorable laws in the manifestations of the historical structure. History is multi-aspected. Some events may appear to be cyclical repetitions and fluctuations of a preceding era. But it is certainly possible to learn from the story of historical dynamics. It is essential to utilize the resources of science for achieving progress in human societies.

Physical science, in spite of the conception of the uncertainty or indeterminacy of electronic behaviour, supports the notion of determinism so far as the operation of laws in the universe is concerned. But humanist idealism is opposed to any notion of inexorable naturalistic determinism in history. So will it be opposed to any hypothesis of climatological determinism in history. It does not hold that history is a conjunction of contingencies or a series of miracles. History proceeds according to certain probabilistic laws. But the human being is a creative agent. He is not the mere reflex of the forces and relations of production. He has certain autonomy and individuality. Often he finds himself in incongruous alienation with the social, political and natural forces and situation. But it is through his efforts to conquer this externally-rooted alienation that he realises his personality and his self.

Evolution and Humanism

The religious scriptures propound the cult of special creation of the world by an omnipotent God. Geology and biology, on the other hand, adhere to the notion of the gradual evolution of rocks and the various phyla, genuses and species. Neo-Darwinism would ascribe to the human species its roots among the primates. The origin of life has been a mystery still. A plastic responsive sensitiveness to the external stimuli, a capacity for assimilation and coordination coupled with respiratory inward activity and reproductive potency characterize the functioning of life. Life or *prana* is a dominant category of Hindu psychology and is regarded as a mighty cosmic force in the Atharvaveda (II, 4). According to the Vedanta, life represents the operation of a transcendent-cosmic being as force and there is continuity of life from the animals to man. According to the *Kathopanishad* even trees (sthanu) have lives. The discovery of the roots of life in the qualitative refinements of protein and other microorganisms appear fascinating to a section of scientists. The explorations of the DNA and RNA and the study of the genetic code are posing serious threats to the adherents of the transmission of Samskaras (merits and demerits) from one existence to another.[1] Philosophical humanism does not seek to offer resistance against the corroborated conclusions and verified propositions of science. It is fully committed to the view that no ban can be imposed on the creative potentialities of mind and it is willing to revise its foundational statements in the light of advancing scientific researches. It will, however, maintain a spirit of critical scrutiny even towards the natural sciences. Darwinism with its support of natural selection replaced the Lamarckian conception of the transmission of acquired characteristics. Hugo deVries' concept of mutation and the laws of heredity of Mendel (1822-1884) have further refined classical Darwinism.

Some attempts have been made by philosophers to incorporate newer dimensions in the evolutionary method. Bergson stressed the dynamism of the creative *Elan* in the evolutionary progression. Alexander and Lloyd Morgan have emphasized the emergence of newer categories in the evolutionary drama. Matter, Life, and Mind are three such dominant emergents and, further, there would be the emergence of the Deity.[2] Aurobindo

1. Contrast Sri Aurobindo, *The Ideal of the Karmayogin*, p. 53 : "He [the stress of the Hidden Intelligence] is in the seed of man and in that little particle of matter carries habit, character, types of emotion into the unborn child. Therefore heredity is true but if *prajna* were not conceded in the seed, heredity would be false, inexplicable, impossible." The light shed on genetic transmission by the notions of "genotype" and "phenotype" and chromosomes is much more sophisticated than in the psychology of Sri Aurobindo.

2. S. Alexander, *Space, Time & Deity*, Vol. II, p. 348 : "For any level of existence, deity is the next higher empirical quality. It is therefore a variable quality, and as the world goes in time, deity changes with it."

has stressed supramental evolution and is sanguine that beyond mind there would be the revelations of the potencies of the supermind resulting in the transformation of surface terrestrial consciousness. Whitehead's theory of Organism with its notion of Eternal creativity and the twofold primordial and consequent nature of God is an independent philosophy of reality and processual flux and is further removed from the notion of materialist-mechanical evolution. Philology and linguistics have posed further challenges to the concept of biology by making significant the question of the first origins of speech. Furthermore, Phenomenology has not renounced the adherence to the notion of the apprehension of "essences" of things and will not accept the mechanistic mode of evolution.

To the political philosopher evolution, specially in the form of social Darwinism, accepts the devastating doctrine of the struggle for survival. The notions of competition and brutal exploitation have been sought to be reinforced by evolutionism. There is also a trend towards reductionism, in the evolutionary methodology, inasmuch as the higher is genetically explained in terms of the lower. But idealist political philosophy feels that once a qualitatively predominant change has taken place it acquires an autonomy of its own and cannot be reduced to the category out of which it has evolved.

Humanism and Dialectic

The dialectical method signifies various types of intellectual technics and processes. In the sense of a disputationist, argumentative dialogue, the dialectic was used by Socrates to point out contradictions in the arguments of the opponents like Protagoras, Thrasymaches and Glaucon. The concept of Apoha as formulated by the Buddhist logicians and the Kantian concepts of paralogism, amphiboly and antinomy are also illustrations of dialectical argumentation. Hegel also makes a distinction between negative dialectical reason and positive speculative reason. Aristotle regarded the demonstrative method as standing on a higher plane than the logical method of the dialectic. Implication (*arthapatti*) and subsumption (*sambhava*) can also be included in the dialectical art of argumentation. Plato in his *Republic* regarded the dialectic as the highest science of universal ideas which could be pursued after having obtained advanced scientific competence. Furthermore, the dialectic, as opposed to immutability, signifies motion, change and dynamism and in this sense Heraclitus, Buddha, Marx, Engels, Lenin and Bergson are dialecticians. Opposed to the notion of slow evolution, the dialectic stands for intermittent breaks in progress, leap, jump, catastrophic movements and the transformation of quantity into quality and vice versa. At a cosmological level, it is and may be said that the antagonism between Ahriman and Ormuzd, Yan and Yin, Good and Evil[1] (in Manichaenism), Deva and Asura, God and Satan or Buddha and Mara may be regarded as illustrating dialectical polarity.

Humanism adheres to all modes of enquiry, communicative dialectics and analysis which can advance the frontiers of knowledge. Perception and inference, free dialectical communication or *shastrartha*, sympathetic understanding of the values and norms of the role-takers, imaginative reconstruction of situations and empathic projection, history and tradition, implication, induction and generalisation, deductive syllogistic argumentation, comparative aesthetic and economic evaluation and moral assessment, textual exegesis and documentation, field experimentation and rational criticism of scriptures and testaments are accepted by it as legitimate sources for the origination and validation of knowledge. The only touchstone is that any evidence adduced must not run counter to the criterion of reason and must be amenable to intellectual criticism and verification. In the conflicting encounter of intuitions and propositions reason is the sole torchlight. The welter of dissonant voices can be harmonised only through the arbitrament of reason. Intuitional wisdom and supramental gnosis will also have to face the bar of reason if they are to elicit public approval. The Socratic dialectic is a permanent vindication of the autonomy of critical challenging reason.

1. George Catlin, *The Story of Political Philosophers*, p. 576.

But there is nothing sacrosanct about the triple mode of arrangement of events and propositions in terms of thesis, antithesis and synthesis.[1] The dialectical method of Socratic-Platonic argumentation is acceptable to the humanist in the sense that a good deal of truth is elicited through dialogues, debates, discussions, argumentations and counter-argumentations. But there cannot be only three modes of proposition-formulation as vehemently sponsored by Hegel and Marx. There can be two or four or seven or even more modes of predication. The *Syadvada* concept of sevenfold forms of predication has been considered as an invitation to intellectual scepticism which refuses to make categorical statements. It is possible, nevertheless, to accept the position that different predications are possible regarding the diverse real characteristics of the object. Thus *Syadvada* does not teach subjective relativism or scepticism but is a recognition of the possibility of multiple predications regarding the diverse aspects of an object.[2] It rids us of the Hegelian mystery round the number three in the dialectical mode of argumentation. Reality is a multi-moded, multi-aspected infinite, eternal, vast transcendent-cosmic continuum and to assert that the predications of thesis, antithesis, and synthesis exhaust the modes of predication regarding it only reflects a limited frame of reference. What appears as an antithesis to one investigator may be a synthesis for some other. The constitutional divine right monarchy of Teutondom was a synthesis for Hegel. But Marx would regard

1. Lester Ward supported the concept of synorgy or the systematic and organic collaboration of the forces of nature is the sequence : collision, conflict, antagonism, opposition, antithesis, competition, interaction, compromise, collaboration, cooperation and organization.— *An Introduction to the History of Sociology* (1948), p. 175.

2. Reconciliation or synthesis is a basic philosophical problem. The Upanishads wanted to reconcile the *brahman* and the *sarvam* (all). Plato sought to reconcile the ideas and the multiple objects. Aristotle wanted to synthesize form and matter. The Christian theology aimed at reconciling grace and fell. St Augustine wanted to reconcile the city of God and the earthly city. Kant wanted to reconcile the juxtaposition of phenomena and noumena. Hegel wanted to reconcile being and becoming. Bradley aimed at reconciling appearance and reality. Similarly spiritual humanism aims at reconciling absolutism and moral personalism.

it as an antithesis. The classless organisation of society based on the association of producers would be the synthesis for Marx. But for some others this may be only an antithesis, the real synthesis being by the creative advance of the unalienated human self. To Marx, the Greek civilization was the product of innocence but to Whitehead the whole of modern philosophy is only a series of footnotes on Plato. The earlier version of the dialectic considered Gandhi as a bourgeois reactionary, later on, through reassessment he was promoted to the status of a social emancipator. Thus it is evident that the dialectic method lacks the definiteness and rigorous exactitude of a scientific method.

Humanism and Existentialism

Existentialism has been traced to St Augustine and Pascal. Kierkegaard, Berdyaev, Heidegger, Jaspers and Satre are its leading modern spokesmen. Humanism and existentialism are similar in crusading against the abstractions of a scientifically-oriented objective civilization and in advocating the primacy of the subject over the object and also maintaining the fundamental identity of the knowing real subject and the existing apparent subject. Both are opposed to the exaltation of generalizing universalism and plead effectively that the unique individuality and radical personalism of men be given due recognition. Thus ethical and spiritual humanism has some points in common with the philosophy of religious existentialism. Both react against mechanistic materialism and vitalistic objectivism.

Kierkegaard[1] found that the rational idealism of Hegel had no place for devout pathos and religious subjectivism. The

1. Soren A. Kierkegaard (May 5, 1813—November 11, 1855) is hailed as the greatest Danish philosopher and the promulgator of the creed of Christian religious existentialism. He had obtained a Doctor's degree by writing a dissertation entitled *On the Concept of Irony*. He flourished as a rebel against Hegel's dialectic. Temperamentally he was contemplative and an introvert. He was intensely melancholic and subjective and declared almost a war on objectivization in the realms both of society and cognition. He had studied the Bible. He had also read some of the Greek literary works and the tragedies of Shakespeare. He was also

intricate logical categories of Hegel culminating in the Absolute, negate that sense of duality of the human being and the Deity on which ethical notions are found and thus the Hegelian system does not contain enough scope for the justification of moral conduct. Kierkegaard had made a deep study of Hegel's *Logic* but regarded it as intellectual jugglery. Cognitive reason, at best, is only one aspect of life. Mere ratiocination and conceptual disquisition can lead only to paradoxical generalizations. Will and feelings are also essential as the antithesis of reason. If one seeks for a philosophy to help him in his struggles of life, he will find Hegel's *Logic* as a poor guide. Hegel did not remain confined to logical judgments and syllogisms. He wants to comprehend within his system also the historical manifestations of the Spirit and ethical disquisitions. But in his attempts to provide a philosophy of history, historical events lose their specific empirical identity and only logical categories predominate. Historical events and personages do not remain recognisable individual entities but are merged almost in a philosophical sea of concepts. Although Hegel is a dialectician and is concerned with dynamism like Heraclitus, eventually, there is not much difference between his absolute idealism and the monism of Parmenides. Philosophical humanism also reacts against the absolutism of Hegel. If one adheres to the notion that in the process of self-manifestation, the Absolute Idea receives completion then it has to be maintained that the Absolu.e is not perfect and an imperfect developing Absolute is a contradiction in terms. Kierkegaard earnestly seeks a philosophy

influenced by Martin Luther's individualism. Johann Georg Hamann (1730—1788) of Konigsberg, a fiiend of Kant, als had scme impact on the Danish author. Hamann found more wisdom in poetry, myths, allegories and linguistic symbols than in the perfection of logical reason and science and his strictures against reason had impressed Jacobi. Kierkegaard's works reveal his profound sense of agony and desperation at the sight of temporal malformations. As an author, he reacted against the official Christianity of the day. Hegel died when Kierkegaard was only eighteen. The latter developed some opposition to the imposing system of Hegel's absolutist dialectic when he attended Schelling's lectures in 1841-1842 wherein the conceptual architectonic of Hegelianism was attacked. Trendelenberg's logic also provided him some materials for refuting orthodox Hegelianism.

of life but in Hegel's dialectic he finds only an exhibition of concepts. Later on, Kierkegaard also repudiated Schelling's absolutism. Nevertheless, it has to be acknowledged that Hegel's attempt to formulate a dialectical philosophy did influence Kierkegaard to some extent. The latter's system begins in a revolt against Hegelianism but some of the elements of even the inadequate dynamism in it, although inadequate according to Kierkegaard did influence him.[1] But while Hegel provided, according to his own light, the certainty of rational philosophy, Kierkegaard gave only paradoxes. Life is afflicted with so many critical demands that decision-making becomes an exercise based not on intelligent marshalling of communicable objective evidence but on *ad hoc* terms. Humanism, to the contrary, accepts the notion of rational determinate decision-making for building the edifice of a perfection-oriented polity and socie y. It wants to replace guesswork and patchwork by the categories of the logical understanding.

Christianity gave to Kierkegaard the message of the deep significance of the moral individual. In the Biblical story of the redemption of Job he found consolation. In the story of Abraham and Isac, one finds the glorification of the wrath of God and of submission to Him. These religious stories deepened the faith of Kierkegaard in God's compassion. Deeply conscious of his own personal sin, prior to his profound religious transformation, Kierkegaard preached the neutralization of egoism based on rational arrogance. But humanism considers obsession with sin as a morbidity. Kierkegaard was acutely aware of his own sufferings and frustrations and he interpreted the world as characterized by despair. To some extent, thus, he reminds us of Gautama Buddha, Augustine and Schopenhauer. He was pained to find that there is no

1. Kierkegaard's deep subjectivism and intense self-consciousness influenced several later thinkers. Karl Jaspers, Karl Barth and Martin Heidegger, were influenced by his method of philosophical comprehension. Karl Barth who strengthened the movement of "Critical theology" in Germany and Switzerland was influenced by him. Thus the critical theology movement had been indirectly influenced by Kierkegaard. With the issuance of the English translation of his works, his influence is no longer confined to Denmark, Sweden and Germany but is being felt also in France and America.

place for the implementation of the moral teachings of Jesus Christ, St Peter and St Paul in the present day world. It was essential, hence, to revive and restore the transforming character of Christian teachings. There were two schools of Christian thought prevalent at the time. The historical and critical school advocated an exegetical, textual and interpretative approach. The second school hailed Christianity as a permanent ethical gospel. Both these approaches had primarily viewed Christianity as an intellectual instrument according to Kierkegaard. He, on the other hand, wants to interpret Christianity, as a meaningful philosophy of life meant for the enhancement and perfectibility of human character. But he believes that the Christian gospel can never be fully vindicated in temporal manifestations. Time is incapable of manifesting the splendour of the Christian wisdom. Eternity alone is its guarantee. Unlike Kierkegaard, philosophical humanism is not tied to any one religious revelation. Because of its cognitive orientation, it will not accept the trinitarian formula and the theological dogmas of sin, salvation by faith and transsubstantiation. Philosophical humanism is far more appreciative of the historical and scientific modes of comprehension than Kierkegaard.

Many arguments have been advanced for proving the existence of God. The cosmological argument was sponsored in the Upanishads and the Nyaya philosophy. Anselm propounded the ontological argument which was lightly treated by Kant, although Hegel supported it. But according to Kierkegaard, truth cannot be discovered by intellectual dialectics. The Divine Incarnation can manifest the immanent truth. Human reason and symbolical representations are inadequate to grasp the perfect truth. Only the deep layers of subliminal subjectivity can reveal the truth. But philosophical humanism, is far more appreciative of the role of critical reason in the advance of the frontiers of knowledge. It will like to scrutinize the intuitions and insights gained by subjective inwardization and contemplation. Hence to it the religious subjectivism of Kierkegaard is inadequate for comprehending the absolute integral truth. But in its crusade against the abstract formalism of the Hegelian dialectic and the dehumanizing character of the scientific worship of objective external nature, the religious existentialism of

Kierkegaard and Berdyaev partly shares the spirit of the ethical and spiritual humanism.

There are some notable differences between existentialism and philosophical humanism. First, while Kierkegaard's existentialism is based on the historicity of a specific revelation, philosophical humanism is based on the fundamental primordial principle of an absolute Existence which is consciousness. Secondly, while Kierkegaard accepts the notion of immersion in the inner depths, humanic activity and contemplation are synthesised. Thirdly, while existentialism is attached to revealing the experience-generating aspects of *Augst* (anxiety) and *Forcht* (fear, terror), humanism pleads for the conquest of *dukkha* and *bhayam*.

Nor can the existentialism as represented by Berdyaev and Sartre escape the criticism of the humanist. Existentialism appears to be infected with deep inadequacies.[1] It is partly irrational in its approach and has no faith in communitarian participatory mass democracy and rational progress. Its quest for the authenticity of personal experience and decision-making is not capable of realization on any broad level. To the humanist, the rise of existentialism is partly correlated with the growth of social and economic contradictions which are concurrent with the advance of gigantic metropolitanism and technocracy. Its inner retreat[2] proceeds from the non-recognition of the fatal flaw in modern society stemming from the simultaneous juxtaposition of immense wealth and mass agrarian privation. It has no message for the alleviation of the penury, destitution and misery of the workers and peasants. Hence existentialism appears as utopian and as a species of "fatigued

1. H. J. Laski, *The Dilemma of Our Times* (London, 1952), pp. 139-44. It is somewhat surprising that Laski should have counted Sorel and Ortega Gasset among the spokesmen of existentialism — *Ibid.*, p. 139.

2. Jean-Paul Sartre, *Being and Nothingness : An Essay on Phenomenological Ontology* (E.T. by H. E. Barnes, London, 1969), p. 29 : "... anguish is the mode of being of freedom as consciousness of being; it is in anguish that freedom is, in its being... Kierkegaard describing freedom in the force of what one lacks characterizes it as anguish in the face of freedom. But Heidegger... considers anguish instead as the apprehension of nothingness, contradictory; ..."

scholasticism"[1] because some values as proximate goals of action have their intimate relations with socio-economic processes.[2] To the humanist, to seek a transcendental or revelatory or intuitional root for values is not plausible in the eras of critical science and rationalism. He is not refuting the private sanctity of transforming religious experiences but he is urging that these have no large-scale capability of generalization and public inspection. Hence they cannot claim sociological relevance to the modern world which is subjected to so many contradictions and pressing challenges.

Humanism and the Behavioural Sciences

The human person is not pure intelligence. Through study, meditation, writing, teaching, intuitional insights, role-performance, and other types of experiences, it gains information which are systematized into knowledge. Thus it is not plausible to conceive of it as pure *noesis* or unadulterated *sattva*. Volition is also an integral aspect of the human person.[3] Unless physically incapacitated, a man wants to do something. Through participation in novel activities, he enriches the nature and bounds of his experiences. He also craves for emotional satisfactions. There are certain basic drives or character-constituents and permanent wishes which he wants to satisfy. Without such emotional gratifications man's nature is dwarfed and stunted. Hence at least a partial gratification of libidinal and attitudinal complexes is essential. The extra-cognitive aspects of the human psyche have been conceptualized by the Upanishads in their notions of man as *shraddhamaya* and *kamamaya*. The reactions of a man in course of intersubjective interactions have a good deal to contribute to the moulding of his personality. When a man reacts to a situation it is as a total complex and

1. *Ibid*., p. 149.
2. "Values are born, in fact, of the ability to satisfy mass-demands; they wither away as that ability diminishes."— H. J. Laski, *Faith*, *Reason and Civilization*, p. 66.
3. Cf. F. H. Bradley, *Appearance and Reality*, p. 200 : "For our Absolute was not a mere intellectual system. It was an experience overriding every species of one-sidedness, and throughout it was at once intuition and feeling and will."

not as any specific segment. The totality of reactions reveal the complex mode of experiencing of man as a physical, vital, emotional, cognitive, ego-gratifying and delight-loving complex structure.

Philosophical humanism considers psychic phenomenology as expressive of the total personality of man and hence it does not regard the tension between the instinctive, concupiscible, affectual and emotive sides of a man's inner being[1] and his rational, deliberative and cognitive dimensions as permanent. Mind, intellect, Ahamkara and Chitta, (or the three of the four Vyuhas — Samkarshana, Pradyumna and Aniruddha of the Pancharatras) are not separate sectors of the physiological organism. Man's inner functioning is a dynamic perpetual process of formation of perceptions. There is no physiological sanction for the autonomous habitations of the mind and the intellect (Mahat or Vijnana) in the inner regions of the body. The neurological functioning is conceptualized in terms of Manas and Buddhi. There is no valid foundation for a rigorous hipartite or a tripartite faculty psychology but certainly the cerebral system is the basis of the modes of functioning known as cognition, determinate volition and conation or feeling. In this sense philosophical humanism is integral and not sectoral. Intuitional self-awareness, overmental perception, phenomenological understanding, supramental gnosis, dialectical noesis, and ratiocinative consciousness have no watertight separate localities of their own. They are all aspects of the intricate functioning of the brain structure. Conscious life is dependent on cerebral activity. It is possible through prolonged meditation, concentration and deep absorption in the subject-matter of enquiry leading to total withdrawal from external distractions to find out meanings and truth which are beyond the normal range of apperception of the common man. But there is no ontological hiatus between rational cognition and spiritual wisdom. The unconscious, the subconscious, the ultra-marginally

1. Aurobindo's conception of a transmigrating, evolving, subliminal, Chaitya Purusha, which is born out of the Divine (the son of God) and stands behind the manifestation is too occult a notion to receive any corroboration from experimental psychology.

conscious, the supraliminally conscious, the conscious and the super-conscious as layers of apprehension are all integral aspects of the functional dynamism of the brain.[1] Even the so-called super-conscious dimension involving the immediate direct awareness of the supreme transcendent is concretely experienced at the level of the mental functioning and the notion of the merging of the subject and the object is only a poetic mode of communication.

The appreciation of *rasa*, the realization of *dhvani* (sound), poetic embellishments and rhetorical implications and the cognition of the Sphota of words and sentences are also the functions of the dynamic mental mode. The differential types of optical, acoustic, gustatory, olfactory and tactile sensations are also related to the brain organism.

There is no anatomical-physiological foundation for the hypothesis of the habitation of the soul in the pineal gland or the heart[2] or the pericardium (*puritat*) or the cranium. The soul or self is the conceptualization of a man's total personality.[3] But the conception of the soul as a substantial entity invested with the heavy load of impressions of previous existences which can be recollected in the deep inward experience of the highest super-consciousness, and as oriented towards a further habitation in some super-terrestrial realms of hell, purgatory and paradise where it can experience either perpetual perdition or time-bound heavenly bliss or even perfect beatitude and swim in a vast ocean of delight and supergnosis is beyond scientific modes of investigation and hence not amenable to inter-subjective validation and verification. Immutable being and

1. The human brain, enclosed in the cranium, consists of (A) Cerebrum, (B) Corpus callosum, (C) Pineal body, (D) Vermis, (E) Cerebellum, (F) Spinal Cord, (G) Medulla oblongate, (H) Oculomotor nerve, (I) Pituitary gland.

2. "In the heart, truly, is the self (*atman*). Here there are those hundred and one channel. To each of these belong a hundred smaller channels. To each of these belong seventy-two thousand branching channels. (*hita*). Within them moves the diffused breath."— *Prasna Upanishad* (E. T. by Hume).

3. Cf. S. Radhakrishnan, *An Idealist View of Life*, p. 261 : "The soul is the actuality of the organic body in man, even as vision is the actuality of the eye."

multiple cosmic determination are integral components of the Supreme Real. Impersonal indeterminate existence and polycentric multiform becomings are equally real aspects of Reality. Humanism, thus, is not a philosophy of transcendence. Nor does it postulate the negation of volition, conformation (samskara) and emotion. It only teaches the mobilisation of mental and physical energy for the glorification of man and his ideals. But it also wants to go beyond terrestrial immanency. The earth is the theatre of man's concrete social and cultural actions but physical, chemical and biological processes like radiation, gravitation, refraction, combustion, intus-susception, respiration and reproduction do not constitute the optimum field for the manifestation of human energy. Man has to go beyond them. Through meditation, concentration and deep absorption man can release creative altruistic forces and synergy for collective development, total social amelioration and cultural regeneration. Thus it is possible to go beyond fear, cerebral disorders and disenchantment, nervous breakdown, corroding anxiety and psychosis and obtain strength for the neutralization of stagnation, pain, affliction, malady and disorder. Humanism, thus sanctifies the concept of human ideals and their healing, regenerative and transforming power.

At the level of critical logic, personality is unreal according to the absolutistic school of Vedanta. The supreme real being the Absolute, all other distinctions are temporary and illusory.[1] Even in the Samkhya conception of the multiplicity of selves or Purushas there is no explication of their variations and differences from one another. According to Buddhism also, the psycho-physical personality is unreal. It has, hence, to be transcended and even negated for the realisation of Nirvana. The modern behavioural sciences, on the other hand, emphasize

1. Both Aurobindo and Berdyaev emphasize the spiritual character of the individual person and maintain that the real and not the empirical nature-worshipping individual is creative force. But there is greater stress on creativity and activism in Berdyaev than in Aurobindo. Aurobindo maintains that the true spiritual Atman is behind the flux of forces and the personality acting through nature is a formulation and emanation of the transcendent impersonality.

the concept of ego-functions like sense perception, conscious thought, memory, control of motor action, harmonization and taking recourse to projection and regression. Humanism is in agreement with the modern behavioural sciences in not acknowledging any verifiable evidence for the ontological substantial reality of a soul or Purusha. But it believes that the totality of the empirical personality of man has to be developed through a conservation of physical, mental, moral and spiritual energy for the pursuit of one's Karma. A life of the synthesis of Karmayoga and Jnanayoga is the only method to achieve distinction through which one can cast influence on the world. Martyrdom in a noble cause is the supreme way of casting the impact of one's personality on the temporal fluctuations of the world.

Man's full growth has been retarded due to various bio-psychical factors. There are inhibitions and restraining and impeding factors due to hormonal imbalance and other neurochemical, psychobiological and physiological malfunctioning like psychomotor retardation and catastrophic overaction. One can witness psychiatric phenomena like emotional retardation, irreversible emotional instability, nervous convulsions, fantastic autism and various types of phobias. Trauma, dementia praecox, obsessive-compulsive, depressive and anxiety reactions, stupor psychosis and psychoneurosis are the inevitable consequences of an unjust, irrational social order characterized by terrific cut-throat competition and rampant jealousy. There are enough evidences of the growth of psychoneurotic symptomatology in an affluent society and even post-industrial civilization. Frustration, phobias, restrictions, inappropriate identifications and maladaptive orientations result in organising alienation. Alienation is bound to increase in a society that loses the organic moorings in spiritual and moral values. Desperately frustrated persons constitute dangers for the democratic regime. Totalitarianism is the necessary consequence of the accentuation of alienation. Humanism pleads that the new behavioural and psychobiological technics should be utilized for the growth of community-oriented behaviour so that the psychological bases of alienation can be neutralized. For the development of sensory capacities, certain physiological technics can be utilized. Modern physiological psychology will sanction an epigenetic and functional interpretation of behaviour. Instinctive reactions and indeterminate perceptions have to be replaced by or transformed into goal-oriented behaviour defined by preconceptions. The release of tensions and the getting over of hypochondria, guilt-feeling melancholia and anxieties is essential if the psychic energy is not to be wasted in useless and deviant functions. Humanism is firmly committed to moral personalism and total egalitarianism and hence inhibitory and paradoxical behaviour are not encouraged by it. On the other hand, it wants the fixation of psychic energy upon dynamic moral stereotypes in the process of the psychological evolution of man. Mere repression would not serve the purpose because as the Gita says — *nigrahaḥ kim karishyati.* Only a generalised diffusion of moral and spiritual sentiments can result in the suppression, and not extinction of cathetic malfunctioning.

Humanism as a Philosophy of Life

A dynamic gospel of spiritual activism is the necessary logical implication of a philosophy of absolute idealism. Pessimism and ascetic renunciation may suit certain souls who are of an ectomorphic constitutional build and have a detached orientation to life. A life of hedonism, physical and vital gratifications and hectic activity satisfies the mesomorphic type of people. The endomorphic type may like to live in adjustment with the collectivity. But the philosophic humanist does not feel attached to mere phenomenal activism. He has a cognitive bent of mind and he wants to know the absolute Truth. He thus wants to synthesize in his life Karmayoga and Jnanayoga.

A system of humanist ontology and epistemology must provide inspiration to a man in agony. Mere linguistic discussions and logical enquiries have their use in academies and seminars. Logical positivism and logical empiricism are not philosophies of life as they have no dynamic *elan* for human regeneration. Humanism seeks the expansion of the range of awareness for the appreciation of the frontiers of the multidimensional man. This can be possible either through disinterested action or through philosophic and scientific contemplation. In the conceptualization of the two triads — (i) Bharati, Ida and Sarasvati and (ii) Mahi, Hotra and Sarasvati, the ancient Indians attempted to glorify a life of dedication to the pursuit of universal encyclopaedic knowledge. If Plato stood for the ascription of rational and authoritative decision-making to the philosopher king, the ancient Vedanta conceived of universal and transcendent Reason (Sat = Chit) as the being of the ultimate Real. In Indian culture Rama, Krishna, Janaka, Shivaji, Tilak, Gandhi and others illustrate the path of Karmayoga. Buddha, Yajnavalkya, Mahavira, Samkara, Ramanuja, Tulasi, Dayananda, Vivekananda, Rama Tirtha, among others, illustrate the contemplative mode of life. There is no real contradiction, however, between the lives devoted to Karmayoga and Jnanayoga. It is only a matter of emphasis. The Karmayogin also wants to cultivate a detached orientation and disfavours hectic kinetism and a recourse to reckless endeavours. The Jnanayogin disfavours introversion and an attitude of indifference to the maladies of the world. The essence of life is to enrich the cultural heritage through one's own unique achievements and attainment of excellence.

Humanism does not exalt the conquest of political power. Power and sovereignty, it regards as means and instruments to be used with caution and moderation for the eventual promotion of intelligence and a sense of sanctity of life. Kautilya was content to be the adviser of Chandragupta Maurya and led a life of curtailment of wants. The person who illustrates in his life the flowering of Rita, Dharma, Satya and Sila was to be accorded higher deference and veneration than the holder of authority. Thus the glory of human life is conceived as consisting in self-abnegation, the neutralization of vanity, cupidity, irascibility and anger, magnanimity of heart, moderation, and the pursuit of equity and justice. Aristotle stated that animals were created for the use of man but Buddha, the highest embodiment of compassion was willing to sacrifice his life for the sake of animal welfare. In the second canto of the *Raghuvamsa,* Kalidasa has portrayed Dilipa as willing to sacrifice his life for the sake of a cow. If compassion be the criterion for judging the advancement of universalist altruistic culture, then the Hindu-Buddhist culture is unparalleled in the world.

A gospel of universal compassion cannot be charged with being abstract. It shows narrowness to call it "morbid",[1] "spirit-weakening"[2] or smitten with "premature decrepitude"[3] or "bearing the stamp of senility."[4] The Vedic-Buddhistic philosophy of life is a dynamic call for the acquisition of the virility and vitality[5] of the body and mind so that a universalism-oriented existence can be prolonged for one hundred years and even beyond. Physical immortality is an infantile aspiration. Death cannot be conquered but a life of disciplined moderation nurtured by medical resources and physical exercise can, generally, bring longevity. The conceptualization of different kinds of Pranas is a testimony to the quest for dynamic vital energy. A gospel of life oriented to the dynamic realization of the Virat or cosmic power of predetermination immanent in the universe and its incorporation in the life of the nation, society and individual is not the cherishing of an idle conformist routine. Contemplative absorption does not amount to immersion in a dull mysticism. If India could produce a Panini, there is no reason why she cannot produce a Newton and Einstein. The *Ramayana* of Valmiki is bigger than the *Iliad* and the *Odyssey* combined. The *Mahabharata* which is four times the size of the *Ramayana* and bigger than the Bible, the *Iliad* and the *Odyssey* taken together cannot but be regarded as the standing monument of constant hard efforts at the cultivation of genius. Hence the support to a positive world-affirming scheme of values for the realization of national identity and integrity and for the emancipation of

1. A. Barth, *Religions of India*, p. 137.
2. *Ibid.*
3. *Ibid.*, p. 136.
4. *Ibid.*, p. 137.
5. The wisdom of the Veda consists in promulgating a philosophy of dynamic spiritualism, as in Hegel and Gentile. The Vedic cosmogonic accounts illustrate the notions of *tapas* and *Ikshana* and contain elements of vitalism. The word Visvakarma glorifies cosmic action. The vedic psychology teaches the cultivation of noble sentiments (*siva samkalpa*). The Vedic philosophy of life has partial similarity to the cult of "heroic vitalism" propounded by Carlyle, Nietzsche, Bernard Shaw and Oswald Spengler.

mankind from the infecting contradictions, alienations and psychoses is a call for the mobilisation of all types of energy inherent in man-in-nature. Humanism stresses the significance of the dynamic moment (kshana). The concrete moment has stupendous significance. Life is made up of such moments and hence every moment has to be utilized. Every moment, qualitatively, is of equal significance with any other moment. Hence the recognition of the immensity of the concrete moment as an unique, never to be repeated, opportunity for the engaging in strenuous activity for self-realization and altruistic good is essential.

Humanism teaches the cultivation of the spirit of optimism. Amidst encircling gloom and sorrow, it pleads for the incorporation of the spirit of conquering youth aspiring after gaining novel experiences with vigour, zest and vitality. The spirit accepting the pressing challenges and heroically responding to them is essential. Humanism symbolises adventurousness, quest, a spirit of enquiry and scrutiny, a plastic responsiveness to the rising demands of the situation and an organic capacity for assimilation, adaptation and adjustment. These qualities have to be retained for life. They make life interesting and enjoyable. A capacity of youthful mental resilience prevents the stagnation and decadence of the human spirit. Anything that makes a person sick, cowardly and weak has to be consciously avoided. There has to be a deliberate cultivation of the free interchange of ideas and the simultaneous pursuit of classicism, philosophy and the natural sciences is desirable. Humanism pleads for the enhancement of physical and mental powers in order to master the ever-pressing challenges. Without physical vigour, mental decadence also sets in. Only a vigorous mental alertness and a capacity to determine our lives in response to the ideals of a noble existence can give us the necessary fervour, vitality and zest without which life becomes a dull tale of insignificant details. But a vital fervour (*prana-sakti*) should not degenerate into living dangerousness. Humanism urges a quest for physical and physiological health, security and job-satisfaction through the pursuit of a vocation in the social universe. But this material pursuit has to be supplemented with the quest for rectitude, integrity, human dignity, and a transcendent interest in the satisfaction of the immanent desire to know the meaning and value of life in the cosmos.

A philosophy of integration is essential for the modern world. Whatsoever be the realm of one's activity, from political and judicial participation, to painting or philosophizing or contemplative absorption it is essential to concentrate our energies upon the task. That is the way to achieve happiness. Happiness has its secret in integration. The path to integration is the concentration of our volitional, emotional, physical and vital energies and only through such concentration is the realization of happiness possible. A running after flimsy and fluctuating criteria can never give lasting peace and happiness. Integration postulates a wholeness of attention. It is necessary to have one foot firmly planted on earth for the realization of terrestrial prosperity, mundane satisfaction and the redemption of the debt to the ancestors. There should be enough material commodities for the gratification of the appetitive propensities of all the inhabitants of the country. But it is also essential to soar to the heights of philosophical contemplation of the Absolute substance or cosmic-transcendent Reason. Without vision and idealism no great civilization can be built. A satisfaction in the engrossment in the normal pursuits of everyday life is not enough. A transcendence is required. Hence if we have to look to the earth, we have not to forget the visions of the heavens. The range of our vision has to cover *dyavaprithivi*. That is the only way to attain individual happiness and to build the edifice of a worthy and noble civilization and an ethically-oriented culture. It is imperative to harness our energies for the realization of that goal. The propensities for consumer satisfaction and the acquisition of political power have to be duly satisfied but they have to be integrated with the other worthy and noble pursuits.

Idealist humanism inculcates a spirit of boldness, courage and strength in facing the challenges and terrific struggles of life. Free India has witnessed the multiplication of the opportunities for the citizens. But still there is a vast gap and widening chasm between the openings and opportunities on the one side and the expectations, aspirations, claims and felt needs on the other. Thus the critical areas of decision-making will be numerous specially in view of the economic malfunctionings in the system and the possible emergence of international crises. But the protagonist of idealist humanism is sanguine that the teachings of the great political philosophers of the East and West on the concept of man as a moral and spiritual subject must have their impact on providing the enlarged frame of mind and the strength of will needed to ride over the crises and challenges.

Critique of Economic Determinism

The command over economic resources is a great factor in human life but is never the sole factor. For certain individuals of a heroic and prophetic mould it may not be even a great factor. But if we talk in terms of a long-range sociological context, we can say that for the vast number of human beings it is an important factor. Money, certainly, is a basic force. It makes the struggle for existence easier. The quest for money has been responsible for the immense strides made towards the conquest of nature. But money is only one factor in social existence however important it might be.

According to the ancient Vedanta, man is governed by three dominant quests — *Vittaishana*, the desire for wealth, *putraishana*, the desire for progeny and *lokaishana*, the desire for fame, esteem, prestige and honour. Modern sociologists and social psychologists have also tried to identify some of the prime motivating factors in human life. Pareto discusses the 'residues' of combination, persistence of aggregates, sociality, personal integrity and sex. He also refers to the significant role of economic interests and environmental factors in human history. Some other thinkers discuss the primary wishes, the prepotent reflexes, and drives of men.

Man is a complex being. He has a physical side of existence and in the attainment of satisfactions relevant to the appetitive and physiological aspects, property, certainly, is a very important agency. But man is also an emotional, aesthetic, moral and spiritual being. He wants autonomy, spontaneity, contemplation of truth and goodness and finally absorption in spiritual depths and heights. For the realization of these diverse emotional, intellectual and spiritual capacities, money can be only a very subordinate category. We must eat before we can contemplate upon truth but eating is not the causal factor for the attainment of truth. Buddha condemned the path of extremism. It is true that before he could attain the knowledge leading to *Nirvana*, he had to eat the sweet dish prepared by Sujata. But it would be fantastic to say that partaking of the meal was the cause of the attainment of liberating knowledge. It is a fact that before one can make advancements in the mental realms, he must have the necessary means to satisfy the desire for food and shelter. But physiological gratifications are only the elementary conditions of doing something higher and nobler. In themselves they can provide only pleasure which has a sensuous orientation. Happiness is a higher category than pleasure and depends on the integration of will and intellect.

If we turn over the pages of history we find that the dominant role-takers did not crave for wealth. Akbar would have been happy to provide a governorship of Bihar or Bengal or Gujarat to Rana Pratap. But Pratap refused all monetary allurements with disdain. He roamed in the woods and jungles of northern India and testified to the undying valiant spirit of man. Was Shivaji in quest of money? The heroes and martyrs of Kurukshetra and Thermopylae (480 B.C.) were not in search of money. Moses became a prophet when he prayed to God. The makers of early Mauryan history — Chanakya and Chandragupta led a life of stern simplicity. They cared more for the good of the country than for money. Buddha and Tilak and Gandhi cared more for truth than for money.

If somebody were to say that I have referred to the extraordinary men, I may point out that even in the lives of ordinary men a tiresome pursuit of appetitive covetousness leads to frustration and neurosis. Happiness lies in the reduction of wants and not in the endless quest of monetary satisfactionis. In the industrial countries of the world a sense of despar segmentation and delocalization of the psyche from its natural moorings are overtaking people even though there is unprecedented prosperity. Modern civilization has made life easier but highly complicated and competitive. The inventions of science have made the future existence of human civilization itself a doubtful proposition. Perhaps it may be essential to turn towards the old spirited and moral values stressed in Indian and Greek philosophy. Some of the western thinkers like Schopenhauer, Schlegel, Emerson and Thoreau have also testified to the worth of the wisdom of the *Upanishads*, the *Bhagavadgita* and other scriptures which teach the significance of simple life and disinterested action.

Humanism as Ontopolitics : Man as a Moral and Spiritual Subject

Behavioural research in the social sciences does not accept *manas*, *buddhi*, *ahamkara* and *chitta* as substances. There are only mental and intellectual processes.[1] Nor is there any evidence for a tripartite division of the soul into the rational courageous and appetitive parts. Nevertheless, the predominant theme of philosophical humanism that man is a moral and spiritual subject need not be given up. Psychological researches are bound to make us revise our earlier notions regarding soul, mind, rational intellect and understanding. Several areas of modern research are also deepening the human dimension. Ergonomics[2] or biotechnology is sponsoring a human factors approach even in engineering. Qualitative and quantitative personnel requirements information, is now being considered a necessity for the success of project engineering and for handling the involved problems of a man-machine system organization. That the empirical man as we find him today has developed certain moral aspirations and spiritual values, no scientist can deny. Amidst the diversity and plurality of interpersonal confrontations, there are individual and social evidences that confirm the emergence of the moral synthesis in man leading to the dynamization of the steady intellect

1. In the light of physiological psychology, the categories, thinking mind, dynamic mind, externalizing mind, vital mind and mechanical mind (Sri Aurobindo, *More Lights on Yoga*, pp. 24-25; *Letters, first series*, pp. 175-80) only stress modes of mentation and do not imply layers of mind as an ontological entity. Nor is there any evidence for the habitation of the physical mind in the throat-centre, (*Ibid.*, p. 28). Or of mind as a mental substance living "either in an inert torpor or an immobile science" (*The Life Divine*, Vol. II, p. 16).

2. *Ergon*=work and *Nomos*=law. Other synonyms of ergonomics are bioastronomics, biodynamics, bioengineering, manned systems technology.

(*Vyavasayatmika buddhi*) and responding to the intimations of a chastened conscience (*Antaratman*). Even the egoist, the narcissist, the sadist, the masochist, the paranoid, the hypochondriac, the anomic and the psycho-neurotic are not to be given up as permanently lost souls. Even they manifest a continuity of recurrent patterns of conduct and can be made amenable to the energisation of the forces of inner cohesiveness and common goal-gratification.

Ontological humanism accepts the conception of man as a spiritual and moral subject. The physique of man is constituted of physical and chemical energy and on that basis performs biological functions.[1] Man's personality has a biological and vital base but in the course of evolution, man has also developed significant psychological dimensions. For carrying on the social existence he adheres to certain social norms and moral values. In the Indian Smritis, Puranas and specially in the Buddhist and Jaina schools, there is a detailed catalogue of moral values that is of great worth. Max Muller and Deussen have noted the significance of the Vedanta as an inner-directed philosophy of life and as a foundation of pure morality. The Buddhist code of ethics incorporates into its Dharma a marvelously perceptive insight into virtues that are meant to curtail the pretensions and selfish projections of the ego. The conquest of lust is one of the cardinal notions of ancient Hindu and Buddhist ethics. These schools stress the enhancement of the moral aspects of human personality. Morality is not merely the partitioned or individual side of social ethics. It (morality) is the realm of conscious practice of self-abnegation. Social norms aim only at interpersonal accommodation, harmony, reconciliation and adjustment. But when man wants to go beyond the realm of the reconciliation of claims and counter-claims and deliberately looks to the practice of those norms which regard personal sacrifice as a higher category than the recognition of one's due

1. One of the prime concepts of the ancient Indian psycho-physiology is the theory of five pranas—*prana* (respiratory), *apana* (alimentary), *samana* (metabolic), *vyana* (circulation) and *udana* (special senses). Later five more pranas—*naga*, *k urma*, *krikala*, *devadatta* and *dhananjaya* were added. In books of modern anatomy and physiology, there is no recognition of the fivefold-tenfold pranas. At best they are functional and not entitative.

but limited claims, he can be said to be operating in the realm of morality. Thus while the key concept of sociality is justice, the dominant category of morality is the quest of the sacrifice of the ego. When parents are ready to sacrifice their own interests for the well-being of their children, they can be said to be traversing the realm of morality. Thus while the notion of ego-recognition belongs to the province of sociality, morality aims at the pursuit of self-sacrifice as the higher category.

Morality has its roots in culturally preserved values. These latter, according to the believers, are derived either from revelation or from the superior intuitive wisdom of the prophet or the divine incarnation. But to the intellectual, one dominant source of morality is the steady intellect. The rational dictates of the steady intellect teach us that unless we make sustained efforts at our ego-curtailment, society cannot have a stable homostatic existence. But society is neither super-organic nor super-individual. It has no collective spiritual consciousness or separate ego.

Man *qua* man is a social being. But as a moral subject, he has to be in pursuit of the curtailment of egoistic interests. As a spiritual subject, man is an integral organic entity representing the focalised unity of diverse experiences. But he can be said to be a spiritual being when he realizes that eventually all humanity and even all creatures are to be made the objects of compassion because all of them are equally amenable to physical extinction at the time of death and are equally subjected to all types of pain and psychological grief. This recognition further broadens his realm of compassionate role-performance. In the sphere of spiritual awareness, he may apprehend all beings as the portions or reflections or appearances of the one fundamental unitary-organic Reality. Thus the position of man as a moral and spiritual subject gains significance in the modern world of claims, opposed systems of rights, maladies and anguishes.

The acceptance of the notion of man as a moral and spiritual subject has been the prime gospel of idealism. Buddhism, Jainism, Stoicism, Christianity and Kantianism have emphasized the pursuit of a virtuous life. The spiritual dimension of life and the cosmos has been emphasized by the Vedanta, the Samkhya, the Nyaya and the exponents of modern idealism.

But the spiritual conception has been challenged by the various schools of materialism, vitalism, neomechanistic biology, pragmatism, naturalism, Marxism, Freudianism and hedonism. There is, of course, no scientific evidence for the independent ontological existence either in the atomic or infinite dimension of the human soul or psychic being or self. Although some Yogins and mystics claim to have the certitude of immediate experience regarding the soul or self, that experience not being capable of public verification, does not have general evidentiary value. But even the materialist will grant that man has a social and moral dimension which cannot be considered as a mere reflex or as an epiphenomenon of matter in motion or as the qualitative emergent of molecular movement. Qualitatively, man's social and moral dimensions have now almost assumed a recognizable existence as contrasted to matter, mass and energy. The materialist, the mechanist and vitalist would be willing to acknowledge that man's spiritual dimension is the organic, essential totality of his existence. But spirit as the totality is not the mathematical summation of the physical, the psychological, the social and the moral dimensions of man. It is an integrating principle which teaches the dedicated pursuit of the phases and aspects of the multi-dimensional man. It is only the heightening of the spiritual dimension which provides solace to man in times of trouble and deep frustration. When in periods of critical agony and in face of death, man refuses to yield and bow down he is vindicating the superiority of the spirit. Thus spirit is the totalizing or integrating principle. Since there is no available concrete evidence of the transmigration of souls, or for an atomic mind which leaves the body on cardiac arrest for the present, we have to be content with ascribing a limited temporal span to the spirit. In other words, the annihilation of the body virtually amounts to the annihilation of the physico-vital base of the spirit. If one adheres to the metaphysical position of Absolute consciousness as the Reality, it may be possible to hold that at death the personal spirit merges into the Absolute consciousness.

The acceptance of the philosophical position of man as a moral and spiritual subject postulates, at the sociological level, a quest for a just society which rises above narrow sectarianism, parochialism and the pursuit of egoistic interests. An ethical and spiritual idealism cannot sanction the exploitation and the suppression of the weaker sections. But it will not adhere to the gospel of the violent liquidation of the expropriators. At the economic level, it will pursue those technics and methods which can make possible the realisation of the personality of all persons possible. Hence it will try for the liberalisation of both capitalism and communism. Unlike either, it will not be governed by a quest for the abundances of goods and for the maximization of appetitive satisfactions. Economics pertain to a vital but only one aspect of life and should not be transformed into an all-governing mechanism. At the political level, ethico-spiritual humanism derives legitimacy from uncoerced consensualism and adheres to the doctrine of natural right to life and liberty. It also accepts the tent of the judicial review of legislation and administration and the decentralization of power.

Philosophical or spiritual humanism is a comprehensive integral world-view. It adheres to the concept of divine humanity[1] and holds that the Atman is irreducible to the qualitatively differentiated motion of matter or energy. It wants to remove the despicable social and economic situations which reduce more than half of the population to an existence of penury which, in turn, breeds numerous maladies and alienates the individual from a stable community life. It wants to utilize the technics both of Yoga end psychoanalysis to cure the maladies of man. It holds that ethical notions are not the mere rationalizations of class interests but have an element of categorical and apodictic imperativeness about them. If society and the individual would lightly treat the moral laws and govern their actions by mere sensuous criteria, humanity can only head towards disaster.

1. Cf. the Biblical statement : "this mortal must put on immortality"... "mortality swallowed up of life"— Cf. Kant, *Religion Within the Limits of Pure Reason*, III, 1, 7 : "...the universal religion of reason, and so into a moral, that is a Divine community on earth,..."

The quadruple goals of man can be thus illustrated :

(I) Individuation as
Ego-assertion (Tamasika, Rajasika and Ahamkara)

(II) Reconciliation of social tensions, cleavages and struggles (Lokayatta Samavaya) by the enhancement of sociation.

(III) Moral Awareness of the dignity of the person through the practice of Sila (*Yama-niyama*)

(IV) Realisation of the vanity of lust and cupidity in force of the certitude of death and the consequent generation of a feeling of identity with the universe (*Ekatvam-anupashyataḥ*).

CHAPTER II

ETHICAL ABSOLUTISM AND HUMANIST VALUES

The Scientific Methodology and Ethical Absolutism

Whenever there has been the advance of positivism, scepticism, naturalism, anthropological relativism and quantitativism, there has been a natural reaction against that. Vedantism, Buddhism, Plato, Christianity, Kant, and the Indian idealists have sponsored the view that political behaviour cannot be understood and corrected without stress on moral values. The work of evaluation is an enterprise in premium-putting. Whenever one puts a premium on some thing in comparison to another, he is evaluating that as higher than the other one. Values constitute a broad category. Ethics as the science of moral norms, standards, maxims and postulates is concerned with one broad domain of values. But value is a more generic term than morality and ethics as there may also be religious values of the holy and aesthetic values of beauty. If man is a moral and spiritual subject then he has to have some standards and goals of action. Humanism is committed to ethical absolutism because it regards the right as the good and stresses the practice of virtue as altruism. Mere scientific and sociological relativism based on cultural pluralism does not satisfy it. The sensualism and sentimentalism associated with some aspects of the fifteenth century Italian Renaissance also do not appeal to it. It takes the question of the validation and justification of the ethical criteria and standards very seriously and pleads for a rationalist and intuitionist approach to ethics. It is thus opposed to fanatical scripturalism, moral positivism and hedonism as well as to ethical neutrality in the social sciences.

At the outset one can differentiate the two levels at which the question of ethical neutrality in the social sciences has been discussed in the works on methodology. First, there is the academic problem of allowing a teacher to present his own ethical imperatives and ideologies in the university classes. The humanist is a liberal in this sphere and he would allow a conservative and a radical to teach jurisprudence, social philosophy and economics to the university classes. He would only grudgingly tolerate, however, the continued systematic inculcation of one's own valuational preferences in the classes although sometimes the student-respondents would be in a position to make allowances for the exaggerations and overtones of such a teacher whose commitments are known to them. But in the name of academic freedom he would not like that communist teachers be permitted to teach the students such lessons as lead to the weakening of nationalistic urges and the glorification of antidemocratic technics. In the class-room the humanist would essentially appreciate the dedicated pursuit of the "task"[1] assigned to the teacher at a specialized level because the university hall is neither a pulpit nor a platform. Furthermore, in consonance with a tolerant academic attitude should be the policy of editors for the research journals wherein they should be ready to accept the contributions of scholars professing different economic and political ideologies.

Second, there is the ongoing question of value imputation or judging the satisfactoriness or unsatisfactoriness of a policy or a work of art or a philosophical or sociological treatise. In this sense one can evaluate the excellence or otherwise of the Smritis of Manu and Yajnavalkya, Homer's *Iliad*, Shakespeare's *Othello*, or the works of Dayananda, Tolstoy and Tilak.[2] One can even take into his purview the experiences of Gautama

1. Cf. Max Weber, "The Meaning of 'Ethical Neutrality' in Sociology and Economics," *The Methodology of the Social Sciences*, E. T. by E. A. Shils and H. A. Finch (Glencoe, 1949), p. 6.

2. *Ibid.*, p. 1.

Buddha, Teresa and Ramakrishna. Through empathic projection and social enquiry it is possible to know the meaning, the logic-psychological implications and the circumstances of the historical origin of the works taken up for analysis. But such a work of historically-oriented value-interpretation based on empathic understanding and sympathetic projection is only the prelude to the rational task of deciphering and conceptualizing the major causes of cultural, social, economic and political phenomena. This process of rational causal explanation conjoined with value-analysis is the task of the social and cultural sciences. An evaluative analysis proceeds on the assumption that truth-value or *satya* as 'warranted assertability' is a comprehensive notion and both psychological understanding and causal explanation are oriented to eliciting truths about reality from different angles, of course.

Value-analysis may be said to involve a hard task. A distinction will have to be made between different kinds of propositions. Hypotheses, tested propositions and inductive generalizations will have to be differentiated. A distinction has also to be made between words and sentences which can be either positive or negative, hypothetical or disjuncture or apodictical, categorical or assertory, factual or appreciative, particular or singular, and in any one of three modes of predication—*abhidha*, *lakshna* and *vyanjana*. The correlation of the immediate prescribed solutions with the more ultimate values or, if possible, with metaphysical notions like the Bhuma or Chiti is desirable. This kind of correlation involving the explication of the ultimate fundamental values involved in any critical or controversial situation is a task to which the humanist social scientist can address himself *vis-a-vis* the politician who is the decision-maker. Besides furnishing to him the relevant data on the basis of which the latter can make his decisions with regard to priorities, payoffs, outcomes etc., the more urgent task of the social scientist is to clarify to the decision-maker the compatibility or otherwise of the various ultimate value-issues involved in the different theoretical responses to a situation. Decision-making involves the perspective of the instrumental task of converting inputs into outputs in the context of the social system, the economic system and the political system.

It involves the question of sub-systemic and systemic correlations of the various categories of the system. But the task of keeping in view the perspective of value-preferences of the community is no less urgent because, contrary to the assumptions of the eighteenth century French materialists, man is not a machine. Thus it may be said that the decision-making issue appertains to the realm of correlating both the ultimate metaphysical notions and the ethical imperatives of the culture-community with the party manifestoes and concrete solutions proposed. The Cabinet or the chief executive is concerned with the task of exercising the will power in making decisions which will be implemented. But the task of the Planning Commission, advisory boards and committees of experts is intellectual insofar as they are concerned with reasonable or unreasonable choice and the determination of feasible or impossible alternatives. Another value-interpretative work will be to deduce further implications from the solutions proposed and then judge their feasibility for actual operation. An adequate policy analysis involves the cost computation of alternative strategies and also the evaluation of the outputs in terms of their possible qualitative impact on the moral fibre of the citizens. The important task thus is to analyse the results and consequences expected to follow from the pursuit of the policy suggested and to evaluate them in terms of the priorities laid down by the society. This value-interpretative work may further lead to the discussion of the interrelations of the solutions proposed with the generalizations and hypotheses in kindred realms of enquiry which have a bearing on them, through the pursuit of a multi-disciplinary approach. The process of the understanding of values may also involve an awareness of the distinction between instrumental (*Sadhana sampat*) values and intrinsic values (*Sreyas* and *Nihsreyas*). The personalist idealist would not ascribe to the sovereign state and its agencies operative in the political system any intrinsic value. But he would be willing to accept that the state has, indeed, an enormous role in the coordination and implementation of the instrumental values for enhancing support for the realisation of welfare, security, rational social good and total development.

Value-interpretation is linked up with the work of formulating explanatory political theory. Political science is not a mere axiomatic science based on the deduction of relevant propositions from the assumptions regarding the psychodynamic motivation of man. For understanding the aspects of political behaviour, the motivational and cultural determinants of human action cannot, even for the time being, be put off from consideration and the aspect of rational political action be alone emphasized. The American quantitative behaviouralism now being increasingly oriented to computerization and cybernetics is far removed from a knowledge of the concrete reality of the third world. But analytical quantitativism is only a fictional and heuristic mode of science. The quantitative character does not enhance, rather, sometimes it undermines the character of a discipline for being an empirical explanatory science of social action because the qualitative and moral aspects of a situation are not amenable to quantification.

It is possible to differentiate methodologically conceived ethical neutrality for promoting objective scientific enquiry, from moral indifference. When the exact social scientist is concerned with problems of empirical causation, he may behave as being ethically neutral but that does not mean that he is to operate in his role as a citizen also as being morally indifferent. The social scientist has to concern himself with the problem of moral relevance of the issues being subjected to understanding. Max Weber had stressed the notion of a value-free social science in the context of the post-Bismarckian Kaiserite Germany. By stressing freedom from values for the social scientist he was fighting the cause of liberalism and historical economics against Kaiserism. Some American positivists and behaviouralists have also stressed the value-free approach in order to build a scientific theory where a differentiation has to be made between prescriptive propositions and factual empirical propositions. In face of the existing deep commitment to the values of liberal democracy in America, the cry of a value-free social science has not done any damage to the American democratic framework. But in the developing countries where the tradition of institutionalized democracy is weak, the plea for a value-free social science may turn out to be an escape from the assumption of committed positions in the battle between dictatorship and democracy.

While discussing the problems of ethical neutrality in the context of objectivity, quantitativism, increasing scientificity and the growth of a positive rationally-consistent social science, the critic cannot afford to ignore the lessons and values of history. India's vast historical epochs stretching for over four thousand years contain a rich legacy of lessons for the political scientist. Political philosophy cannot be divorced from historical consciousness. Political philosophy and political sociology as the disciplines concerned with political conduct—conduct including regularized patternized behaviour, attitudes, and thought, have to proceed through historically-rooted, conceptual constructs in the task of discussing social causation and finding out the motivational, valuational and institutional-normative determinants of action.[1] These constructs have to have also historical foundations because social sciences have to corroborate their conclusions with historical illustrations as the vast data derived from history need not be ignored. The question of values is linked up with that of cultural relevance of historical lessons and the task of future nation-building. No nation can afford to ignore the values enshrined in the treasure-house of history. Hence humanist political philosophy supports a critical use of the historical method for the study of political values. One basic weakness of the humanism of M. N. Roy and Jawaharlal was to build a model of scientific ethics almost uprooted from the vast historical heritage of India.

The problems encountered in historical logic, appear in a form different from that of the natural sciences. History, generally, is based on the study of particular idiographic events and personalities while the physical and natural sciences deal with the nomothetic, the generalized and the typal.

1. Erich Fromm, *The Sane Society* (London, Routledge & Kegan Paul, 1963), p. 12, differentiates between sociological relativism which is widely accepted by social scientists and *normative humanism*. He says : "... there are Universal criteria for mental health which are valid for the human race as such, and according to which the state of health of each society can be judged. This position of *normative humanism* is based on a few fundamental premises."

In discussing the problems of historical causation and relevance a distinction has to be made between explanation in terms of causally operative antecedent factors and the Aristotelian principle of teleological dependence. Causal explanation involves the pursuit of the immanentistic method dealing with the *samaveta karana* and the totalizing cumulative method dealing with the *asamavayi karana.* The former would be more concerned with the manifestation of inner or immanent forces responsible for change, transformation or revolution, like the soul or spirit of a nation and the forces and relations of production and their outward consequences. The latter, on the other hand, would, be more concerned with external foreign invasions and their impact on the inner entity.[1] These two types of historical investigations, emphasizing either the internal or the external factors which have a causal impact on the other phenomena, are to be distinguished from the concept of teleological relevance which has a futurist goal-orientation. While causal probe and explanations will be concerned with the unravelling of what has happened in the past, teleological relevance involves an awareness of the future potentialities of an object for the amelioration of the human race. Thus philosophical humanism would even look forward to futurist astropolitical notions. An idealistically-oriented and historically-rooted political philosophy will include three types of intellectual formulations a theory of calculable political behaviour based on a knowledge of the roles of past and present actors, an empirical probe into the concatenation of political dynamics and a theory of politically-relevant moral values which have a meaning in shaping the future.

The concept of physical, social and historical causality may be differentiated from that of moral responsibility. Causality is a term of empirical science and involves a probe into the concatenation of relevant categories which are to be imputed efficacy in bringing about an event. But the notion of moral responsibility involves the question of human dignity and freedom. It may even be said that the humanist would advocate the revival of the notion of man as a responsible agent with a

1. In biology epigenesis is opposed to preformation.

goal-mechanism of his own, as differentiated from his undignified transformation into a mere means that has been witnessed in some of the authoritarian and autocratic systems.

Because of its cold formal rationalism and quest for objectivity, science cannot provide an integrated code of morals. In its historical career, science has, generally, been associated with agnosticism, atheism, scepticism and relativism. Hence a social system based merely on science can never go beyond the concept of pragmatic morals for collective betterment. A scientific sociology sometimes amounts only to the enshrinement of expediency. Science tends to neglect the sense of reverence and devoutness associated with moral precepts specially in the Hindu-Buddhist culture. But humanism stresses the flowering of the moral and political autonomy of man through a life of industrious initiative for the realisation of the inherent potentialities which can be manifested through endeavours for the conquest of inhibiting complexes and crises. Both sociality and isolation are needed for a full life of Karmayoga and Jnanayoga which are the paths for the realisation of humanist values.

Some exponents of poly-culturalism preach the cult of cultural relativism with the necessary implication of the advocacy of ethical relativism. Some advocates of dialectical materialism stand for poly-logism and would maintain that each class has its own logical modes and methods of argumentation. On the other hand the position maintained here is that at least some ethical prescriptions are absolute, and are relevant to all mankind. Liberty, equality, justice, fraternity and global fellowship, fearlessness, self-control and compassion are the seven fundamental political and moral values that may be deemed almost as absolutes. It is true that some support to ethical relativism has come from the biological theory of evolution which maintains that the ethical norms of the descendants of *homo sapiens* are only sociological constructs devised for meeting the challenges in the struggle for existence and consequently there is nothing ultimate about them. For millions and millions of years the earth was inherited by molluscs, fishes and reptiles. The evolutionist would maintain that man is only a late intruder on the evolutionary ladder and he has the arrogance to project his moral values as the ultimate absolutes. Without entering into the confused jungle of evolutionary zoology it has been maintained here that political discussions and norms-setting have to have some framework. When Americans propound that their political system is better than that of the Russians, what are the theoretical grounds for such an assertion ? Russians sponsor similar claims regarding the superiority of classless communism to a bourgeois plutocratic democracy. For deciding among rival alternatives we have to have consensus on some standards for judging political systems if we want to go beyond political and anthropological relativism.

There is no contradiction involved in the advocacy of ethical absolutism and ontological spiritual absolutism. The metaphysical support to one primal, self-explanatory, supreme infinite consciousness which is the *weltgrund* (*sa paryagat*) postulates the maintenance of a system of norms in our limited world which will make the teleological realisation of the supreme spirit as Perfect Good possible. Since an unholy conduct breeds alienation and generates anxiety it cannot be recommended by the absolutist. Without the subjugation of moral evil and demerit one cannot get rid of pain. For getting emancipation from terror, gloom and anguish it is essential to pursue the path of virtue. The implication that since the ultimate Being is beyond the categories of good and bad, right and wrong, hence we cannot postulate a parallel set of ethical ultimates need not be logically pressed. The ethical ultimates are only conceived or postulated ultimates. Hence the theodicy of *bhuma* is not affected by the cosmodicy of Dharma as eternal morally-oriented natural law.

Sources of Idealist Humanist Ethics

The humanist is not an uncritical admirer of scriptural revelation, prophetical inspiration, angel's intervention, legislator's code, commentator's exegesis, canonist's argumentation, historical traditions, pontifical mandates, infallibility decrees, credal concepts, the decalogue and the sermons at Sarnath and on the Mount. He has a scrutinizing approach and subjects all historical heritage to the critical standpoint of reason used for common good.

The sacrificial cult of ritualistic observances also does not satisfy the humanist. The various sacrifices and chants—Ahina (daily), weekly, Dvadasha (twelve day), Darsa Paurnamasa, Rajasuya, Asvamedha, Vajapeya, Pariplava, Uktha, Udgitha, Gayatra Sama or Traishtubha Sama, do not satisfy his mind and emotion.

Nor is the humanist bound by the authoritarian creed of force and might. If the strong scoundrel uses his physical might[1] or the potency of an armed squadron to subdue a recalcitrant foe, the humanist considers it as a slur on humanity. The exploitationist gospels of the White Man's burden, Fuhrer's vision, racial myth, *jehad* and crusade, forcible proselytization, indoctrination and brainwashing, the cult of the leader as a charismatic superman with the right to impose his will on the people and the Machiavellian concept of the incontrovertible reason of the state have no appeal to the humanist. For learning wisdom he does not have to go to the owl like Asvatthama,[2] nor to the fox and the lion like Machiavelli's prince nor the Egyptian Sphinx. Thus the dictation of a positive morality by the exponents of state power would be opposed to the humanist spirit. For the humanist, the chastened human conscience and the steady intellect (Vyavasayatmika buddhi) constitute the true sources of moral criteria.

It is not possible to relegate all ethical values and norms as regulative maxims for the rationalization of an exploitationist social order. All ethical norms do not represent the mental fabrications of cunning priests and unscrupulous apologists of the *status quo*. Some ethically-oriented norms may seek to legitimize a social order based on exploitation and terrorization of the suppressed sections. But it will be an exaggeration to relegate all ethical norms as the rationalizations of the relevant and congruous criteria for the maintenance of a polarized society in the interests of the dominant minority of elites.

The humanist looks to the court of internal conscience or the (*antaratman*) or the Daemon. He is not a pragmatist believing

1. Cf. *Mbh.* Poona ed., XV, 38, 23.

2. He learnt from the owl who was devouring the eggs of the birds the lesson of wiping out the sons of the Pandavas and Draupadi.

(*Mbh.* Poona ed., X, 1, 51-52).

in expediency and worshipping success at all costs. To him truth is a higher value than the egoistic gratification of appetites. His aim is not vegetative lustfulness but a rational synthesis of all the information obtained by the functional neurological system of man. He looks for a rational code of ethics which traces the roots of the solution of moral dilemmas in the conscience and steady intellect of man. It is very true that even conscience and the criteria of consubstantial reason (steady intellect) are cultural emergents but they have attained their present conduct-governing status after centuries of struggle and evolutionary endeavours in the pursuit of the conquest of social alienation and the elimination of spiritual poverty and represent the cummulative results of encounter with diverse types of challenges. The moral sense, or synderesis, in man, which manifests its energy in approving or detesting attitudes and actions, although a cultural emergent, has assumed in the course of centuries the character of an autonomous sense. It cannot, hence be equated with the aesthetic sense. Nor are Cudworth, Clarke and Wollaston faithful to the heritage of ethical civilization in propounding a dianoetic theory equating the moral and the logical faculties. It is possible for man to have an intuition of the essences of the moral concepts which regulate life. Thus the code of conduct sanctioned by idealist humanism is removed both from the pessimism of Hardy and Hartmann and the supermoralism and aristocratic elitism of Nietzsche. It is oriented to the eradication of self-centered propensities. It does not seek the Aristotelian creed of *eudaimonia* but wants a harmonious growth of action (*nivrti*) and renunciation (*pravrti*) oriented to the perfection of human faculties. Thus the vegetative creeds of cyrenaicism, hedonism, sensationalism and sensual naturalism run counter to the creed of rational ethics supporting the claims of conscience.

The humanist appreciates the existence of at least partial order in the world. It may be difficult to prove an absolutely immanent and transcendent moral order in the world. But even if there be no ontological ultimate Being, for purposes of human good and rational social perfection we may agree on the projection of some values as psychological ultimates. Truth and reason may be such psychologically objective values.

Humanism, hence, would not subscribe either to gross or refined hedonism which preaches the sufficiency of the goal-gratifications of the individual ego. Nor would it find satisfaction in the felicific calculus based on the computation of pain and pleasure with reference to their propinquity, intensity and duration. It would reject the identification of justice with the pronouncements of the sovereign political superior which it would hold as an invitation to opportunist expediency and the apotheosis of the politics of manipulation, force, fraud and corruption. Only an ethical standard and cannon of validity based on the sanctity of the chastened human conscience will satisfy it. Only the conscience and steady intellect can provide the criteria[1] that will challenge the arrogant pretensions of the holders of power.

The moral instinct may not have been implanted in man by an omniscient creator for the maintenance of his world. But certainly the categorical imperatives of a universal good and the treating of all men, nay all creatures, as emanations from the same Infinite Consciousness and Existence excite our deepest awe and admiration. The moral norms have chastened man, softened his cruelty and barbarity, and raised him above animal selfishness. Hence the moral foundations of civilization have to be preserved from extinction. The quest of the universality of values will strengthen the necessary foundational security and certainty of civilization and save it from dehumanization, alienation, *anomie* and spiritual catastrophe.

Human development demands a constant re-evaluation of traditional ethics. Some irrational elements which are meant to stabilise a non-egalitarian socio-economic structure have to be eliminated from the domain of a coherent political philosophy. But some of the central moral elements may have to be reemphasized. The main theoretical question of discovering the congruence of the concrete social situation and the pattern of

1. In Buddhism there is great stress on the eradication of greed (*lobha*), hatred (*dosha*), stupidity (*moha*), pride (Cf. Greek *megalopsychia*), false views, doubt, sloth and torpor, distraction and agitation, sensual passion, shamelessness, recklessness and malice which are regarded as the hindrances and *kleshas* (depravities).

ethical norms would, of course, be always there. On occasions, certain compromises may have to be made, in an imperfect world, with the moral principles, e.g. when the safety of the physical person or the realisation of the common good are involved. But that should not be an argument for preaching the equal scientific status of all moral norms in the name of sociological and cultural relativism. Nor is relativism a ground for propounding total nihilism in the realm of moral discussion.

Humanism and Values

Natural sciences and some forms of historiography may be concerned only with hard, brute, facts and events. They may disdain to adopt a valuational attitude to the subject matter under review for the sake of dispassionate analysis. But humanism is opposed to pushing the fact-value dichotomy to extremes. The uppermost concern of the investigator has to be the promotion of the rational good of all human beings. This preeminent valuational concern has to govern all intellectual enterprises. A supreme concern for truth and objective reporting of facts is the indispensable foundation of scientific knowledge. Humanist social science will study the congruence or incompatibility of the different ethical and religious teachings. How does Buddha differ from Kapila ? How does Kautilya differ from Hobbes ? How does Confucius differ from Montesquieu ? These are questions that cannot be given up as be'ng indeterminate or unanswerable. The attempt of the exponents of logical positivistic analysts to expunge certain dominant metaphysical and ethical questions as beyond the purview of the linguistic philosopher, humanism deems as unfortunate and as an enterprise calculated to harm the expansion of the frontiers of knowledge. The unhindered unconstrained spirit of questioning has been the root of all advance. Scepticism regarding the received body of traditions and a restless zest for exploring into the unending frontiers of knowledge has been the basis of all creativism. Man cannot refuse to ask questions regarding the source of values. Who has implanted in the great values like truth, non-violence, chastity, liberty, equality, justice, fraternity and fearlessness? Were they implanted in man at the genesis of creation by a sempiternal Godhead or are they the crystallized conceptual resultants of biological and socio-economic struggles for survival ? Values provide inspiration for the pursuit of our enquiries. We discuss the congruence of economic priorities with cultural values. Hence values cannot be totally expunged from scientific enquiries. Even in choosing subjects of investigation for research in physics and chemistry, the research scholar is guided not merely by the requirements of theory but also, at least indirectly, by concerns for their relevance to human welfare. We do not fully know reality-in-itself but to the extent that we attempt to know it our concern is valuationally governed. Whatever promotes the creative release of human powers of free endeavour has a deep valuational side and has a premium upon it. In view of the fact that different socio-cultural aggregations sponsor different emphases on valuational categories, the humanist will not refuse to engage in an evaluative disquisition upon them. A quest for a society where the virtues of human dignity, universsality and spiritual equality will be maintained and fostered makes imperative the search for the valid criteria of political existence. A non-committal analysis of the operative mechanics of the political system is fruitless without a concern for human welfare and decency. A phenomenology of values is one of the prime foundational prerequisites for a developed society. This postulates a transcendent frame of reference needing the probe into the sources and validity of values through perceptive determinate philosophical reasoning called in the Bhagavadgita by the name of *Vyavasayatmika buddhi.* The ground-norms of any developed society are constituted by the accumulated heritage of the criteria of moral validity developed by the seers and prophets of the past. These again are being constantly tested and scrutinized in the course of social evolution. Hence there is the requirement of a trans-empirical frame of reference not in the sense of eschatological or transcendent norms but in the sense of those norms which transcend the bounds of any existing social structure.

Integral humanism seeks to synthesize claims and aspirations of the individual ego with the duties towards and obligations to the broader social and political collectivity. The latter, of course,

1. *Mbh.* Crit. ed. XII/139, 94.

are not group minds or group souls with their ontologically real personality. But for the functioning of the national political system a reconciliation of individual rights and duties with the responsibility to the broader aggregations has to be achieved. Egoism and altruism together. A spiritual and moral humanism nurtured in the philosophical traditions of Indian metaphysics stresses certain key notions. It pleads for the limitation and not the neutralization of the demands of the individual. An exaggerated dose of egoism is bound to generate antipathetic forces in retaliation. Humanism postulates an expansion and extension of consciousness through the incorporation of creative altruistic sentiments in the human psyche. The Bhagavadgita has categorized the elements constituting *sattviki dhriti* and *sattviki buddhi.* These can very well be the accompaniments of the humanist philosopher and citizen. The Buddhists have laid down the way that should be followed by an aspirant who wants to realize bodhi gnosis and *nirvana.* The exaltation of compassion (*Karuna*) is the permanent contribution of Buddhism to the moralization of human civilization. Mystics have pointed to the possibility of the union of consciousness and the merging of the selves in an absolute Existence but humanism which is basically cognitive in its orientation will emphasize the progressive intesification of solidarity, fraternity and cooperative sentiments through the curtailment of egoistic excesses.

Humanism adheres to the separation between the sphere of legality marked by coercion and automatism and that of morality marked by disinterested spontaneity. But the question arises — can not there be conditions amidst which it may be valid for the state to take recourse to some coercion for the eventual promotion of morality ? The humanist's answer is in the affirmative and he would support his view on grounds of the consequential release of moral energy on the part of a considerable section of the population. In enforcing measures for compulsory secondary education it may appear that the state is taking recourse to some kind of coercion on the guardians. But looked at from the standpoint of the future good of the student population and the Directive Principles of the Constitution, that coercion is justifiable because it ultimately makes the students better qualified for participating in collectivity-oriented activities leading to the promotion of the common good. Similarly, measures for the restraint of freedom of contract on the part of the capitalists and labourers may appear coercive and thus tantamount to interfering with their spontaneous action. But such actions do release the shackled moral energy of the producers and consumers and make them effective participants in activities leading to the promotion of common welfare and national good. Hence from the view of the larger interests of society it can be said that compulsory education measures and other policies imposing restraints on the freedom of contract of the capitalists, landlords, oligarchs and monopolists are indirectly oriented to the promotion of moral life among the citizens. On the basis of such ethical notions idealist humanism supports coercive measures for enforcing at least relative (if not total) prohibition and also the social equality of the backward and scheduled sections of Indian society.

Humanism and Non-Violence

One fundamental contribution of the Jaina, Buddhist and Vaishnava ethics to world civilization is the concept of Ahimsa or non-injury. It has been stated by adverse critics that the Jainas carry this concept almost to ridiculous extremes. Suffice it to mention that this concept had vital influence on Mahatma Gandhi who made concrete applications of this motion in the social and political fields. It may also be pointed out that as an ideal, the Jaina concept of Ahimsa represents a profound goal for the contemporary and futurist humanity. It is true that from the phylum protozoa to the phylum chordata and its subphylum vertebrata (or craniata), we find a deep-rooted struggle for existence going on in which violence, bloodshed and conquest have played and do play a leading role. But if we will look at the evolutionary story a little critically, then we find that the strength for survival in the race for existence should not be equated with violence. In the evolutionary progression, big animals like the mammoth and the reptiles like dinosaurs have become extinct. Although non-practicable at an absolute generalized level, the ethics of Ahimsa represents a fundamental concept which can serve as a regulating ideal for human behaviour.

Non-violence is both an individual virtue and a social technic. In the earlier courses of the evolution of the ten phyla from the protozoa to the primates and the hominides, violence has been a dominan technic assuring natural selection in the struggle for survival. But violence is never the sole means for existence. Cooperativeness and rational adjustment have also played their legitimate part. Humanism does not stand for the total abjuration of violence in the present day chaotic state of social and political affairs. India cannot afford the ridiculous luxury of unilateral disarmament in the face of threats to her borders. Nor can capital punishment be taken off the statute book in the face of mounting internal murders and the rampant vulgar display of force. But the onward advance of culture based on the efflorescence of moral values demands that through education, socialization, acculturation, reciprocal accommodation, mutual appreciativeness and an expansion of the brotherly ethic of love, the role of violence in civil, social, political and international political system be weakened. Even dialectical materialism is curbing its earlier deep commitment to violent proletarian revolution and is slowly becoming attached to detente and coexistence. Even the Chinese bellicosity is undergoing at least some modifications. With the advance of industrialism, the western nations are also realising the futility of the empty display of unending force. The humanist sees meaning in the Gandhian theory that one great merit of non-violence is that it does not breed retaliatory counter-action.

Conclusion

Political science has to be teleological. It is a science of ends which are to be progressively realized. The political scientist has not only to analyse ends but has also to set and endorse ends. All great and active political thinking has been teleological. Plato and Aristotle, Locke and Rousseau, Kant and Green had set a higher job for political science than merely being the positive knowledge of administration, voting, the dynamics of parties and other categories and aspects of empirical political behaviour. Politics has to be guided by moral values. The human personality or the essential Atman and the empirical phenomenal Jiva has to be respected. In face of dominant collectivism and the repudiation of the Vedantic and Christian anthropology which has resulted in the submergence of the individual and in the exaggerated emphasis on the conquest of political power, the recognition of the autonomous moral claim of the individual can alone strengthen the democratic fabric. Moral values have not only to be cherished at the intellectual level but have to be realised also at the instrumental level. Confronted with the challenges emerging from the mass society, the industrial society, the disintegration of man in the era of gigantic structures and the crude vulgarization of the Darwinian biology in support of conquest and exploitation, political science has to devise ways for safeguarding human autonomy and spontaneous creativism.

CHAPTER III

THE METHODOLOGY AND CONCEPTS OF IDEALIST HUMANISM

The Multi-dimensional Man and the Multi-disciplinary Approach to Political Philosophy

Ethical and spiritual humanism is multi-dimensional in its approach and its aim is to synthesize the information and knowledge derived from different sources. It is true that in the olden times great geniuses and scientists did not start their intellectual work with the formulation of hypotheses and their testing. Their method was more *ad hoc*. But now, the scientific method is being more and more oriented to the testing of hypotheses. There are certain important steps in the scientific procedure. The first is large-scale observation of the relevant data. The observation must be impartial and objective. It is possible, to a certain degree, to use controlled observation also. Mass observation technics have also been used by certain British social scientists.

John Stuart Mill formulated his famous fivefold experimental method—the method of agreement, the method of difference, the joint method of agreement and difference, the method of concomitant variation and the method of residues. These five-fold methods may be considered philosophical or logical according to the modern scientific procedure. Modern scientific researches, specially in the fields of physics and chemistry, are based on laboratory experiments. Such experiments, however, have only limited relevance to geological and biological researches. In the social sciences also it may not be possible to use experiments on a large scale.

Kelvin used to say that one does not know a thing unless one can measure it. Measurement provides an element of definiteness as it makes knowledge exact. Communication also is made easier thereby because the hearer understands exactly what a speaker wants to communicate. Hence it is advisable to introduce as much of measurement technics as possible in the social sciences. It is very true that there are certain significant qualitative aspects of behaviour which cannot be expressed in quantitative and mathematical terms but that does not mean that even in those sectors where we can use measurement, we should not do so. The acceptance of a substantiated hypothesis or the non-acceptance (rejection) of a hypothesis which is not corroborated by evidences and data obtained through observation and experiment and subsequently systematized is to be deemed another stage in the scientific procedure.

It is true that in numerous fields of human behaviour we may not have the exactitude and definiteness which are associated with knowledge in the physical sciences. Nevertheless, there are certain aspects of human action about which we can talk almost in terms of semi-quantitative exactitude. Marx and Marshall have also been supporters of the partial incorporation of mathematical technics in economics.[1]

The statistical method is not identical with the scientific method. The latter is a wider category and includes in its purview the methods applied in geometry, physics, chemistry, biology etc. In some form or the other, the scientific method was partially used by Aristotle, Hobbes, Spinoza, Darwin and Herbert Spencer. The statistical method deals with probabilities and averages and is based on sampling. The scientific method,

1. Raymond Pearl had studied the problems of population and mobility and had arrived at the conclusion that labour migration is slow in the beginning, very much accentuated in the middle and reaches almost a static level in the end. For this proposition of his, he claims as much exactitude and authenticity as can be claimed for a proposition of physics. Pearl's exaggerated optimism is not fully justified but we have to give him some credit for making an attempt to introduce exactitude in the field of social studies.

on the other hand, is a more inclusive term and it accepts the use of mathematical technics and models on a more comprehensive scale than has been possible, so far, in statistics. The scientific method takes recourse also to deduction on a wider scale than the statistical. As a matter of fact, a large number of scientific hypotheses are implications or derivations from the more inclusive general theories of science and are used for purposes of their further testing. While statistical propositions deal with averages, scientific theories are sought to be finally based on operational causality which is a deductive conception. In other words, statistics is pledged only to the concept of correlation but the scientific method deals with and is concerned with dynamic causation.

The case study method is based on the analogy of clinical technics.[1] For the application of the case study method, the selection of the cases need not necessarily be representative. On the other hand, non-representativeness should not mean the ignoring of the concept of salience. In other words, the case to be studied must have some importance — either intrinsic importance or importance for the analysis of the group. There are three ways in which these two methods[2] can be conjoined : (i) The case study method may lead to the formulation of certain hypotheses which may, later, be tested by the use of the statistical method. (ii) Secondly, the case study method may be used as a supplement to the statistical, whereby the conclusions arrived at by the use of the statistical method may be further thoroughly tested by an intensive probe through the case study method. (iii) Thirdly, if there is a large number of case studies, the conclusions arrived at through these can be further analyzed statistically. Sometimes the case-study method which does yield significant generalizations is used as

1. Medical methodology is becoming increasingly complicated. For example, in studying virus diseases, the following aspects have to be considered : (i) classification, (ii) nomenclature, (iii) structure, (iv) replication, (v) pathogenesis, (vi) immune reaction, (vii) host response, (viii) symptomatology, (ix) distribution, (x) epidemiology etc.— *A Manual of Tropical Medicine* (Indian edition, 1970), p. 1.

2. Some social scientists like Gordon Allport have tried to bring the case study method and the statistical method together.

a preparatory stage for pilot study projects. The pilot study approach is concerned with the study of a limited aspect or a sector or the total universe. The case study method may be used for the formulation of certain general notions as well as some relevant hypotheses which may be further tested by the pilot study schemes. When the pursuit of the latter approach indicates the emergence of some fruitful results, then one can embark on elaborate social survey projects.

The sociological method as used by Small, Park, Burgess, MacIver, Sorokin, Mannheim Wirth, Ogburn, Parsons etc. is concerned with the study of modern societies and their workings. Its fundamental concepts are society, association, community, wishes, interaction, accommodation, reference group, class, etc. The anthropological method, on the other hand, is primarily concerned with the study of the pre-literate and tribal cultures. Its attention is focused only upon those cultures which have not been exposed to the various categories of technological civilization. The second difference between the sociological and anthropolitical methods is that the former is concerned with the intensive study of some limited aspects of modern social structures. It emphasises the detailed study of specialized aspects of the lives and behaviour of groups and social entities. The anthropological method, on the other hand, is more totalistic and integral in its approach. It wants to study the total aspects of a tribal culture. In order to understand even one aspect of tribal behaviour like religious motivation or patterning of coordination or subordination, it advocates that all the aspects should be studied as a totality. Only thus can it be possible to study even one aspect of the system. Thus while the sociological method is sectoral, the anthropological is configurationist.

Another dominant approach to political and social analysis is the functional. In the ancient and medieval periods, philosophers were mainly concerned with finding out the nature of the fundamental substance out of which the manifold plurality originated. Some of them held that fire is the original substance, others referred to water or air or *Apeiron* as the primal substance. In the Middle Ages also the Christian theologians were concerned with the nature of the soul, its beatitude and its relation to God. The ontological and epistemological approach to philosophy as developed in the early ages was, generally, the main pre-occupation of cosmologists till about the eighteenth century. It is not that they were unmindful of the functioning, or the modes of the processual dynamism of the primal substance. But, by and large, it is correct to say that the structure of substance and the analysis of its various levels of manifestations engaged the attention of thinkers for a considerable period. Since the nineteenth century, however, the rise of Lamarckian and Darwinian biology has emphasised the notions of use, operation, action and functioning, etc. While the earlier cosmogonists were concerned with the genesis and structure of substance and the external morphology of different species, the biologically-inspired thinkers have been concerned with the changes in structures brought about by the functioning of the organism in the natural environment and the ecological complex. Thus the emphasis now is on functions and on the changes brought about through the use and disuse of organs as in Lamarckism or on the modifications and their perpetuation brought about by the process of natural selection.[1] But it must be emphasised that while there has been increased emphasis on the study of the dynamics and the operative mechanism of organisms and entities, the study of structures has not been given up in modern natural and social sciences. In medical science we can say that while physiology is concerned with the functioning of the organs, anatomy, cytology and histology are concerned with the internal structure of the body, the cells and tissues. In modern functional psychology we find that the old notions of mind and soul have been given up and experimental psychologists are concerned more with intellection and mentation than with the intellect and mind as objective entities. It may even be correct to say that to a certain extent the old Buddhist theory of stream of consciousness (*Vijnana-Santana*) is being re-stated, substantiated with more sophisticated technics, of course, by modern psychologists of the behaviouristic profession. Behaviour is a category related to concrete entities. The

1. In mathematics also we find the development of what is called the functional theory.

research worker may deal with an individual's behaviour or group behaviour or crowd behaviour but the items comprised under behaviour are concerned with concrete specific entities.[1] Marxism has also been functional in its approach to the extent that it points out the contradictions of the capitalist system as found in its working. It was one of the charges of the democratic thinkers that Marxian communism concentrated its attention mostly on the study of the inadequacy and defects of democracy and was unmindful of the organisation of the communist social, political and economic systems. But Soviet economists and management experts have studied the dynamic aspects of the Russian socio-political system and economy. It is certainly true that we do not have any historical example to show the functioning of the political and economic theories of Guild Socialism and Syndicalism. It has to be acknowledged, however, that Guild Socialism did address itself to the organisational aspects of the commune which was supposed to replace the modern state. In his *A Grammar of Politics*, Harold Laski was also partly concerned with the organisational aspects of the pluralist society. He discussed a number of economic and political institutions which were to characterize the society patterned on pluralist notions of dispersion of sovereign authority. In public administration also we find that more emphasis is now being placed on the study of the functions of the various organisations. Management agencies are being studied with reference to their working. Deriving inspiration from the functional approach, the sociological school of jurisprudence as formulated by Pound and Holmes has emphasised that legal norms should not be studied in abstraction or isolation. Their genuine significance can be found only if the functioning of the economic and social systems is taken into full consideration. Without such

1. A pattern, on the other hand, is a generalised type, and is a heuristic or a hypothetical concept. The conception of pattern represents a generalization abstracted from numerous concrete items. There can be a pattern of behaviour, a pattern of action, a pattern of bureaucracy, a pattern of state interference and so on. An attempt to study patterns has been made by Parsons in his tenfold variables—specific-diffuse, universalist-particularist, ego-affective and ego-neutral, ascriptive and achievement-based and self-oriented and collectivity-oriented.

correlation, the study of jurisprudence remains formal and abstract. Even in some of the recent studies of the High Courts and the Supreme Court in India and in the United States, emphasis has been sought to be placed to some extent on the functional and behavioral aspects of judicial administration. The composition of the judiciary is certainly important but more important from the standpoint of the social and political system is its way of functioning in the concrete universe. It is thus becoming increasingly clear that the functional approach is a dominant aspect of the modern social and behavioral sciences.

The structural-functional approach as developed by Parsons in sociology is methodologically somewhat more comprehensive than the functional approach of writers like Finer, Ogg, Munro and Zink. Parsons has discussed the structure of the social system, the cultural system and the personality system, he has also certainly emphasised the study of their functions. It is true that in the modern systems analysis approach as developed by Almond, Deutsch and others we find that considerable attention is focused on the study both of structures and functions but it will not be correct to say that the structural-functional approach is identical with the systems analysis approach. The latter is somewhat more integrated in its approach. The systems study approach takes into consideration some of the technics of electrical engineering like information-transmission and information-retrieval. It also uses the technics of cybernetics, inputs-output models, feedback etc. But the structural-functional approach as earlier developed by Max Weber is somewhat more traditional in its use of scientific terminology. Thus the difference between these three methods functional, the structural-functional and the systems analysis[1] approach must not be lost sight of although it is true that there are fundamental common elements. Philosophical humanism being integral in its approach to political problems seeks to obtain relevant knowledge from diverse sources and is not solely committed to one specific method.[2]

1. The roots of the systems approach can also be traced, to some extent, in Max Weber.

2. Cf. Aristotle, *Nicomachean Ethics*, T, 2 : "And politics appears to be of this nature; ... and we see even the most highly esteemed of capacities

Philosophical humanism is teleological in character because it is concerned with the value and destiny of man in the context of absolute idealism. It is conscious that its advocacy of an infinite consciousness is not based on scientific experimentation but is a postulate of logic for systematizing our experiences. The quest for the fulfilment of perfectionist ideals also is a derivation from the heritage of cultural traditions and cannot be subjected to the models and formulas of behavioral politics. Hence while appreciating the data and information obtained from the various empirical modes of scientific formulation philosophical humanism will try to systematize that knowledge for the realization of the rational good of all citizens.

Philosophical humanism with the view of man as a creative spiritual and moral subject functioning through the process of critical intellection is integral in its approach. In the enlarged perspective of knowledge, hence, it considers the sole commitment to any one standpoint as limited and even vitiating the approach to truth. Hence it is multi-method-pursuing in its approach. It regards the dialogue method or the conversational thrashing out of points as the essence of the dialectic. Dialectic is valuable to the extent that it stresses ceaseless argumentation and progressive reconciliation of antinomies. One service of the dialectical method in its Hegelian-Marxian forms is the pursuit of an integrated attempt at the rational understanding of cosmology, anthropology, phenomenology, art, religion and philosophy. The attempt to understand the problems of the social and political realms in the context of cosmogonic and cosmological formulations and the probe into the physical, chemical and ecological factors governing and motivating human behaviour appeal to humanism. They help in the formulation of an integrated comprehensive world-view which is of special significance in the epoch of growingly narrow specialization. History as the record of the experiences of a nation is valuable for providing knowledge. It is the storehouse of the collective experiences of a nation and thus has more

to fall under this, e.g. strategy. economics, rhetoric; now since politics uses the rest of the sciences, and since, again, it legislates as to what we are to do and what we are to abstain from, the end of this science must include those of the others, so that this end must be the good for man."

lessons to teach than the speculative geometry of an utopian writer. Although not a positive quantitative science, historical knowledge is valuable because it emphasises the contextualization of a proposition within a larger relevant framework because apart from the contextual environmental framework, political knowledge becomes rootless. Thus Aristotle, Polybius, Vico, Montesquieu, Burke, Hegel, Marx, Spengler and Toynbee are significant as political theorisers because they study politics in the framework of history. Indian political thought cannot afford to renounce its connexion with historical contextualization. Our history does not begin only some centuries ago. A civilization and culture with more than five thousand years of recorded history cannot afford to neglect the immanent message of its cultural continuity. Even at the pragmatic level it can be stated that without knowing about Bismarck one cannot appreciate the currents of the German political system. Similarly, without knowing about Lenin and Stalin one cannot understand the contemporary Russian political system. Hence a student of political science must know history. It will not be an exaggeration to say that without some knowledge of Shivaji, one cannot genuinely appreciate the intricacies of the contemporary Maratha political system. But humanism holds that an awareness of and an attempt at the appreciation of the dominant historical traditions does not imply a clinging to unfounded traditions. The philosophical approach is integral because it stresses the explanation of the limited generalizations of natural and social sciences from the standpoint of the creative moral and spiritual subject. Thus political science has to be both historical and philosophical in its methodological pursuits. Nor can it neglect the urgent necessity of the solution of the contemporary problems. Having clarified its own cosmological, psychological and ethical views, humanism seeks to address itself to the solution of the pressing problems of man on the earth as well as of astropolitics.

Ours is an age of immanentization. The modern world is based on extensive commodity production. The political system is focalized by the sovereign state with its three adjuncts of the army and the bureaucracy and the fiscal structure. Since the Renaissance there is a stress on rational enquiry into the problems of the cosmos, the earth and society. Political enquiry in the age of immanentization is overworked with the analysis of the processes, forces, patterns, functions and constraints of the sub-systemic components of the system. These aspects of political investigations are comprehended under the empirical, scientific, and applied dimensions of political science. But there is also the philosophical tradition concerned with the values of man as a spiritual and moral subject. For immediate social relevance, humanist political science, necessarily, has to concern itself with the probe into the dynamics of concrete situation.[1] The perennial tradition of the spiritual and moral values will become petrified unless it can provide the *elan* for immediate national regeneration and reconstruction. Armed social and political revolutions cannot be checked unless concrete opportunities are provided for the realization of the moral and political personality of man at a global level. The concepts of Ramarajya, Dharmarajya, the city of God on earth, the

1. According to Karl Mannheim *Freedom, Power and Democratic Planning*, pp. 3-21 & Chap. XIII the main symptoms of the present day crisis are :

(i) New social techniques making for minority rule in large organization like the army, factories etc.

(ii) The neurotic complex of power.

(iii) The growth of monopolistic economy and the total displacement of the local, self-sufficient, non-profit economy of the handicraft and agrarian communities.

(iv) The decline of self-regulating small groups.

(v) The lack of coordination between business, bureaucracy and voluntary associations.

(vi) The disintegration of co-operative controls.

(vii) Disruptive effects of class antagonism and the irrationalism of mass society.

(viii) The disintegration of personalities — growth of the anxieties of the self.

(ix) The disintegration of consensus and of religious bonds — dual morality as a source of insecurity — the crisis in valuation.

(x) The growth of organized thought as in Jesuitism and Marxism. The growth of the manipulative approach to thought.

(xi) The segmentation of intellectual functions.

(xii) The delocalization of the mind — the tearing of thought out of its context.

Satyayuga, the rule of the philosophers or of the priests of the positive society will be considered as idle utopianizations of the apologists of an old order unless the political systems can solve the problems of the day. Thus political science has to have both theoretical and philosophical as well as positive and functional.

Ontopolitics and Empirical Political Analysis

There are two major challenges to an idealist humanist political philosophy today. One is that emanating from the empirical and quantitative orientation of the American political scientists who want to build middle-range and narrow-range propositions regarding systemic and subsystemic functioning and behaviour. They want to build rigorous research designs and execute research projects with as much rigour and precision as possible with the help of statistical tools. Some of the extreme exponents of the empirical approach will like to cry a halt to all historically-oriented philosophical enquiries in political science. They would interpret the latter as the infiltration of subjective bias, opinion statements, personal proclivities, prejudices and predilections into the discipline which hinder the pursuit of objectivity in a scientific work. They propound that the days of great system-building are over and we should be content with intensive micropolitical investigations of the small and specific problem of limited areas. The philosophy of humanism, on the other hand, is concerned with a synthetic holistic orientation towards the specialized knowledge derived from the empirical branches of learning. The data, the propositions, the tested hypotheses, the models etc. as devised by the empirical political scientists are important. But they need further clarification as well as a philosophic synthesis. The work which Kant did in the realm of critical philosophy by his attempt to bring together the empirical mode of analysis based on intuitions and the twelve categories of the understanding and the transcendental synthetic framework based on the ideas of reason has also to be done in the social sciences. The vast amount of information that is being collected by the data banks, the numerous institutes of applied social science research and the statistics departments of the governments have to be classified with reference to the new light that they can throw on morally-oriented motivation and empirical human behaviour. Political philosophy as a humanist critique of the propositions and abstractions of empirical behavioral political science has a deep relevance today. It is true that specialization is increasing and it is not possible to be an Aristotle or a Hegel or a Spencer today; nevertheless, the deep-rooted demands of the human mind and soul for systematic knowledge and some penetrating insight into the nature of the cosmos and the value and the destiny of the sensitive human individual cannot be suppressed. The human personal beset with the agonising maladies of the present day world does demand some fundamental value-pattern which can provide meaning to his existence. The student of political science cannot rest satisfied only with middle-range or low range propositions and conclusions regarding voting behaviour in some rural and metropolitan areas or some studies into the role of the strategic elite or oligarchs in some modernising countries. These are not enough as items of political knowledge. Hence the approach of humanist political philosophy whose fundamental task is to organise the ever-expanding body of empirical information into interlocked propositions relating to the goal and destiny of the human individual in the macropolitical system is important.

Empirical analytical research has made meaningfully significant the study of power, authority, force, control and dominance as the key concepts for the understanding of the political process. But humanism as ontopolitics conceives of man is a moral and spiritual subject and hence it considers the Machiavellian concept of man as selfish and greedy and the Hobbesian concept of man as being governed by an irresistible craze for power, more power and more and more power, as the depictions not of the normal political man but of the psychoneurotic and alienated megalomaniac characters. The common man does have legitimate political aspirations but the overmastering passion of manipulating the will of others according to one's own whims is characteristic of a perverse megalomaniac and a sadist. The normal political man, unless he is to be considered psychopathic, does have altruistic sentiments and is moved by feelings of transcendence of egoism for common good. Vena, Ravana, and

Duryodhana or Machiavelli's prince, Carlyle's here and Hegel's world-historical individuals are not specimens of the goal-gratifying political man but are tragic and pathetic deformations. Nero and Nahusha, Catherine and Karala Vaideha represent the degeneration of pragmatic expediency into reckless violence and crude manipulation. For personal quests of vengeful wrath, they are ready to deprive humanity of much that it holds dear. The basic problem of idealist humanism, on the other hand, is to resurrect the picture of man as a moral and spiritual subject. The realization of the five basic values—liberty, equality, fraternity, justice and fearlessness (*abhayam*) is the dominant need of the present era. We are heading towards gigantic organizational structures and in this vast network of complexity, the reinforcement of the moral and spiritual endeavours can be the only antidote to alienation which is bound to grow in a world full of mighty and lustful political cynics and megalomaniacs. Idealist humanism being comprehensive in orientation is not confined to the pursuit only of the quantitative and empirical technics of political analysis. Sympathetic understanding, the imaginative appreciation of the difficulties of people below the poverty line, the enhancement of the growth-capability of the normal educated man, for the aesthetic evaluation of works of art, literature and history and the recognition of the cognitive capability of man to maintain a transcendent frame of reference whereby he can also inwardize the sentiments of the abnegation of power, are also stressed by humanist ontopolitics. Hence there is no ground to assert that the analysis of power and authority is the sole business of politics as the art of Dandaniti.

The modes of historical and moral-cultural comprehension and the analysis of the texts of political philosophy are not palatable to the exponents of empirical political science. The empirical political scientists, however are weak in one area—their knowledge of the development of science is rather inadequate. They loosely refer to concepts of the various natural sciences but they seldom have penetration into their intricacies. Some exponents of the systems analysis school talk of cybernetics and automatic control theory and plead that homeostasis should be attained in a political system just as homeostasis is illustrated in the case of the physiological organism or the thermostat. But it should be noted that basic automatic control theory is a highly sophisticated branch of communication engineering. Similarly the exponents of the systems analysis school talk about positive and negative feedback. But the concept of feedback also involves a reference to the terms of electronics like plate circuit, grid circuit and so on. It is strange that while earlier critics had been mocking Herbert Spencer for having applied the notions of the regulatory, controlling and circulatory system borrowed from biology to the political sphere, there is no attempt to challenge the incorporation of these newer sophisticated notions of electronics and physiology to the political system. A system is defined as a dynamic structure characterized by interdependence amongst its parts and sustained by the multi-functional operation of its various units and of its sub-systems. There is motor-energy transmission in a mechanical system for the conversion of inputs into outputs. But can any political scientist experimentally prove that the political world is characterized by such operations in its structural system ? This is only a figment of the imagination to say that the political universe is a system in a technical sense. In physics, the molecule and the atom are regarded as systems. In Chemistry, the crystal is regarded as a system. In astronomy, the solar universe is regarded as a system. In each one of these cases there is a structural unity, dynamic interdependence among the units and an all-governing control mechanism. But to say that the political universe is characterized by such subtle processes is certainly an unwarranted application of the terminology of science to the political world. The biologically-oriental nineteenth century political scientists were guilty of applying concepts like the inheritance of acquired characteristics or natural selection or struggle for survival or endocrinal and respiratory functioning to the political world and they were ridiculed. The modern exponents of cybernetics and systematics make a similar attempt and conceive of the political system in democracies as characterized by communication structures which are comparable to nerves in the physiological organism. But I think that the formulation of such notions is merely an analogical exercise.

It may delight us for a moment but it is absolutely removed from a genuine portrayal of the political reality. The systems analysis approach as practised today by American political scientists belongs to the same category of analogical methodology as that of the earlier organic school.

A basic problem which creates an agonising psychological situation for a sensitive thinking individual is that of the relation between naturalistic determinism and moral and spiritual autonomy. A citizen may not refrain from asking the question as to whether his will, impulse and actions are determined by some more massive impersonal forces or whether he is the wielder and, maker of his own destiny. This question cannot be relegated merely to the domain of religion or metaphysics. Even in making administrative, political and personal choices, the individual is perturbed by such questions. When he is adversely affected by some administrative decision in his office he feels like philosophising as to whether the punishment meted to him is the consequence of his own actions or whether some superior agency of force is responsible for that event. Such problems do make pertinent, the philosophical modes of explanation of even politically-oriented human actions. An idealist humanist may interpret even political actions in terms of a divine determinism. On the other hand, an exponent of materialism or motionalism would interpret them in terms of concatenation of forces, some of which may be amenable to human explanation while some may escape the bounds of his knowledge. What I am trying to emphasise is that we cannot rule out thinking about the nature and goal of human decision-making because decisions have vital influence on our individual, social and political destiny. Whether the statistical analysis of a set of variables and collected data satisfies the participant in the political game or whether he is anxious for insight into more ultimate, even indeterminate and imponderable causes for satisfying his conscience are significant in the life of an individual. Thus the philosophical thinking on administrative and political decisions which are normally supposed to pertain to political science has relevance to the political investigator. It may, hence, be maintained that decision-making with the value-structure of the community in mind as well as reflections on the proximate and remote consequences of actions of the participants in the political game do make relevant the philosophical mode of enquiry. Thus one significant area in which humanist political philosophy is still relevant to our days is the rational meaning of decisions arrived at. The mechanics and dynamics of decision-making and its functional and environmental prerequisites pertain to the domain of empirical and behavioral political science but reflections on decision-making in terms of its historical and axiological context as well as the desire for finding deeper meaning into the decisions arrived at, would involve modes of argumentation which have been associated with humanist political philosophy. In its course of historical evolution, idealistic political philosophy has been discussing the goals of the individual, his destiny as well as the meaning of social and political events. Thus it may be maintained that critical reflection upon decisions and the consequences of political actions is a task which makes hominocentric political philosophy in the traditional sense still relevant to our days and reveals the inadequacy of empirical political science.

Another important area in which humanist political philosophy is still relevant to modern times is the discussion of the meaning and value of historical and ethical traditions. Even when there is advance in rationality, objectivity and modernity there are vital areas of the human universe which are governed by traditional ways of action. The entire question of social restraint and permissiveness is governed by traditions. Man, to a great extent, is a creator of social and cultural traditions. So far as the antique and genteel traditions are concerned we cannot rest satisfied merely with imbibing them and socializing ourselves according to them. Valuational judgment which reveals the creative spontaneity of man becomes of uppermost concern when a person is placed in a context characterized by tensions among the diversity of traditions. He is to choose between them and not be dwarfed and determined by them. Choice oriented to the growth of human potentialities and autonomous spontaneity involves valuational interpretation, for example, the traditions emerging from the Ramayana and the Mahabharata may enjoin two disparate kinds of conduct upon an individual. He may be advised according to one type of tradition to engage in a course of action, characterized by self-abnegation. Rama, for example, typifies self-abnegation and the renunciation of political power and determinate legal sovereignty. On the other hand, the traditions sanctified by Krishna may enjoin upon the struggling individual a course of action characterized by economic acquisitiveness and the ruthless conquest of power. The sensitive individual will have to choose among these two traditions and he will have to consult his rational faculty. Thus decision-making among alternative courses of action supported by different sections of the traditional heritage will also involve humanist philosophical enterprise. The political philosophy of idealist humanism will provide to the citizen not only an awareness of the continuing heritage of traditions but will also train him in the logical apparatus whereby he can formulate the moral and rational criteria of choice among them. The Ramayana and the Mahabharata, by and large, are supporters of enlightened philosophical monarchical system. The modern Indian citizen, on the other hand, adheres to the concepts of participatory democracy and political legitimacy derived from the verdict of the electorate. Here again, humanist political philosophy and its criteria will be relevant to the individual in his decision as to what type of political system is he going to support ? —Whether he will stand for idealist humanist socialist democracy or for enlightened paternal monarchy ? Such critical analysis goes beyond the range of empirical political science.

Ontopolitics and Historical Materialism

The second major challenge to the humanist political philosophy as traditionally understood stems from the various exponents of dialectical and historical materialism. The latter regard Marxism as the only scientific social thought today and the other systems of political speculation and political wisdom it will brand as ideological mystifications trying to support the *status quo* and to ignore the sordid game of exploitation of the underprivileged sections like the wage-earners, the poor peasants and the other small-scale traders and landless workers. According to the Marxist mode of analysis, polylogism and the convergence of multiple intuitions and sociological standpoints have no meaning. They believe in the entire satisfactoriness and adequacy of the proletarian logic. Hence, in power, the exponents of totalitarian communism like to suppress all dissentient system of protestant ideologies and pose as the infallible armed popes of the proletarian testament.

The challenge to humanist political philosophy from the side of Marxism is deeper than that emanating from American empirical theorists who are direct or indirect defenders of the capitalist economy and of competitive political pluralism. The latter have developed their structural-functional models and game models in the context of empirical liberal capitalism which in spite of its glaring defects at the sociological and economic levels has sponsored the concepts of social tolerance and freedom of expression. They believe in the solution of problems through intellectual discussions, mutual give and take, bargaining, and negotiations. The heritage of liberal democracy is bound to make the science of empirical political behaviour liberal and appreciative of the profound values of integral hominocentric political philosophy. Its rootedness in the traditions of Locke, Jefferson and John Stuart Mill will make empirical behavioralism appreciate that a political philosophy based on the great classics has a profound role to play in the creative advance of human civilizations. But the Marxist attack on the liberal heritage is trenchant, drastic and disruptive of the values of civilization. The intellectual edifice of historical materialism has been built by the efforts of thinkers and leaders like Marx, Rosa Luxemburg, Plekhanov and Lenin who had no tradition of liberal democracy in their own countries and who had slender appreciation of the values of methodological criticism in philosophical enquiries. Marxism as practised today in several countries of the world has become equated with a totality of technics and methods for the ruthless suppression and even destruction of every school of thought that is different or alien from the officially recognised ideology. It is true that during the twenties, thirties and forties Russia evoked the esteem and admiration of some liberals, who felt elated at the dynamism, buoyant optimism and vigour of the Russian society. But the academician cannot swallow the misdeeds of

Stalinism in action. He has nothing but deep disdain for the Russian purges and forced confessions resulting in the judicial murder or imprisonment of almost all the leading anti-Stalinists. The brutal assassination of Trotosky in his Mexican exile and the cruel liquidation of hundreds of thousands of Kulaks can receive only denunciation at the humanist's hands.[1] During the forties some socialist humanists like Laski, were committed to the Marxist ideology.[2] They were sanguine that the fundamental ideals inspiring the Russian Revolution would provide the intellectual and spiritual *elan* for the transformation of a class-ridden society.[3] Humanist political philosophy, on the other hand, flourishes only when there is a battle of ideologies and confrontation of antithetical propositions and the organon of reason is used for the analysis of the categories of understanding devised by the different schools of thought.

Dialectical materialism, certainly, is the expression of deep resentment against the exploitationist and extortionist technics of bourgeois capitalism. Hence, as a prophecy, it has become a symbol for the crystallization of the resentment of all suppressed sections against the iniquities of an unjust society. Hence, ever in predominantly agricultural countries it has a profound appeal. Humansim also has all sympathy for the agonies and deprivations of the suppressed sections. But it considers armed struggle for the capture of the governmental machine as the last technic and not the first preferential choice. It shares with Marxism a deep antipathy against exploitation in any form. It will refuse to mortgage the body of man to the cruelties of the tyrant, the oligarch, the landlord and the Pharaoh. It also refuses to mortgage the mind of man to the fabrications of the cunning bishop or priest. It feels that the great challenge posed by the over ten thousand pages of the writings of Marx makes essential the mobilisation of concentrated efforts to make possible a

1. H. J. Laski, *The Dilemma of Our Times*, p. 181.

2. "The men who seek, through the ideals of the Russian Revolution, to revitalise the values of our civilisation, submit their dream to tests of reason and of logic which, so far in history, have rarely maintained its splendour when its first rapture has died away." —*Faith, Reason and Civilization*, p. 166.

3. H. J. Laski, *Faith, Reason and Civilization*, p. 201.

reign of freedom, peace and plenty for the poor people of the underdeveloped world. The problem of bread is urgent but a situation should not be created when bread and freedom become alternatives. The message contained in the seven words — 'Give me liberty or give me death' is also vital.

In India we have a vast legacy of freedom of thought. If the key concept of empirical democratic American behavioralism is developmental socialization, and if the basic theme of historical materialism is proletarian organization, the key concept of Indian culture has been *moksha* or emancipation. Emancipation postulates the full growth of individualism by the destruction of all kinds of impediments, restraints and fetters. Only the free investigation of reality by uncoerced thought-processes can provide release from the tentacles of alienation, anxiety and neurosis. The Indian concept of *moksha* is even more vital than the freedom of thought envisaged in the context of the schools of Western liberal democracy which were nurtured with the heritage of Christianity. In spite of all its humanism and its quest for the ethics of compassion, Christianity has not been as tolerant, in practice, as Hinduism. The Hindu-Buddhist culture is based on the highest possible recognition of freedom of thought. Kapila, the supposed founder of the Samkhya cosmology, is regarded as having repudiated a personal God but, still, he has been venerated in the Indian tradition as a great primeval Rishi. Gautama Buddha challenged the orthodox cosmogony and theology, derided the substantialistic character of the soul, repudiated the doctrine of the infallibility of the Vedas and hurled great counter-blasts against the contemporary ritualistic liturgy and the ceremonial codes and practices. Nevertheless, he was exalted as a superior superman or even as the incarnation of Vishnu. The Mimansakas like Jaimini, Sabara, Kumarila and Prabhakara denied the efficacy of God and Jainas repudiated theism but their views were not suppressed by a resort to arms. The intellectual freedom of opinion contemplated in the Hindu-Buddhistic tradition is one of the most priceless legacies for the sustenance of democratic and humanist values in India and the world. This legacy of Hinduism and Buddhism in the shape of tolerance and accommodation (Samavaya as it is called in the Asokan inscriptions) is the intellectual context in which idealist humanist political philosophy can flourish. In Athens also Plato could formulate his radical views in the context of the atmosphere of intellectual freedom. The Sophists were great exponents of freedom. Socrates became a martyr for vindicating freedom of thought and expression. The British school of empirical philosophy was also developed in an atmosphere of freedom. The free unhindered expression of opinion and of preferential statements is the key to the expansion of knowledge and is a prime democratic notion. The humanist dimension of political philosophy fully committed to freedom as the antidote of alienation is, oriented to enhance the vitality of civilization. The diverse kinds of intellectual responses to the pressing challenges of the contemporary world have to be synoptically viewed for their critical appreciation and synthesis. What is essential is not ecclesiastical and political conformism but a critical and comprehensive response to the contemporary agony. Hence there can be no demand for only other commitment except to truth. A religious congregation and ecclesia may enforce conformity. An authoritarian party may also demand commitment. But a University cannot clamour for commitment. It is a place for the preservation of classical heritage and the advancement of modern learning Hence the only commitment that it can demand is integrity in the pursuit of knowledge. Dispassionate investigation, objective analysis and accurate reporting can alone be the method pursued by political philosophy. The cultural heritage of India has ever enshrined the path of free investigation. It does never aim at the annihilation of the opponent or the condemnation of the dissenter in a concentration camp. It teaches the increasing appreciation of a comprehensive mode of enquiry. Hence an attempt should be made for the construction of a political philosophy which is synthetic in its comparative evaluation and appreciation of the Vedic Buddhistic and modern Indian traditions. It will try to examine and evaluate critically dialectical materialism, Maoism, the subtle logical argumentations of Green, the exalted idealism of Bosanquet, the illuminating exegesis of Barker, the socialist thought of Cole and the sociological analyses of Sorokin, MacIver, Mannheim and Laski. The insights gained from the

West European and Scandinavian experiments cannot also be ignored by idealist humanist political philosophy.

Spiritual Humanism Political Obligation and Satyagraha

With its teleological conception of politics oriented to the enhancement of common good, humanism is opposed to the contractual concept of obligation. If the Spinozistic formula of the equation of right with power be correct, then the power of the sovereign may inhibit the exercise of his rights. But Hobbes eliminates this limitation and ascribes absolute power to the sovereign. The politically organized forms of sovereignty can be either monarchical or aristocratic or democratic, still the preference of Hobbes is for a monarchical form of sovereign polity. But Hobbes's enunciation of the absolutist theory of contractual obligatoriness suffers from several weaknesses. First, if there were no preexistent rights in the state of nature recognised by an imponent sovereign, then it does not seem logical to hold that the institution of sovereignty can lead to the emergence of a complex system of rights. Secondly, according to Hobbes, obedience to the sovereign depends on a particular principle of the law of nature that covenants should be maintained. But if the state of nature is a condition characterized by the war of each against all (*bellum omnia contra omnas*) it is illogical to conceive that it can ever be the situational foundation upon which can arise the moral doctrine that covenants should be always fulfilled. Hobbes's nineteen natural laws are only psychological and logical maxims of prudence and to attribute their existence to a prepolitical state of nature when free and equal persons were battling mercilessly against each other does not appear convincing. Thirdly, according to Hobbes, the contract can confer only *natural* right, because *legal* rights are subsequently sanctioned by the sovereign who is instituted by the contrac .

The possibility of a confrontation between the organized authority-structure and the protesting human being cannot be ruled out. According to humanism the only sound course is to adopt the view that a successful rebellion is not wrong if instituted for the sake of common good. The usual charge against the social contract theory that is bad history is also significant because humanism adopts an evolutionary approach to the question of the origins of institutions. At the logical level, the real flaw of the contractualist approach to political obligation is that this theory seeks to justify a system of rights and obligations independent of the dynamic functionality of an organized and institutionalized social structure. Humanist idealism on the other hand, conceives of the evolution of law-abidingness as being closely linked up with the growth of habitual obedience to social norms which inculcate that obedience be rendered to associations which confer advantages upon the citizens through their functioning. There can be, hence, no valid sanction for an authority-wielding regime except that it is a part of man's social nature to obey a group if it provides to him some utility which he could not obtain unaided. Thus not the fear of the mighty leviathan but the growth of cultural norms and social norms that strengthens the sense of obligations.

Philosophical humanism refuses to accept the statist formula that legal and political obedience is based on coercion or on the fear of the rod of the absolute state with its inalienable, illimitable, determinate sway over citizens. Nor does it trace obligation to a contract with Manu and Prithu agreed upon in remote times by the patriarchal ancestors of the human race to surmount the problems engineered by the dominance of human perversity and bellicosity. Obligation for it has only one rational source and that is the habit of citizens to receive satisfaction from the performance of his duties to the state and from the latter's due discharge of its functions. The state is not a divine idea on earth, nor is it an autonomous personality. It is a mechanism for the transaction of common business of the citizens and hence obligation to it can be based only on the citizen's satisfaction over the role performance of the state. The permanent right of the individual to resist any law or ordinance that goes against his higher reason or *Antaratman* cannot be negotiated in a democratic system, least of all by one searing by the ethics of Satyagraha. But it must be stressed that the inalienable right of resisting unjust commands, promulgations, decrees, ordinances and laws is a last resort. Normally the political, parliamentary and judicial methods of the redressal of grievances should be taken resort to. Attempts have to be made to mobilise public opinion and legislative opinion for the acceptance of the demands of the resisting individual. Only after the exhaustion of political and judicial methods, should Satyagraha be resorted to by persons who have created a climate of confidence in their sincerity and conscientiousness. The corrupt use of Satyagraha by hoodlums and anti-social elements to get redressal of irrational grievances and to elicit ego-oriented concessions is the degeneration of a noble instrument. Even Socrates, the greatest resister of the Hellenic world refused to flee from prison for personal safety. Satyagraha has to be prevented from posing a contingent threat to political and social homeostasis because the jeopardization of the system will only bring confusion and chaos and endanger civility, decency and valuational sentiments. Philosophical humanism accepts the need of Satyagraha, in the socio-political system but only as a last device to be resorted to by citizens of proven integrity and high character. Ethical rationality demands that Satyagraha does not degenerate into a perverse technic for uncivilized conduct. Self-immolation practised in recent times in two or three developing countries smacks of the spirit of feudal femininity of the medieval times and cannot be encouraged by a theory oriented to the advance of reason, science and human fellowship.

Spiritual Humanism, Sovereignty and Natural Right

Associational life is increasing in the world today. The state also is an association and is not identical with the community as imagined by the Greek and the German idealists. Pluralists like Figgis, Follet and Barker challenged the discredited notion of the monistic absoulte state and its pretensions. But pluralists, in the course of their tirades against Austinian positivism misconceived of the nature of the political system because they neglected the pivotal role of a coordinating agency. The notions of public service state, welfare state, socio-capitalist state, mixed economy and positive state have been propounded and they have rendered necessary the re-interpretation of the state in terms not of a constraint-imposing mechanism but as an agency for serving common rational good (*lokahita*). Its ideality is to be expressed not by success in war but in terms of its capability to promote public welfare and associational good.

There were historical and theoretical factors for the relative absence of the concept of sovereignty of state in the ancient and medieval world. Positive law-making was not yet considered a business of the political superior. He was concerned with tax-collection and occasionally with the recruitment of soldiers. In the relatively undeveloped state of technology it was difficult for the state to penetrate into the interior regions for enforcing obedience. Hence custom, tradition, folkways and *mores* had dominance in the socio-political system. In several civilizations there was cherished the belief in the higher binding power immutable eternal, divine laws and the positive laws of the monarch in contravention to those natural laws were deemed to be invalid.

Humanism is libertarian in its orientation. Hence the Austinian—Burgessian notion of absolue, inalienable, uncontrolled, sovereign omnicompetence sounds incongruous with its assumptions. It also refuses to accord total sovereignty to the fifty one per cent of the members of a parliament or a legislative assembly. At the legal level, it would be satisfied with the establishment of a synthesis between the doctrines of parliamentary sovereignty and judicial supremacy. At the political level, it accepts the doctrine of sovereignty of the people. But the people are the final and ultimate repository of power. They legitimise the authority of the members of the parliament and act as watchdogs over them. Alert citizenship which prevents the people's representatives from tame acquiscence in a leadership cult is the essence of democratic behaviour. It is an implication of the doctrine of the ultimate political sovereignty of the electorate that in exceptional cases a non role-performing representative, can be recalled from the legislature. On a limited scale, initiative, referendum and plebiscites may also be permitted for the dynamic and effective realization of the sovereignty of the people.

At the still more ultimate levels of theoretical speculation, humanist idealism would look to Truth or Right or Rita or Natural Law as the sovereign even behind the sovereignty of the people. For the mathematics of practical politics, the parliament may be the sovereign and the people as the great community may provide the social and political bases of communitarian legitimacy to that. But from the standpoint of the reasonably perfect society marked bv the efflorescence of human potentialities, the loyalty of a sane moral person can only be to truth and eternal law which is beyond mathematical calculation, political bargainings and the pluses and minuses of assembly forensics. Man as a creative moral and spiritual subject can render obedience neither to any Caesar, nor to any prophet but only to immanental law. Hence in terms of a futurist utopia it can be said that an assembly or a parliament cannot bind the conscience of a Socrates, a Gandhi or a Laski. Man's final and ultimate loyalty can be only to the infinite eternal Consciousness and its immanental manifestations in terms of Rita or higher law. Hence eternal natural laws which lay down the criterion of the moral distinctions have an uppermost status and man can pay unequivocal deference only to them. The human spirit cannot bow to any other being agency or authority. Democracy accepts that the rulers and the ruled must keep on changing. An uninterupted exercise of power and dominance by any one group is antagonistic to the democratic spirit. Ethical humanist democracy too, at the ultimate level, would consider obedience to the immortal laws of perfection or Rita as to only fundamental guides. This kind of deference does not negate the socially accepted distinctions of right and wrong or good and bad but places them in the context of higher truth.

Idealist humanism based on loyalty to right and truth and popular sovereignty has no place for any claim to unwarranted charismatic authority. A charisma based as some extraordinary contribution to social welfare and cultural regeneration is understandable. The ancient and medieval conception of charisma based on extraordinary self-discipline has a certain meaning. The charisma of a Gautama Buddha, a Ramakrishna and a Gandhi is understandable. But a charisma based on sheer physical force, robbery or predatory instincts has no place in a democracy. A competitive pluralist society oriented to the change of the ruler and the ruled at stated intervals can have no place for claims to extraordinary charismatic authority. A self-acquired charisma is understandable but an imposed, manipulated and dramatically manufactured charisma is opposed to humanist equalitarianism. A pluralist communitarian democracy is to be governed by rules, regulations, functional norms and judicial writs and not by the whims, visions and obsessions of megalmomaniacs. The ascription of any charismatic deference to constitutional codes, rules and norms would be tautological or even meaningless because these can also be changed in course of time. Democracy aims at the governance of men by the evolution of cultural and institutional codes and the diversity of social norms. It has been demonstrated that in the developing world charismatic authority has been taken recourse to because of the weakness of institutionalized role sets to meet the challenges of the times. But the crude display of vulgar technics to inherit, to manufacture and to transmit charisma in 1971-1976 in our land, should serve as a warning to all humanist intellectuals.

Humanism being a gospel of moral personalism and ontological individualism, believes in natural right. It does not dismiss the world as an illusion, delusion or hallucination. The terrestrial world is a theatre of concrete action for the achievement of moral, social and political rights. It is true that the individual human being is subject to terrific fear from accidents and the inexorability of final extinction. But at a social, political and economic level, terrestrial existence is bound to continue and man will aspire after the increasing release of energy for the realisation of a better future. Hence humanism is committed to development and growth of liberty, equality, fraternity, justice and fearlessness. It therefore, accepts the philosophy of inalienable natural right. It does not worship the omnipotence of the totalitarian Leviathan which results in the alienation and robotization of man. In place of the apotheosis of the charismatic power of the individual leader or the dictator or the party it is committed to a philosophy of limitation of power. The free movement of the individual is to be highly cherished. Man should have freedom of movement and the right to pursue a gainful vocation. Interpersonal relations are to be governed by the efflorescence of creative citizenship, social ethics and participating community life. The regimentation of all aspects of life under the iron governance of a party or a state is not palatable to it.

The support to a teleological conception of natural right is based on the postulate that for the development of the inherent potentiality of man and the attainment of the perfection of personality, certain claims have to be deemed to be inalienable or natural. We have to recognize the notion of natural right in a moral and psychological sense, otherwise there will be nothing to inhibit the emergence of fascism and totalitarianism. The latter flourish on a mere mechanical conception of man and conceive of him as a mere means and instrument for effectuating the will of an autocrat or a monopolistic party. If man is an Atman and a citizen of a kingdom of ends then his natural right to life has not to be compromised. But this right cannot be had merely by petitioning and asking. One has to be prepared to fight for it. The power-holders would not like to capitulate and hence Tilak had said that one has to make sacrifices for getting his right recognized and respected. Only if a person does his duties and leads a life of dedication can he obtain the moral authority and the will power to fight for the assertion of his inalienable natural right. The belief in one's natural right to life and liberty makes necessary permanent chance of collision between the holders of sovereign power and the dissenting individual.

The individual's natural, inalienable right to life is justified in the ultimate analysis because it antedates the existence of the states. During the days when families, clans and tribes were the preeminent social aggregations, the right of the individual to life was fully recognized. But there were certain limitations in the sense that individuals belonging to different clans and tribes were not granted the advantage of this right. The Vedantic conception of the Atman, the Roman conception of equity, the Stoic philosophy of immanent Reason operative in all human beings, the Buddhist emphasis on the Aryan Ashtangika Marga and the Christian conception of an all-perversive human commonwealth have resulted in the recognition of the conception that man *qua* man is a moral and spiritual member of the human society and does not derive his right to life from any external source. The immanent and inherent right to life should be only rarely interfered with even during the situation of a war or internal emergency. The prestatal inalienable, natural right to life was legally recognized by the state after its emergence. Hence the state does not give the right to life, it only recognises it. The Buddhist concept of compassion would even go a step further and plead for the sanctity of the life of all creatives. The Vaishnava ethics would also concur with the Buddhist standpoint because it subscribes to the Gita concept of Sarvabhutahita (good of all living beings).

There is one fundamental difference between the orientation of the Western idealists and the basic values of the philosophy of the Samkhya, Yoga and the Vedanta. According to Green the philosophical justification of the right to life consists in the human body being the vehicle for the performance of activities leading to the realisation of common good. It is the prime gospel of Hinduism, on the other hand, that the spirit or Atman is sacrosanct in its own right. It is a divine spark, a sacred being and moral self. Hence while the ultimate justification of the right to life lies according to Hinduism in the innate sacredness of the human being as a divine self or rational-spiritual continuum, in Green's thinking, it is its instrumentality in the realisation of social good that imparts validity to the right to life. It was unfortunate that so vital a right as the inalienable natural right to life was sought to be negated in some circles during the dark days of the Emergency in India.

Justice

Justice is an immanent notion of the human heart. Man craves for justice. Some religions formulated to conception of eschatological justice. A just omnipotent God could not be reconciled to the notion of unredeemed justice. Hence if justice was not done on earth, it had to be vindicated after death. At the elementary level, justice means the settlement of disputes and conflicts according to the canons of impartiality, objectivity and rationality. The personnel of the judicial organization—the Sarpanch, the Munsiff, the Sessions Judge, the High Court Judge and the Supreme Court Judge, must be guided by the sole consideration of fair play and a total equalitarianism in the award of due punishments. They should be guided by the Constitution, the existing penal code and the recognised canons of legal interpretation. Of course, the judges are expected to be aware of the trend of sociological and political forces in the country. But in deciding cases they do not have to be guided by the manifestoes and the resolutions of the national executive of a ruling party. There should be speedy disposal of cases because justice delayed is justice denied. At the sociological level, justice inculcates the governance of social, political and economic relations by the criteria of dueness and equity. The concentration of wealth on one side and rampart penury on the other has no moral foundation. Justice however, never contemplates the physical liquidation of the exploiters. Even against the recalcitrants, the legal and moral processes have to be harnessed. The equality of opportunity is a vital element in the realisation of social justice. The right to earn a decent livelihood according to one's ability and professional competence is the dominant concept of economic justice. Political justice implies the incorporation of the canons of civility, decency, participatory democracy, creative citizenship and the total development of the faculties and potentialities of a person, so that the human adult can lead a life of liberty and fearlessness. It is thus amply evident that justice never cherishes the enshrinement of the existing situation. It is opposed to justifying the existing as the rational. It wants a constant revision of the existing structure in order to make it more meaningful. Hence it is irrevocably opposed to the conception that would regard a particular church as the communion of saints or the capitalist order as a permanent institution directed by the invisible laws of Providence. Justice demands that the essential idealism of the triumphant divine city or the ideal Ramarajya should be operatively realised on this earth for the well-being of all human beings.

Theory of Punishment

Humanism accepts a philosophy and ethics of tolerance, cooperation, mutual trust and universal acceptance. Hence it does not uphold a retaliatory theory of punishment. Some of the barbaric forces of penal action like the mutilation of limbs, blinding or drowning would not be sanctioned by it. Nor would it sanction the resort to ordeals by fire or water which have the support of some of the Dharmashastras. Only slightly less violent in character than the retaliatory theory is the retributive theory. By and large, both the theories accept the formula of tooth for tooth and nail for a nail. The researches in modern criminology, psychoneurotics, psycopathology, neurobiology and forensic science tend to support a reformatory theory of punishment. Even the Gandhian formula of undergoing self-punishment for changing the brutal heart of the criminal would corroborate the reformatory theory. But society as it is constituted today is far from being perfect. Hence humanism would not be opposed to coercive technics for bringing the criminals and anti-social elements to their senses. For serious offences, capital punishment and imprisonment for life have to be maintained on the statute book. Where there is valid proof that a person is guilty of cold-blooded murder, the judge must not hesitate in awarding the death sentence to the criminal. The general formula is that punishment should be commensurate with the guilt incurred. Hence the theory of deterrent punishment which demands very heavy punishment in order that the offender's fate may teach a lesson to others, need not be accepted. In some countries punishment in the form of mutilation of limbs or flogging or capital punishment is awarded for the crime of rape or theft. Such a punishment does not offend our natural quest for justice but seem somewhat incongruous with the philosophy of humanism which has not despaired of the redemption of even to worst offenders. Thus, humanism while aiming at the practice of the reformatory theory will, in practice, in a world full of contradictions and cruelty will, for the present, be satisfied with the retributive theory. Deterrent, it will consider as an extreme and violent form of the retributive and the retaliatory theories.

It has been the dream of some sociologists that with the socialization of the means of production and the extinction of exploitation and political authoritarianism, there will be a radical transformation for the good in human nature. Patanjali, Buddha and Gandhi also held that with the energisation of efforts for the practice of Yamas and Niyamas and specially Ahimsa, the altruistic, compassionate dimensions of human nature will flourish and human civilization will enter upon a transformed path of creative large-heartedness. Humanism considers these noble sentiments as exercises in utopianization which teach the transcendence of contrarities for the quest of a perfection which does not seem realisable in the near future.

Humanism and Conservatism

The quest for social mobility reveals the inadequacy of historicist conservatism, bureaucratic conservatism and capitalist conservatism because these three ideologies look with hostility upon notions of liberalism and radicalism. The humanist is critical of Bismarck's, Disraeli's and Churchill's historicist conservatism. Bismarck was a proponent of blood and iron and even sanctioned imperialism to some extent. Disraeli was a conservative imperialist. According to humanism, in the coming era conservatism and imperialism must become things of the past. Asian, African and the Latin American nations should have full opportunities for growth. Hence the humanist who is opposed to orthodoxy, revivalist fanaticism and expansionist virulence cannot support conservatism. He appreciates the role of Churchill, in the mobilisation of the forces that resulted in the final defeat of Hitlerism. But he feels that Churchill's imperialism and his opportunist antipathy against Russia were narrowly conceived. Churchill had earlier tolerated Salazar and Mussolini. In the triumph of the Italian Duce he had found elements that could counterbalance the "bestial appetites and passions of Leninism".[1] With all his rhetoric and his linguistic brilliance, Churchill, the arch-imperialist had no positive gospel for the redemption of European humanity. He was only anxious to contain Russian communism and for that he was willing to devise plans for an European economic union and for military collaboration with the United States. His flaw was that being absorbingly captivated with the ideal of a traditional Britain, he failed to realize that imperialism abroad and a triumphant aristocracy at home had lost all chances of success in the context of the emergence of newer political and economic forces in the post-world war period which demanded a universalist approach. The humanist has certainly to reconcile a passionate quest for individual freedom and academic autonomy with planning for full employment and growth, He cannot afford the luxury of conservatism.

With his intense emotional involvement in the successful

1. H. J. Laski, *Faith, Reason and Civilisation* (London, 1944), pp. 93-94

consummation and implementation of the social democratic ideology, the humanist is bound to cross swords with the gospels of Roman Catholic counter-revolutionism and hierarchical elitism. T.S. Eliot's[1] conception of a hierarchical, aristocratic Christian culture and society appears as a romantic nostalgia for a forgotten past.[2] To Eliot, Karl Barth and Niebuhr, the Church is the guardian of sacred values. To the philosophical humanist, whatsoever be the personal, inward and emotional worth of mystical religious experience there could be no public and scientific objectivisation of that experience. A man of faith might derive satisfaction from religious intuitionism but the havoc-engendering social and economic contradictions of a polarized society cannot be solved by the gospels of imaginative flight, introspective catharisis and religious atonement. Hence according to the humanist, Eliot's conception of culture appears narrow, inhibited and unrealizable.

Humanism And Internationalism

Just as spiritual densified gnosis (Vijnanaghana or Citi) is the dominant theme of Indian culture so also other cultural cycles cherish principal themes of their own. The Semitic cultures have a profound consciousness of an omnipotent God and prophethood. The Chinese ethical and social philosophies adhere to the notion of Tao. The Greeks had a deep notion of proportion and the Romans of law. The Christians adhere to a Trinitarian formula. Other civilizations have cherished similar other formulas. The nation-state is a necessary stage in political evolution. It neutralizes, if fully adhered to, the vestiges of casteism and feudalism and the corrosive aspects of internal violence. But the efflorescence of humanism on the global scale demands that the future world order should not annihilate diversity and multiformity but should seek to stress the foundational principle of human unity on moral, political, sociological and economic considerations.

The external framework of a technological civilization is slowly creating the foundations of a world order. Under the

1. T. S. Eliot, *Towards the Definition of Culture* (1948).
2. H. J. Laski, *The Dilemma of Our Times*, (London, 1952), pp. 118-35.

League of Nations and the United Nations there has been the growth of cooperation in several non-political fields. World public opinion is now slowly being built against the untrammelled assertion of the sovereignty of a state. At the time of the Suez Canal Crisis, the Conservative Government in London had to yield to the pressure of British and world public opinion. Slowly the foundations of a world order are being laid. The formidable emergent challenges from the stratosphere, biosphere and ecosphere are bound to make the hardliner and the chauvinist also think in terms of an international order and peaceful co-existence. According to philosophical humanism, the nation-state is not the final phase of political evolution. World history need not persist to be a theatre of global annihilation. Any glorification of force and war as done by Heraclitus, Machiavelli, Hegel, Nietzsche, Treitscthe, Bismarck, Bernhardi and Clausewitz can only bring global annihilation and total nihil. History bears evidence to the havoc-generating impact of pan-Germanism, pan-Slavism and pan-Islamism. Hence the quest for armed regional pacts ostensibly under the legal cover of the Article 52 of the U.N. Charter does constitute a threat to peace. Peaceful co-existence can alone be the antidote to the triumph of bipolarisation, tripolarisation or quadripolarisation of the world. Imperialism, whether political or economic or ideological, constitutes an invitation to war. But war need not be made the final arbiter for settling mutual counter-claims. Negotiation, conciliation, mediation, arbitration and other peaceful technics must be increasingly resorted to The border-disputes between India and China centering round the forcible occupation of nearly fifteen thousand square miles of Indian territory and the Arab-Israeli conflict can be peacefully settled. But all nation-states have to to satisfied with some curtailment of their sovereignty. The United Nations, constituted as it is on the basis of great power dominance in the Security Council, cannot be the basis of a genuine world state on federal pattern. Some positive steps can be taken for the reform of the United Nations whereby the permanent membership of the Security Council can be raised to fifteen and the powers of the General Assembly can also be enhanced.

Humanism has to find its political culmination in an

international order. Amidst the persistent threats of aggressive chauvinism, fascism, totalitarianism, Ceasarism, military coups, plutocratic oligarchy and imperialistic neo-colonialism, only the dedicated quest for global peace and justice for the realisation of a new humanity can save civilization from dismal disaster and perilous doom. The quest for detente, peaceful co-existence and economic cooperation, receive their consummation only in the realisation of a world order recognising the cultural individuality and unique souls of the various nations. Even if there is no immediate ideological and structural agreement on the realisation of a world order, there should be no ground for pessimism. A pragmatic and behavioral commitment to the peaceful solution of the tension-generating issues in world politics will slowly strengthen the basis of world order. The recognition of the concepts of self-determination of peoples and an irrevocable commitment to the outlawry of war will prepare the essential background for a global order. The unmitigated emphases on the cult of state omnipotence has resulted in the propagation of the notion of sovereignty by Bodin, Hobbes, Blackstone and Austin and the other positivists which justifies the recourse to armed adventures for the settlement of disputes regarding national interest. The imperatives of a world order, on the other hand, demand the revision, and possibly even the renunciation, of the view that armed conflicts are legitimate for the vindication of national right. The acknowledgment of the individual as a subject of international law makes imperative the universal recognition of human rights whose transgression will autonomically attract the interference by a world body committed to a communality of legal and political objectives. If nations sincerely desire the safety of humanity from nuclear annihilation, the pacific settlement of disputes is essential. The problems of international economics pertaining to investment priorities, balance of payments, exchanged oil have to be amicably settled. The quest of institutionalized essential internationalism is not a mere spiritual and moral aspiration emanating from romantic sensibility or enthusiasm but it is an urgent legal necessity for safety of the human race itself. Even if there is no existing world community, the quest for an international juristic order need not be delayed on the academic ground that a sense of community is a precedent of the organisation of law.

Total disarmament at this stage may appear utopian. Hence, in the interest of the world community, opinion may be concentrated on the control of nuclear energy. A comprehensive nuclear treaty for banning future tests and the destruction of nuclear stockpiles is essential. Steps should be taken to reduce the manufacture and sale or transfer of conventional arms. For reducing the wide gulf between the industrial and the developing world the gap between the two has to be lessened. In their arrogance, the industrialized countries may boast that their wealth is the product of their hard and protracted labour and hence why should they share it with the indigent nations of Asia and Africa. But the economic logic is not so simple. Even the much-advertised hard labour of the Americans has been supplemented with and expanded by the hard physical labour of African slaves. Besides historical antecedents and a moral and psychological spirit of sharing, the compulsive logic of modern sociology and economics make imperative a world order for the realisation of global brotherhood of mankind. Thus the formula of inalienable absolute sovereignty conceiving of the nation-state as an autonomous guardian of moral values which has the supreme right of asserting its sway in the court of world history through blood, iron, electricity, atom and hydrogen, has to yield slowly to the formula[1] of one world association based on mutual regard and the appreciation of each other's cultural contributions to the human family.

The spirit and letter of the Universal Declaration of Human Rights which has been incorporated in the constitution of several states has to be implemented for the promotion of genuine internationalism and the commitments made under the Helsinki Agreement of 1975 and the International Covenant on Civil

1. Cf. Alexander Pope, *An Essay on Man.* VI, 361-369 : "God loves from whole to parts : but human soul must use from individual to the whole. Self love but serves the virtuous mind to wake, As the small pebble stirs the peaceful love; The centre moved, a circle straight succeeds,

Another still, and still another spreads.
Friends, parent, neighbour first it will embrace;
His country next; and next all human race;"

and Political Rights, 1977, should be strictly fulfilled. The resistance of the totalitarian and semi-totalitarian and monarchial systems to the recognition and implementation of human rights has to be transcended. South Africa, Rhodesia and Albania are three glaring examples where basic human rights are being flouted. The Amerindians or the Red Indians in the U.S.A. are a vanishing race. Their identity demands urgent protection. Human rights have a higher moral sanctity than the legally guaranteed right of citizens. They are not meant only for the limited purpose of dismentling the old edifice of imperialistic colonialism but aim at safeguarding the humanist heritage. Hence the protection of human rights by an international agency has to be effectuated. As an immediate program, the U.N. Commission on Human Rights has to be strengthened and activized. For the consummation of a global order based on non-aggression and peaceful co-existence, public opinion has to be mobilized for peace. If schemes of socio-economic reconstruction are more urgently attended to at home, disarmament will, to some extent, at least follow. The failure at the economic front goads some ruling groups to embark on a policy of war in the quest of an external scapegoat on whom to release the pent up emotions of rage.

Freedom is indivisible and any attack on freedom in any part of the world is a challenge to all freedom-loving peoples. Hence a conjoint approach to problems of world peace is essential. A federal approach to economic and political problems raging in the world is the only legitimate technic for the maintenance of peace. But the pursuit of the federal institutional approach demands the genuine growth of a "federation of mind". No single nation or group of nations can pose to be the custodians of world peace. Hence the building up of peace areas and a peace-oriented approach are essential. But peace has to be attained with honour and justice. There need be no acquiscence in a policy of exploitation and injustice.

Conclusion

While empirical and behavioral political science is, generally, engrossed in the structural — functional study of the components of a political system which are conceived as being in a state of constant interdependence and thus being organically linked, humanist philosophy seeks to emphasize the valuational dimensions of the political system. The mere study of the processes of the empirical universe is not sufficient. The enunciation and popularisation of the ideals of a good life which will provide the evaluative criteria for judging the role-performance of the system in operation is a legitimate intellectual enterprise. The empiricist may retort that we have had enough blueprints of good life in the past. But it has to be emphasised that each age will need its own blueprints for defining and clarifying its ideals, objective and priorities. Ours is an age of alienation,[1] contradiction, frustration and cynicism. There is a growing mechanization of life and a consequent despiritualization of the socio-political structure. The growing challenges make essential the fresh definition of goals. It is a poor consolation to seek refuge in the gospel of ethical relativism. The existence of different value-patterns and regulative norms makes urgent the task of evolving certain criteria which will help man in the clarification of his goals and in differentiating the universalist from parochial and communal consideration. How can the spontaneity and creativism of man as a moral and spiritual subject be preserved in an age of automatism, depersonalization, organizational bureaucratisation and partisan consideration is a vital task for the political scientist. It is true that there was no moral idealism behind the Assyrian and the Roman imperialisms and the predatory conquest of the Huns and the Mongols. The manoeuvres of new imperialism have been based on financial capitalism and were inspired by the notion of the White Man's burden. But these examples should not be a cause of despair. Buddhism, Stoicism and Christianity did have notable repercussions in generating idealistic currents of thought which had a noble impact on political evolution. Hence to conceive of political behaviour as capable of being influenced by ethical rationalism and idealist humanism is not to be guilty of the charge of utopianising speculation.

While the political scientist would analyze the problems of

1. Perhaps Fichte for the first time used the term *Entausserung* (Alienation).

the present era, the political prophet would make prognostications regarding the future health of civilizations. The future of political science is linked up with the future of human society. The dialectical polarity conceived in the antithesis between Ahriman and Ornuzd, Cain and Abel, or Deva and Rakshasa has to yield place to Samavaya which will be a state of reconciling harmony and universalist compassion. The spirit of alienation and disenchantment has to be replaced by a creative consciousness of dynamic human fulfilment through significant achievement in the fields of social and behavioral sciences, history, poetry, arts, religion and philosophy. Politics will eventually cease to be the sphere of merely the objective spirit manifesting itself in the family, society and the nation-state. An awareness of the creative dimensions of human phenomenology will make its impact felt upon the dull concern with the technics and mechanics of the objective external world. An era of the resplendence of idealist humanism will mean the cessation of power politics and of the cynical apathy to the well-being of others. But idealist humanism does not visualize either the withering away of the state or the consummation of spiritualized anarchism. Constituted as man is, to think that in the near future there will be the dawn of a perfectionist utopia is a kind of enthusiastic chiliasm. The process of governance is bound to be there. It is only possible to devise institutional restraints upon it but it cannot be done away with.

CHAPTER IV

HUMANISM AND THE INDIAN POLITICAL SYSTEM

The Indian Cultural Immanence

Both Spengler and Berdyaev accept the view that culture has spiritual or religious roots and propound the notion of the metamorphosis or transformation of culture into a megalopolitan commercial civilization. For purposes of theoretical analysis it may be useful to maintain an analytical distinction between a mechanical, commercial, technological civilization and an aesthetic, ethical and spiritually-oriented culture. But in probing into the motivational determinants of Indian historical and political evolution, for the sake of semantic convenience, culture may be treated as a comprehensive category signifying the total modes of an individual's and a society's responses to environmental challenges. Thus conceived, it may be stated that the dominant problem of Indian culture is to seek an ontological spiritual unity in multiplicity and diversity. Indian history has been the history of long millenia and not merely of centuries and generations. There have been epochs of battles, conflicts, wars, devastations, waste and frustrations. But the creative spirit of the people that had been responsible for the building up of glorious civilizations in the past is still active and its principal norms and ideas, concrete architectural and sculptural symbols and valuational criteria have been oriented towards the exaltation of moral and spiritual sentiments. It does not conceive of culture as a closed organic unit. Its orientation, on the other hand, has been towards global universalism and increasing synthesis. The renunciation of parochial ethnocentrism has been its fundamental integrating notion. Its key concept, thus, is not iconoclastic rejection, but appreciation and absorption of vital, sociological, aesthetic and ethical symbols in a spiritual frame of universal reference. There may have been some epochs of decline when the valuational quest degenerated into an unscrupulous apology for power and property but the overall impression that one gets from the study of the symbols representations, and literature of India from the days of the Saptasindhu civilization to modern times is an assertion of the sanctity of Yama and Niyama, Tantricism notwithstanding. Humanist politics is based on this recognition. It is true that at times the aspect of multiple diversity became more pronounced and the organic notion of unity was lost sight of resulting in the arrest of national vitality and the minimization of social organic solidarity. Nevertheless the dominant spiritual *elan* has persisted. A historical awareness of the Indian cultural patterns is, hence, a psychological support to the task of nation-building. An awareness of India's vast cultural heritage is an indispensable requirement for alert and active citizenship in this country.

History has been considered as the basic social science and sometimes it is said that history is past politics and politics is present history. History may even be considered as the root of politics as no social science research scholar can have a penetrating grasp and appreciation of his subject-matter without an awareness of the historical perspective. The concepts of social welfare and development as the goals of the political system have also a profound historical aspect. The historical growth of the labour, agrarian and humanitarian movements in the world is a topic of vital concern for the students of the social sciences. Leopold von Ranke, Karl Marx, Max Weber, MacIver and Laski were also students of history. Hence to expose the students and citizens to the historical method oriented to the dynamic assessment of cultural, political, social and economic forces, is an imperative task of nation-building. Dayananda, Vivekananda, Tilak, Aurobindo and Rama Tirtha have repeatedly stressed that a sense of awareness of the cultural continuity is essential to generate a sense of genuine pride in the past and future of the nation. From the days of the Indus civilization and the Vedas to modern times, the perennial stream of Indian culture has been flowing and it will be rendering the citizens rootless if the realisation of the unity of the past, the present and future is lost sight of. A sense of historical partnership will alone impart a psychological dimension to the merely mechanical notion of nationalism based on commodity production and oriented to the promotion of trade. The participation in intellectual and other types of pursuits which promote the growth of feelings of appreciation for historically-rooted cultural immanence is an antidote against mere passive acceptance of or acquiescence in the rules and regulations of an authority-enforcing regime. It imparts a higher saiience to the activities of the ontological individual who does not consider mere acquiescent support-offering to the regime to be his sole task. He believes that his active, dynamic support is essential to impart genuine legitimacy to the ideological propaganda and external legal legitimacy of the political power-holders. A historical awareness of the glorious epochs of national creativism enhances the efficacy of the individual and motivates his involvement in the workings of the political system.

There is an immanent continuity in the cultural and historical heritage of India. This continuity is deeper than the mere temporal continuity maintained through the enactment of certain events on the physical soil of the country. From the Vedas down to the twentieth century there is a cultural continuity visible through the adherence by the people to moral values and religious traditions. Religions emanating from non-Indian soil have also, to some extent, made their influence felt on the land. But the dominant stream whose tributaries have percolated to the lives of the masses has been the Vedic-Buddhistic tradition. The cultural heritage from Amarnath to Rameshwaram and Kanyakumari has been the fundamental base of unity that has sustained the nation amidst its turmoils and challenges.

Hence the study of Indian political, social and religious experiences in a historical perspective is essential. The pursuit of the historical method in the social sciences makes one visualize the nation as a dynamic continuum. The opponents of the historical approach to the apperception of the cultural heritage of the nation point out that the carrying on of the load of the past means that along with the load of wisdom of the ancient days one is compelled to carry on the burden of their errors and irrational prejudices also. It is also said that the Philosophical and literary classics were also the products of their own days and we cannot solve the political problems of global politics in an era of critical transition by the recipes of Aristotle's *Politics* and Kautilya's *Arthashastra.* But the exponents of the historical approach do not want to convert the universities into places for the boastful glorification of the perennial tradition and the past cultural heritage. They only want to use the classics for the chastening of the mind and the enlargement of the heart by exposing the people to the wisdom of the olden days. They are not preaching any repudiation of the critical sense of enquiry and scrutiny. The historical approach to the social sciences has not come to an end with Montesquieu, Hegel and Marx. It has deep relevance to the understanding and explanation of the dominant patterns in the Indian political system. It is open to debate whether the historical structure is characterized by the prevalence of inexorable laws, but there is no controversy regarding the point that history has some significant lessons to teach to the social scientist. So far as the concrete solutions of the problems of contemporary Indian political system are concerned, it is true that they can be solved neither by the formulas of Kautilya and Manu nor by those of Aristotle, Marx, Parsons, Lasswell and Almond. A synthetic historical and humanist orientation is essential for their solution.

The Crisis in the Indian Political System

The period after India's independence has been marked by rise of localism, violence, linguistic particularism, economic disparity, cynicism and pessimism. The unjustified supercession of judges and the throttling of the press between 1973 to February 1977 certainly indicate the creeping of perversity in the political system. Some problems have been solved on paper through the manipulation of statistical figures but the grim nakedness in the countryside of Bihar and other states has its own story to tell. The malady in the country has been differently diagnosed. Some have talked of a crisis of character and a crisis of confidence. Some medically-oriented analysts and biochemists would put the blame on the food consumption habits of the people which produce laziness, lethargy and gastro-intestinal disorders. Some Aristotelians would put the blame on the climate of the torrid zone. Myrdal spoke of India as a "soft" nation whose inhabitants disdain to undergo the processes of protracted toil and hard discipline. Some would blame the corrupt politicians who have exploited the country's resources while others would hold the bureaucrats to be the guilty offenders who have fed inaccurate statistics to the legislators. It must be noted that the disease of the Indian political system can be diagnosed only by the method of multi-factorial dynamics since no single monistic category can be held responsible for all the evils. A complex and complicated disease must have numerous causally operative categories behind it whose confluence and conjuncture result in the eruption of the symptoms syndrome.

In the Indian political system there have been several crises. But the experiences of March 1977 definitely indicate that the system based on competitiveness and plurality can re-assert itself. Even a semi-totalitarianism based on the distribution of favour to a chosen coterie and to some favourite social and religious groups in the nation cannot obtain legitimacy. The teachings of the saints and sages urging for a quest for moral values have penetrated into the consciousness of the masses who, generally, have an inmate revulsion against the perpetration of injustice. The moral quest can gain political completion only in a system characterized by opportunities for equitable and just distribution, the development of the capacities of the citizens for fully participating in a community-oriented democratic polity and the realisation of territorial and national integration. The differentiation of groups and associations is a characteristic of modern development and in India also group formations and increasing development of associational existence are bound to take place. But the painful empirical lesson of Indian history has been that the trend towards diversity has often been strong in this country. In the quest of growth and development, it is essential, hence, to take steps to promote sentiments of national integration and cultural patriotism. The clustering of emotional attachments around the nation can act as a deviant against the deviant eruptions of the sentiments of associational density and loyalty to the region, group and sub-group. The sectorial egos have to be neutralized and thus alone can responsive adaptation to the challenge ridden environment of the day be made. Certain dominant characteristics of and some correctional measures to remedy the dysfunctional elements in the Indian political system will be pointed out below:

Nation-Building and Political Development in Modern India

1. A military system is a deterministically closed one. A totalitarian and oligarchical polity as in the U.S.S.R., Eastern Europe and China is a mechanically and coercively closed system. A theocracy, as in Pakistan and old Tibet, is a trans-mechanically closed hieratic and hierarchical system. Capitalism sometimes is a monolistically closed system. Only an idealist humanist democracy is an essentially open, mobile, liberal and free system. Closed political systems are characterized by entropy, which according to the second law of thermodynamics, tesults in disorganization. A humanist democracy has to be characterized by the growth of trends antithetical to entropy and has to manifest negative entropy by the incorporation of energy from the environment for greater organization and differentiation for vital growth. The homeostasis of the Indian political system has to be, hence, linked with urgent social and economic change. The goals of the system have to be linked with the expectations of the people, the demands of the parties and interest groups, the resources of the country and the feasibility costs of the objectives. The quest for the satisfaction of demands has to be linked up with the enthusiastic support that can be given to the government in the implementation of the priorities. Matters of dispute should be settled peacefully and carrying all controversial issues to the street shows immaturity, jealousy and hostility that may lead, eventually, to the eruption of totalitarianism. The basic values of a humanist political system are liberty, equality, justice, fraternity and international fellowship, and fearlessness. There should

be no compromise so far as their concrete realization is concerned. Although these basic political values cannot be deemed to be as immanentally operative as the laws of motion formulated in physics, yet a consensus of thinking intellectuals may be obtained as to the recognition of the supremacy of these values. The instrumental and proximate values and the relevant technics of their realization in the Indian political system have to be linked with these basic values. American behavioralism and the systems analysis approach have popularized notions like assimilation, accommodation, acculturation, socialization, mobilisation, participation, capability promotion, homeostasis and feedback response. Dialectical materialism has popularized notions like expropriation, conquest of power, liquidation of counter-revolutionists, the dictatorship of the proletariat, democratic centralism, etc. Spiritual humanism is committed to sustained growth and the peaceful redistribution of resources to cater to the needs of all citizens because it is not segmental and parochial in its approach. The political process should be open and the interests of weaker sections like Harijans should be promoted through a leadership that is careful to articulate their interests. Furthermore, the system should take steps to protect the individuals from viral, bacterial, mycological, protozoan, physical and chemical diseases, disturbances and fear.

2. The political system has to be vital enough to generate funds and energy so that the formal and institutional agencies of action can be mobilized. The sentiment that if things go wrong then a charismatic prophet would emerge by providential dispensation and settle matters right is not conducive to the operative efficacy of the system. Citizen efficacy has, hence, to be promoted so that situations of crisis and conflicts can be mastered. If the system fails to respond successfully through correctional feedbacks to antithetical forces, its survival cannot be guaranteed even by people of extraordinary charisma. The real strength of the nation consists in the mobilisation of people's strength througth the decentralized foci of governance. The increasing possibility of role-taking and role-differentiation among citizens and their groups has to be fostered. Even semi-authoritarian controls should be everywhere lessened and decisions regarding the fixation of priorities and the allocation of

resources have to be consensual and the result of collective debates by the legislature, the party leadership and the Cabinet for systemic role-performance.

3. Primacy has to be attributed to national integration as the real foundation for the growth of the political system. The state is a primary and significant association of all the citizens and their children but the political system which is the dynamic institutional and associational expression of the nation is a more comprehensive concept than the state. The cult of the omnipotence of the state, hence, should be substituted by loyalty to the organic nation which is the vehicle for the preservation of the cultural heritage. The loyalty to the nation which represents a partnership between the old heritage and new visions and hopes, takes primacy over the loyalty to the kin groups. The sole commitment of the citizen is to the interests of the nation and not to any group or divisive organisation. At the operative level, one notices a deep feeling of immanent romanticism in India. The old Janapadas and the small provincial units were engaged in internecine conflicts. Even in the Ramayana and the Mahabharata one can notice the exaltation of internal struggles. The issue, in both the epics, of course, was of justice but the participants were Indians themselves. Hence one prime task of the political system is to foster country-wide integration as a counterpoise to the rampant romanticism clustering around divisive and fissiparous slogans. In the West, there have flourished pronounced champions of individualism like Protagoras, Hobbes, Locke, Milton, Paine, Jefferson, Ricardo, Mill and Spencer but at the practical level there has always persisted the strong feeling for the community (*res christiana*). Hence separatist claims on behalf of the individual ego have never sundered the deep feeling for the community there. But in India, at the practical level, there have been a large number of foreign invasions some of which were solicited by the disgruntled and alienated elements at home. In spite of the theoretical adherence to the idealism of the good of all living beings (*sarvabhutahita*), there were epochs of the suppression of the masses and the triumph of selfish oligarchical elites. Hence it is essential to check the degeneration of individual and sectional claims into anti-national enterprises. The magnification of the

claims of the nation as a great community is essential. The essential basis of integration is psychological. A psychological identity-consciousness with the forlorn, humble, deprived citizens is essential. An emotional attachment for the Himalayas and the land fertilized by the rivers emanating from it and further stretching from the Vindhyas upto the oceans around, can provide the psychological feeling of identity-consciousness. The strengthening of the psychological roots of the nation can be brought about by teachers, educators, moral leaders and saints. Politicians sometimes may encourage separation for promoting personality-oriented politics of manipulation and agitation. But teachers who have to play a major role in the task of national regeneration have to inculcate sentiments of patriotism and solidarity among the citizens. The task of nation-building has to precede the task of state-building because the former fosters sentiments of self-abnegation for the realisation of the goals of a higher collectivity. After centuries a political system oriented to the realisation of multi-dimensional Swaraj has been established in the country. The territorial integrity of the system from Kashmir to Kanyakumari and from Gujarat to NEFA, Meghalaya and Mizoram should be established. No inch of territory should be surrendered in Kashmir and Ladakh and on the Indo-Chinese border. For strengthening sentiments of organic nation-building more and more citizens should participate in collectivity-oriented activities at village, block, district, state and Union levels. A participatory communitarian democracy soliciting the favourable involvement of the citizens in its processes by the egalitarian allocation of material resources among them can alone protect the system. Democracy, in practice, in several countries of the world, has manifested several weaknesses. It has resulted in cabinet dictatorship, bureaucratic despotism, the installation of governments on winning only the minority of electoral votes, extremes of partisanship, corruptions in elections, demagoguery, mobocracy and ocholocracy, centralization of power in the capital cities and metropolises, dilatoriness in decision-making and competitive struggles among leaders of machine politics for dominating the political arenas. There is no genuine government by the people anywhere. But still democracy is not worse than any other form of government known to mankind. It is sad to contemplate that the Asian countries where the sun of civilization first rose have now become only the objects of history and the dominant strings of the political drama are being controlled from Moscow and Washington. Education has to foster sentiments of patriotism, tolerance, and political socialization in democratic values in the Afro-Asian World. There has to be the formation of nation-defensive attitudes which can preserve the immanent and expressive values of the cultural system and stress that knowledge is both for advancing the frontiers of research and for promoting collective unity and political regeneration.

4. The basic features of the Indian Constitution like adult franchise, fundamental rights, judicial review and federalism, must not be subjected to ordinary or extra-ordinary parliamentary amendment. They can be touched only if there is the clear verdict of the people for amendment.

5. Right up from ancient times it has been demonstrated without any doubt that Indians did not lack in personal bravery and dauntless resoluteness even in face of terrific odds. But it is also a fact that on several occasions their weapons were not fully developed. At a time when the Mughals began to use cannon, the Indians could not meet them on an equal footing with their slightly obsolete weapons. The Marathas lacked naval strength. Hence the modernization of weapons is a very serious task. Researches for the internal development of sophisticated weapons are essential. If the neighbours go on making stockpiles of devastating military potential including nuclear bombs, for safeguarding the precious heritage of the civilization and culture of this land, it is essential in self-defence to manufacture atom, hydrogen and neutron bombs. Idealist humanism is not a philosophy of unadulterated Ahimsa. It believes in justice, equity and mutualistic reciprocity. Hence if the Indian cultural heritage is exposed to the attacks by intercontinental ballistic missiles, realistic strategy demands that the country should be well-equipped both with the conventional and the most modern sophisticated weapons. The defence budget, hence, should not be curtailed.

6. Idealist humanism accepts, however, that the real defence of the country demands the resolute mobilisation of the will power of citizens who are dedicated to the urgent tasks of the

safety of the nation. In ancient times defence was relegated to a particular caste or group. But that notion of parochial military elitism is not congruous with the formidable modern challenges. Behind the trained and equipped military personnel, there should be the united psychological and moral will of an integrated nation fully committed to the realisation of the country as blessed sacred land. The mistakes of the past need not be repeated. From the Hindukush to the Brahmaputra, the land reveals a poignant record of invasion, suppression, humiliation and liquidation of people. Vallabhbhai Patel and Rajendra Prasad had displayed wisdom and remarkable foresight in the resurrection of Somanath which is a symbol of the historical heritage of the land. Today a revitalized resurrected nation is working for the recognition of its legitimate place in the world political system. A vast, comprehensive and developed political system has to be built and strengthened so that the citizens may pursue the values of intellectual ascent and rational enlightenment along with the chastening of emotions for the growth of moral autonomy. If the values of growth and development are to be cherished, the political system has to be well-defended. Defence requires the involvement of the citizens in it through the total mobilisation of their energy for achieving the tasks of national regeneration, development and security. Experiences of the Indo-Pakistani and Indo-Chinese border wars have demonstrated the importance of the view that the nation should mobilise its defence potential also on the popular front. A National Solidarity and Defence Association should be established. Its aim would be to protect national integration, strengthen patriotic sentiments among the youth and prepare a second front for defence purposes in times of national crisis.

7. Kashmir is an integral organic part of the Indian Union. It has been the land of some of the prime exponents of Indian cultural values. It is the land of Kayyata and Mammata. It is the land of Kalhana whose *Rajatarangini* is a classic of Sanskrit political historiography, and of Bilhana. Abhinavagupta, the exponent of the Saiva-Vedantic philosophy of Pratyabhijna, lived there. The semi-encyclopaedist Kshemendra with his *Avadanakalpalata* and other noted works is a monumental figure in Sanskrit classical poetry. Samkara is said to have visited

Kashmir. Kashmir, thus, is a vital part of the cultural and political system of the country and even in modern times it bears testimony to the sacrifices of thousands of soldiers who have shed their precious blood for its safety, integrity and development. The country will not permit any relaxation on the Kashmir front. Citizens from other parts of the country should have the same legal and proprietory rights there as have been guaranteed to them, by the Constitution, in the other parts. The sub-culture, if any, of Kashmir should become an organic component of the perennial stream of the historical continuity of Indian political system. Just as Hyderabad has become an organic part of the Indian polity so should Kashmir become a vital part of the immanent Indian soul and body.

8. Widespread decentralization and dispersion of political power is essential. The governance and the administrative mechanism of the country should be carried on at *five levels* — the federal centre, states, districts. blocks and villages. The division is, more or less, a functionless entity and hence district administration has to become streamlined and development-oriented. The image of the district magistrate as a servant and public functionary needs to be projected. Community Development schemes represented an attempt to concretize the ideal of a better, nobler and more satisfied state of existence for the villagers of this vast land. Gandhi considered the uplift of the villages as of paramount concern. But the objective reviewed is immensely worried over the deplorable state of economy and the lack of feelings of emotional identification with the community which prevail in the countryside. Any general appraisal of their working is enough to convince the critic that they are not the agents to effectuate a fundamental revolution in the attitudes and belief-systems of the rural people. Block administration has, hence, to become more energy-generating. Today corruption is eating into the vitals of block administration. Gram Panchayats have been almost immanent in the Indian social system. With the coming of Independence they were legally re-constituted as the vital bulwarks of the Indian social and political mechanism and the new experiments in democratic decentralization have further enhanced their dynamic role as agents of social and political transformation.

But the infiltration of partisan and caste considerations have made them only the executive committees of the rural elite who are, generally, in league with some of the corrupt and ineffective block officials. To remedy these weaknesses village panchayats have to be made genuine experiments in local democracy and home rule. More funds have to be generated to make them active and functioning.

9. The immanent romantic trend of Indian history and culture must not be allowed to weaken the centre. Hence the advocacy of administrative decentralization must not be interpreted as invitation to weaken the centre. In financial matters more autonomy can be given to the states. But sentiments of patriotism and identity-consciousness with the nation must not lessen. Sub-nationalism does not have to be given any quarter. India is a federation but of the Canadian and not of the American type. The integrating monistic trends of the federal polity should be strengthened in face of the counteracting trend in Indian history towards the constant emergence of centrifugal forces which have sometimes even brought about national defeats. But it is not practical to convert the governmental mechanism into an unitary system. The central government should have enough military power to deal with a recalcitrant state which in the name of state right or autonomy works for secession. The cry for secession should be dealt with as a national crime and treason.

10. The Rule of Law is a cardinal concept of democracy. All citizens should be tried in the same courts of law. Extraordinary Courts to try citizens have no place in an egalitarian democratic polity. The penal structure has to be absolutely impartial. Laws should proceed only from the regularly constituted authorities for framing them. Rule by ordinances is not to become the normal pattern of democratic functioning. Sectoral and class considerations should not be the impelling force behind legislation. As far as possible, laws should have a general orientation. A law enacted to safeguard the selfish interests of a dominant elite is a contradiction of democratic idealism. Laws should have behind them the social support of the citizens. An alert, vigilant and active public opinion is an effective prop for the preservation of judicial integrity and the effectuation of

the rule of law. The rule of law demands the integrity and full independence of judicial functioning. The judicial process should be simplified for the quick disposal of cases. The exorbitant fees of lawyers is incongruous with a democratic system because it acts as inhibitive for a very large number of citizens. The bar has to act as a watchdog for safeguarding democratic processes. Judges have not only to be absolutely honest but should also seem to be honest. They should avoid, as far as possible, social contacts as recommended by one of the Law Commission Reports. Any tampering with judicial integrity will be a terrible damage to the concept of the rule of law which has been one of the prime contributions of the British to the Indian political evolution. Some decisions of the Indian High Courts and the Supreme Court have been of profound significance and have served to reinforce the faith of the citizens in the impartiality and independence of the judiciary. The judgment of the Allahabad High Court holding the former prime minister Indira Gandhi guilty of two charges of corrupt election practice was indeed epoch-making both in the judicial subsystem and the political system as a whole. The induction of the communist authoritarian view of the judicial interpretation being governed by the trend of social policy and "the political wind" will be anti-democrats. The Indian Supreme Court had given a tough fight to the coercive enterprises of the government before the Emergency. A few decisions of the Patna High Court relating to university affairs in Bihar, in 1962 and 1965, were of great significance in mobilising favourable sentiments for the impartiality and integrity of the judiciary in the minds and hearts of the educated elite in the state. It is true that to convince a defeated party of the independence of the judiciary is indeed very difficult if not impossible. The citizens have to be on the guard for maintaining the sanctity of the rule of law. It will be indeed disastrous if, rightly or wrongly, the citizens were convinced that the doors of free and fair trial are closed for them. The rule of law peremptorily demands that social corruption must be eradicated because even the administrative and educational elite emerge from the social set up. Hence not only has the judicial process to be made immune against governmental interference but venality, graft and corruption have to be rooted out from the associational structure itself lest they cast their dark shadow even on the sacred land of the judicial courts.

11. Anomic and anarchical eruptions like mass violence, the assassination of leaders of rival parties, the encouragement to deviant behavior, criminality, perversion, forcible *gherao* of persons in authority and riotous demonstrations have no place in a humanist communitarian democratic system.

12. It is a matter of deep gratification that the parliamentary and state elections of 1977 have restored to the citizen the democratic rights of free existence, the equal protection of law and the safeguards of the rule of law. Since 1971 a criminal conspiracy had been hatched to deprive the citizen of the values and privileges of a dignified life based on critical enlightenment and of a Swaraj based on law. The restoration of the parliamentary system and of the supremacy of the processes of law and judiciary have made it imperative that the mechanics and dynamics of democracy are infused with the ethos of full freedom, and a spirit of common partnership in realising the virtues of fellowship and fraternity. The Indian citizen has been the subject of much ridicule. The old priestly Sanskrit legal codes relegated the vast masses of the populace to an inferior mode of existence. In the Islamic jurisprudence, the Zimmis were, more or less, second class citizens. To the protagonists of an alien imperialism, the Oriental people were immersed in inebriating contemplation and watched with unconcern and patient deep disdain the vicissitudes of political transformation. Although not as mesomorphic and heavily-built as the western man, and not as capable of physical mobility as the light-bodied Mongol, the average Indian citizen is a modest, moderate, goal-satisfying creature and he craves that his political aspirations and economic gratifications should be attended to. In recent times Bihar, specially, has shown a proneness to violence that is ominous. Other states had also their quota of skirmishes, violence, intimidation and indulgence in abusive slogans during the days of Assembly elections. But it was reserved for Bihar, the land of Gautama Buddha and Mahavira, to indulge in a bloody orgy. According to the official version, the death toll in the wake of the elections of June 1977 was

27 but according to unofficial reports more than fifty people lost their lives. It shows that the criminal elements are out to perpetrate dastardly deeds against the citizens and the administrative machinery finds it difficult to cope with the situation. But the administrators will have to protect the lives and liberty of peace-loving citizens by wielding the rod of punishment impartially. No political system can tolerate intermittent sporadic violence.

13. For the institutional strengthening of national Swaraj, a two-party democracy is the most suitable mechanism. A totalitarian monolithic party becomes hegemonist and even destroys the inner democratic functioning of its own structure. Only the competition between two national parties for obtaining the electoral mandate for ruling for a limited period of time can counteract the natural tendency towards party oligarchy and the triumph of leadership in the game to grab power. Even a proletarian party, instead of working for the withering away of the state, begins an unmitigated process of self-perpetuation. Hence the two-party system as the main pattern associated with some other issue-oriented regional parties can be expected to run the democratic state-machine. For the present, the cry of a partyless democracy seems to be an utopian project.

14. In case an existing governmental mechanism fails to deliver the goods there should be opportunities for changing it. The commitment to maintain the democratic political system does not imply that the maximization of energy is needed only for somehow maintaining the system homeostasis. The health, vitality and growth of the system is essential. If a government has become degenerate and is of low legitimacy then there should be ways of changing that. If the representatives become partners in the perpetuation of a corrupt governmental system then *some ways have to be devised for their recall, if over sixty per cent of his electors demand it.* Persons who have forfeited the confidence of the electorate have no moral right to demand any deference.

15. One important method for soliciting adequate public response to and sympathetic appreciation for governmental policies is the release of relevant information. The information-

imparting function is of profound import in a democratic polity. During the emergency there was strict censorship and for some time there was the imposition even of pre-censorship. In the tyrannical and despotic political systems of ancient and medieval times, there was resort to violent imposition of the policies emanating from the top centres of decision-making. But in the nineteenth and twentieth centuries even the most dictatorial and authoritarian regimes cannot but publicize their policies. The polyarchical and democratic polities have, in addition, to frame policies for the realisation of the common good of the system through the appreciation and articulation of the aspirations, desires and needs of the citizens. In this process, political activists, leaders, interest groups, the press, political parties, institutions and associations have a significant role-performance aspect. They provide a linkage and a bridge between the policy-makers and the citizen-respondents. Sometimes the collection of information is thwarted when the decision-makers show irritation at the communication of unpleasant information to them. The Congress debacle in March 1977 elections was, to some extent, a function of the wrong information given by the intelligence agencies to the government regarding the latent attitudes of citizens and the real texture of public opinion. Some philosophers and sociologists have exalted the role of the intuition and the superior vision of the leader in a political system. But intuition cannot function in a vacuum. Unless the data are correct, even a highly gifted leader is bound to commit mistakes. Hitler's blundering adventure against Soviet Russia would not have been possible if the Nazi secret service had offered him a correct appraisal of the armed might of that formidable communist antagonist. For security reasons it may not be possible to share some vital information with the public but there can be no justification for the Indian Government not being accurately posted on the latest developments in Sinkiang, Tibet and the MacMahon Line regions. The humiliating experiences at the time of the Chinese-Indian battle of 1962 would have been avoided if the Nehru government had amassed useful information and shared a part of them with the citizens. The press also cannot escape responsibility. Was it not its legitimate function to collect relevant information regarding these vulnerable areas and offer them to the people? Communication is a key concept in modern social and behavioral sciences. It refers to aspects that seek to accelerate the process of bestowal of legitimacy on the decision-making authorities. In a democracy, communication may eventually become a substitute for coercion and constraint based on sanctions. With the introduction of planning in the country, administrative processes have assumed increasingly significant roles as foci for the convergence of different types of communication. For example, the political executive communicates with the administrative personnel and the people through formal and informal channels also communicate with them. The mechanics, dynamics and impact of communication thus have assumed an increasingly important dimensions. For articulating the expectations, aspirations and grievances of the people and for aggregating their demands in terms of issues which are to become the bases of policy decisions, are needed great political dexterity and tact on the part of the village leaders and activists. Unless there is unconstrained communication between the people and the policy-makers, the political and administrative system will lack adequate support and this will hamper its capability for effective implementation of plans. A large number of decision flow from the block headquarters to the people. This flow of decisions is through the official machinery of the blocks and also through the semi-official machinery of the Mukhiyas. The latter in their turn, may mobilize the energies of activists for this process of communication-facilitation. The process of formulation of decisions at the block level and their communication to the villagers as well as the process of communication of the decisions made by the higher authorities at the state and district levels to the villagers is a multi-dimensional problem which requires the mobilization of the tools and techniques of behavioral sciences for its adequate grasp. In this context, it is desirable to study three aspects of the communication process with reference to decision-making in the block and village areas. First, relevant decisions made at the level of state headquarters, divisional headquarters, district headquarters and sub-divisional headquarters are to be communicated to the block administrators. The latter communicate some of the relevant decisions to the people in the village areas. Secondly, some decisions of local importance are arrived at by the block administrators themselves and these decisions are also communicated to the villagers. Thirdly some decisions are arrived at in the conjoint conferences of the block administrators and the village Mukhiyas. These decisions are also communicated to the people. The appreciation of the dynamics of communication is essential for the understanding of the political system. The following four hypotheses in the field of communication research may be hazarded for being tested by behavioral studies. The Indian plans have not resulted in the emergence of successful information—transmitting activists in village areas. Programmes involving innovations, which may have the effect of changing the existing power structure in villages, are not adequately communicated to the villagers. The Mukhiyas are more interested in communicating money-demanding programmes to the people than in communicating subsidy-granting programmes. The process of feedback of communication from the villagers to the block level being weak, hinders the process of decision-making.

16. The real malady of the Indian economic system which is the vital context of the political system is arrested development due to the continued prevalence of agricultural feudalism and the abject poverty of the masses. In Europe, by the end of the 18th century feudalism was almost extinct. The Russian serfs were emancipated in 1861. By 1865 the American Negroes were emancipated. It is true that Zamindari has been abolished in Bihar but still there is a large number of feudal landed proprietors. The Ceiling Act has not brought about any substantial change in the land ownership structure. The landed families have taken advantage of the loopholes in the legal framework to retain the proprietorship of their land in the hands of their own kith and kin. The major socio-economic evil in the country is that the gross iniquities of the highly unjust and disparate distribution of wealth and land have been amalgamated with the unequal strength and numerical quota of the different castes. If the population statistics and economic resources of the different castes were, more or less, equal then the castes

would have functioned as polymorphic pressure groups counter-balancing one another. But the unequal demographic and economic resources of the various caste groups intensify the evils of feudal exploitation and social particularism and create dangerous situations fraught with explosive dimensions for the body politic. Hence a genuine collectivity-oriented economic policy of allocation of total resources is essential.[1]

17. The students are posing threatening problems for the system. The rowdy youth begin to swear by Gandhian terminology and non-violence only when it becomes clear to them that the government is determined to be relentless. After the elections of March 1977 the youth have been talking in an aggressive tone bordering upon constant threats. A good many of them who had nothing to do with the movement and who were even siding with the Congress Government pose as freedom fighters and great leaders of a revolutionary dispensation. They hurl threats to the university authorities, intimidate bus and taxi-drivers, extort subscriptions from shopkeepers and indulge in deeds of gross indiscipline. It is extremely difficult to carry on an administration oriented to citizen-welfare in such an atmosphere. It is absurd and even perverse to claim that students should be allowed to practise large-scale copying from books and note registers in examination halls and invigilators should not protest. In the Patna University, some invigilators and teachers have been humiliated, abused, manhandled and even assaulted. The manifestation of the inflated ego of some of the students and the infiltration of outside anti-social elements into the ranks of students pose the gravest threat to University administration and even to the civil administration. Peace, it seems, can be maintained only by the show and use of force. The moment there is relaxation of governmental pressure, the anti-social elements masquerading as genuine students assume threatening proportions. Some demands of the students are, no doubt, genuine. There should be more laboratory, library, canteen and transport facilities. The quality of food served in the hostels should be improved.

1. For detailed schemes of economic reconstruction, Ch. VII of this book may be consulted.

The facilities of fellowships, scholarships, stipends and grants have to be enhanced. But if the students misbehave with the college and university authorities and threaten to lynch them, why should the police not enter the campus. If criminal actions are committed, the police are fully within their legal competence to enter the Assembly halls, the Parliament halls and the High Court buildings. If the university remains a place for the cultivation of the sacred vocation of scholarship, it must be kept immune from police ravages. But if that immunity is abused and violence is taken resort to, police entry is bound to be there. Citizens cannot tolerate some criminally-minded student leaders posing threats to the lives of their children and relations in the University campus. Sometimes it is said that teachers and administrators should assume courage and face the agitated mobs. This feeling sounds noble but it amounts to imagining that the teachers and administrators are crusaders and are prepared to become martyrs. Why should a section of citizens be asked to be prepared for self-immolation ? Lord Buddha might have tamed Angulimala — the furious fanatic and the terrible death-dealing robber. But it is on record that a poor courageous principal of the Rajendra College, in Chapra, in North Bihar was slaughtered in the campus. A Vice-Chancellor had been killed in Yadavpur and that had elicited a lot of verbal sympathies. But what about the humiliations of, intimidations to and assaults on other senior teachers and vice-chancellors in Bihar ? Should we ask the teachers to walk armed with revolvers and have their own security guards ? In the Patna College, in 1973, some half a dozen teachers and the Principal were beaten by the police who were chasing rowdy students who, allegedly, had pelted stones on them. Nothing could be done to rectify the grave wrong. To make the story still more humiliating pressure was brought on some teachers to change their statements and in course of the proceedings the defense lawyers asked unbecoming questions from the Principal. The large-scale *politicalization* of the universities leading to the invasion of academic decision-making areas by power-hungry politicians is to be avoided. Certainly the student should undergo the process of *politicization* meaning thereby the cultivation of the awareness, by them, of the significance of political entities, institutions and forces. They also must be exposed to the process of *political socialization* implying that they should learn the values of creative, participant citizenship in the family and educational institutions. But while politicization and political socialization are legitimate psychological processes, politicalization acts as an encouragement to rowdyism and lawlessness among students.

18. Philosophical humanism wants to strengthen Swaraj by suffusing that with moral and spiritual sentiments. The citizens have to have faith in the legitimacy of the political system and the sense of commitment to preserve its unity, integrity and its vast and precious cultural and historical heritage. A deep sense of cooperative reciprocity and brotherliness is a prime motivational determinant in infusing a sense of martyr's spirit for the preservation of the country's Swaraj and culture. Mere political Swaraj has a tendency to degenerate into the pursuit of corrupt technics for the acquisition and accentuation of power. Mere economic Swaraj often degenerates into a tripartite struggle between the capitalists, landlords and workers for gaining ascendancy. The internecine conflicts and cleavages disrupt the homeostasis of the system. It is essential, hence, that the moral norms of conduct so deeply stressed by Buddha, Patanjali and Vaishnavism become internalized as the guiding maxims of the political role-takers.

CHAPTER V

IDEALIST HUMANISM AND PUBLIC ADMINISTRATION

The student of public administration has to be aware of the significance of political sociology, fiscal policy, delegated legislation, administrative adjudication, empirical politics, management science and organisational theory which are making rapid advances these days. The problems of leadership, public opinion, electoral behaviour, mass observation, the dynamics of the legislative process, decision-making, micro-political phenomena, scientific management, bureaucratic behaviour etc. are also important aspects of modern applied researches and they have relevance to public administration. In the transformation of the medieval civilization with its despotism, ecclesiasticism, feudalism and fragmented social sectionalism into the modern civilization of the nation-state with its rules, regulations, norms and orders, the rational-legal civil service has played a strategic role. The bureaucracy in modern political systems has been based on certain generalized categories like fixity of tenure, monetary payment, reasonable chances of promotion, hierarchical span of control and strict job-definition. The old Anglo-Indian bureaucracy was characterized by a dominant legal punctilio oriented to the conformity to precedents and system-maintenance. Philosophical humanism contemplates an era of extensive production, immense introduction of economic innovations and know-how, and large-scale social change and status-transformation amounting almost to a total revolution. In the transformation of inputs into outputs, in the channelization of the feedback responses of the public to the level of decision-makers and in a dynamic reconstruction of society and economy, the civil service has a significant role to play in the developing world. This formidable task demands a new type of bureaucracy which is innovative in its orientation and is committed to the philosophy of socio-economic change contemplated in the Indian constitution. The absorption in matters of promotion and personal preferments and the rigid attachment to operative rules and precedents as the guiding star which only result in immobilism have to be replaced by a missionary spirit of dedication to act as instigators of concrete change for effectuating the dream of a classless and casteless society based on surplus rather than on poverty and destitution. So far as the relation with the changing team of ministerial personnel is concerned, of course, the civil service would be neutral in the matter of portion involvements. But certainly civil servants should set their feet down when corrupt ministers want them to act against their conscience. Furthermore, the civil service must be committed to act as catalysts of political development and its commitment to preserve the fundamental values and the basic structure of the Constitution has to be irrevocable. The motivational internalization of and the emotional identification with the great political and moral values like liberty, equality, justice, fraternity and fearlessness is essential. This will make possible the lessening of anti-democratic and anti-humanist behaviour.

There are some impediments in the path of goal-gratification at the level of administration. These are :

(i) Compartmental attitude in place of a coordinated integrated approach to administrative problems,

(ii) Inadequate channels for the effective transmission of feedback responses from the public to the policy-makers,

(iii) Inadequate cultural socialization of the administrators in the ethics of democratic egalitarianism and the growth of something like an administrative caste resulting in bureaucratic conservatism, inadequate contacts between the administrators and the public and the inaccessibility of the top administrators,

(iv) The Finance Department playing an inhibitive and

negative role towards urgent works of reconstruction and development,

(v) Procrastination and apathy in the quick disposal of business,

(vi) Faulty distribution channels even with regard to essential commodities,

(vii) The constantly advertised allegations of corruption and misconduct of the middle management.

(viii) Furthermore, a devastating force that has disturbed efficiency and exposed the administrators to cruel public ridicule is the growth of unionization among the employees. Just as the growth of student unions has posed numerous threats to the university administration, so has employees unionization disturbed the smooth psychological working of the government secretariat and other places of decision-making. Unionization is to be fostered to the extent that it is a protective device for the pursuit of the economic demands of the employees. But if the employee union is to resort to third degree technics to pressurize and manhandle administrators for getting cancelled transfer and posting orders and for making them sanction the crossing of the efficiency bar and for expunging remarks from confidential character rolls, then the symptoms are indeed alarming and betoken the eruption of malignment tumours in the cardiac and endocrinal systems of the administrative body politic.

A manifesto for the reform of Indian public administration on the lines of the main philosophical notions of humanism can be thus laid down :

1. The humanist will plead for the increasing control of the administration by the public. But public control does not mean that administrators will be accountable and responsible to the members of the public and not to their superiors in the departmental hierarchy and to the cabinet. But it does mean that due deference will be shown to public opinion as an indicative, supportive and directive force in the politics system and that obvious lapses in role-performance have to be avoided. Genuine public grievances expressed through newspapers and the

legislature should be redressed without unnecessary delay. There should be extensive contacts between the administrators and the public where frank exchange of views on the dominant issues of the day should take place. Aggressive dominance, evasiveness in making replies and incorrigible corruption are not congruent with the democratic functioning of the administrative mechanism. Discriminatory application of rules and needless utilization of sanctions also are not to be encouraged. Wherever necessary and possible, the criminal, contractual, personal and tort liability of officers in relation to the citizens must be enforced. Pathological processes generated because of the malfunctioning of the system should be replaced by the removal of bottlenecks in the administrative morphology. Furthermore, there should be the avoidance of psychological constraints which are generated because of administrative arrogance and cocksureness.

2. The concentration of power in the hands of the central government is bound to result in the omnipotence of the cabinet and the bureaucracy. It may, sometimes, result in the exaltation of the leadership cult. It is also possible that the political, military and economic elites may enter into an unholy alliance for the selfish agglutination of power. There is a vicious logic in the scramble for power because power can be retained only by the enhancement of power. Necessarily, the unending rapacity and coercive technics of dominance utilized by the power-holders lead to the diminution of the status of the average man. For centuries, the Indian rural countryside has been the mere object of history because it has been the feeding ground for tax-extortion and the supply of recruits for the army. Furthermore, there is the persistent and painful story of the ravages, depradations and naked use of force by the feudal landholders. The great imperative for a people's government is to make the people conscious of their rights. Every citizen of the Republic is to be invested with rights equal to those of the tallest in the political system. For this, decentralization of power is essential. Only that quantum of power which is essential for the purposes of defence, law and order and the maintenance of the transportation and communication system should be retained in the central and state capitals. Generally, in a humanist commonwealth, political power would be controlled by philosophical and scientific competence

and be inspired with a feeling of reflective sympathy. The perversities of power have to be negated. Power should be linked up with functional role-performance and if people's committees, citizens' committees, gram Sabhas, block level organisational groups etc. begin to perform their tasks in a spirit of dedication, power would have to devolve from the higher layers of the political pyramid to the lower ones. Unless the average citizen shares in decision-making, he cannot experience a sense of efficacy. He would remain pessimistic and apathetic and may even cherish sentiments of resentment against the established regime. But increasing participation in the making of decision regarding the polities and programmes, at whatsoever level they be, would nurture in him the sense of appreciation of the legitimacy of the system. The growth of the cognitive, conative, aesthetic, moral and teleological faculties of man which is the prime goal of philosophical humanism necessarily demands, at the level of constitutional, governmental and administrative centres, the growth of the citizen's personality. Totalitarianism has a cynical attitude towards the common man. It claims to rule in his name and arrogates to itself the wisdom to interpret the will of the people at a higher level than they themselves can do. It tends to exalt the leader and the party as higher than the people. But genuine democracy demands for the common citizen the right to commit mistakes and learn from them. While totalitarianism fosters political adolescence, democracy aims at the growth of the maturity of the citizen.

3. Rural administration is infected with many evils. There is demand of monetary payments by Block officials even for doing routine jobs like the commutation of land rent after the registration of a deed of sale or purchase of land. The petty officers of the Block are in the habit of settling *Gairmazruwa* land with some interested parties if they are paid bribes. There are other evils concerning economic administration in the village areas. The land rent collection policy of the government in several states has been shifting. But, eventually, almost all dues have been sought to be collected. The consequential demand for the payment of land rent arrears results in hardships for the agriculturists. Sometimes the rent collector and the village Mukhia enter into an unholy alliance to charge the property

cess from the people at differential rates. The large amount of money that has been sanctioned for developmental activities in the villages has been very unfairly distributed. Some big villages tend to monopolize the sanctioned funds for an entire block. Thus schemes meant for the eight or nine villages in a block are grabbed by only one or two villages. The clever people who know how to flatter the powers that be tend to corrupt the entire sub-system. During the emergency, the policy of destroying illegal encroachments on public roads was implemented to some extent. There might have been some harshness in the implementation of the policy but the wisdom of the policy is beyond question. Road encroachment is a phenomenon not only of the urban sectors but also of the rural areas. In the villages public roads are used for thrashing the paddy crops and for providing a place for the habitation of the cattle. During the rainy season it is a common phenomenon in the countryside to be seen that roads have been cut and *bunds* or earth structures adjoining the irrigation canals have been damaged. Here also one will find that some rowdy villagers take the initiative in such criminal activities. When crops are growing in the fields one common practice of thieves is to cut the upper portions of the crops containing grains. It is difficult to get redressal for such activities of stealth from the police or the Mukhia. The cow-boys of the neighbouring villages often play great mischief and the grazing of the fields of others is a fairly common crime in the rural countryside. Hence the rural administration needs immediate streamlining. A revitalized rural administration will be a great bulwark of the Indian political system.

4. The civil service has to learn to appreciate the genuineness of public responses to the systemic process of the conversion of inputs into outputs. Outputs have to be preserved from being monopolized by the dominant castes and the financial oligarchy. Along with the older concepts of economy and efficiency, the newer notions of soliciting widespread acceptability for policies of allocation and the correction of the malfunctionings of the administrative system in the light of negative feedback responses are to be governing norms for the civil servants. The higher civil service is not merely to supplyremote control mechanism

from the headquarters and to dispense and legitimize punishment but has to provide corrective measures for getting rid of the apathy and cynicism of the citizens by mixing with them in a spirit of cooperation and fraternity. Thus abstract and impersonal relations have to be supplemented with human and humane relations. A domineering attitude in relation to the public has to be replaced by the humanization of response-patterns. This implies that bureaucrats have to be prevented from building formal and informal pressure groups of their own. This, in turn, postulates a radical change in their behaviour-pattern. Of course, as noted earlier, the rule of law prescribing equality before law, the equal protection of laws and the absence of prerogative courts with extra-or-non-constitutional powers, has to be there but, besides, a brotherly ethic of compassion and deference for the dignity of the 'last' man has to prescribe the bureaucratic norms in contemporary and future India, if a participatory communitarian agro-industrial Gram Swaraj and democratic Gandhian socialism is to be the goal of attainment.

5. The costs of the establishment of the governmental and administrative mechanism have gone up considerably due to prodigal spending, inadequate motivation because of the absence of a spirit of dedication, overstaffing consequent on the operation of Parkinson's law in bureaucratic structures, economic constraints and mounting proliferation of board, commissions and committees. The humanist spirit of simplicity and avoidance of gigantic structures should also be reflected in the reduction of the costs of governance. The idealist humanist will also plead for increasing simplicity in the style of living of the administrators. Conspicuous consumption has to be replaced by the quest for increasing simplicity and self-abnegation.

6. Discipline in the administrative hierarchy should be a function not alone of constraint but of the logic of the situation where all role-takers derive job satisfaction from the discharge of their duties. Mutual esteem has to be shown both by the public and the administrators to each other. A spirit of genuine reciprocity, cooperativeness, mutual trust and the appreciation of the good points of each other should govern the interrelations of the administrative participants and the people.

7. Administrators have to display a capacity for enthusiastic persuasiveness so that their decisions not only are rational and purposive but also appear to be so to the clientele. They should have the capacity to form an integrated perspective of the department as a whole and they should have the capacity for directing their vision towards the materialization of public good.

8. The juridical approach to political science and public administration has been developed since the eighteenth century. In England, Blackstone, Bentham, Austin, Holland and Hewart, in Germany, the theorists of the *Rechtsstaat* and the *Verwaltungsrecht* (administrative law), in France, the exponents of the *droit administratif* and Duguit, and in America, Burgess, Goodnow and Pound have strengthened the juridical approach to political science. In response to the demands of a rising technological-commercial society and in order to supplement the working of the organs of democratic government in the modern positive-service state, the role of administrative adjudication and judicial tribunals is increasing in modern times in India also. The judicial control of administration is a significant aspect of the democratic process both with reference to substantive law and procedures. This needs strengthening of the remedies to preserve fundamental rights. The judicial control of public administration is vitally essential for the realization of the values laid down in the Preamble and the other parts of the Constitution. The undemocratic aspects of the legacies of despotism, ecclesiasticism and imperialism have rendered the average citizen too weak to resist the encroachments of the state. Hence the citizen should be made aware of the judicial remedies like injunction, certiorari, *mandamas*, *habeus corpusy* and *quo warrant*, which are available to him for the enforcement of his rights. Torture to elicit confession can have no place in a system of free law. Fair hearing and a reasonable opportunity to defend oneself is also an imperative need of juristic democracy.

9. The vertical distance between the top administrators and the members of the lower echelons should be reduced. The attitude-complex towards subordinates born of the legacy of paternalism and the resort to coercion should be replaced by that of negotiation. But in the name of an integrated personnel

administration it does not seem feasible to reduce the four-layer civil service structure to two or three.

10. The police administration needs thorough overhauling. The rampant recourse to corruption in matters relating to criminal cases is a standing scandal. Police officers at the station cause irreparable damage to life and property by their failure to act in time when cases are brought to their notice. But for the successful realization of humanist political ideals, it is also imperative to have courageous citizens who can give impartial evidence and necessary clues for the detection of criminals. A rationalized police administration demands the use of wireless communication and forensic laboratories. But costly scientific appliances will fail to deliver the goods unless the police personnel undergo a process of moral regeneration. For instituting cases against people guilty of atrocities against the weaker sections, the police has to be more solicitous. Any attempt at the manipulation of the police personnel for serving selfish ends by leaders of political parties is a criminal slur on civilization.

11. The wide and systematic application of scientific methods is the secret of the efficiency of modern industrial civilization. In place of intuitional, haphazard and confused technics, science stresses the use of experimentally-validated and rational processes that will result in the maximization of the turnover, in the economical deployment of the human and non-human materials of production, in the elimination of waste, in the streamlining of the concatenation of the different entities of the administrative system, in the achievement of targeted priorities within the time-schedule, and in the realization of over-all horizontal and vertical co-ordination among the different areas of the productive and the administrative organization. The quests for rationalization, scientific management, organization and management, etc., are phases and aspects of the use of reason, science and technology in the service of the community. In the Oriental-tropical Indian setup with its centuries old traditions of feudalism, social oligarchies, economic stagnation and antiquated productive methods, the increasing application of scientific technics is one of the prime needs of the hour. Without the application of scientific technics we can neither fight our internal and external enemies nor realise our plan objectives. For the

enhancement of productivity and streamlining of administration, operations research techniques relevant to the minimizing of waiting-line in establishments, production planning, inventory models and inventory control, job scheduling, marketing research with reference to the search for consumers etc. may be experimented with a view to the optimum utilization of material and financial resources.

12. Organization and methods aim to use the one most scientific method for bringing about the end-product of the implementation of public policy in the quickest period. It emphasises strict job-description and analysis and through the emphases on the preparation of Process-chart, Workload-chart, Control-chart etc. it aims to enliven and quicken the tempo of work. It utilizes the technic of procedure standardization both for the establishment and the line activities of the operative agencies. It also emphasises the fruitful management of the physical tools of administration and of the working instruments for the personnel in such a way as to bring about an accelerated disposition to work in a well-organised spatio-temporal set up. But it cannot be denied that the Organization and Methods approach is too mechanical. The Hawthorne Experiments of the Western Electric Company brought increasing focus on the human dimensions of the productive process and since then in the United States efforts have been made to combine the scientific management scheme of Taylorism with the human relations approach which stresses the enhancement of prestige, and the development of psychological and moral ethics of employees.

13. Public and business administration have been enriched by the insights of behavioral approach. The behavioral approach inculcates the role of participant group decision-making. Decision-making with regard to public policies is not a mechanical act; it is, on the other hand, a teleological process informed with a large number of informal, non-cognitive and associative responses. Hence the behavioral approach to public administration may be regarded as two supplements to the scientific management approach.

14. The promotion of morale in the services is also essential. Morale is manifested in vitality and zest in working, in the endurance of hardships and cheerful exposure to risks, threats

and dangers and in a dedicated sense of job-performance. For morale-building it is essential that the employees should have physical capability, the hours and the physical establishment of work should be satisfactory, there should be a harmonious adjustment with the task in hand, the employees should be free from severe complexes, frustrations and mental disease and monetary and psychological incentives should be provided within the limits of the country's slender resources.

15. Sometimes it is said that socio-economic development can be fostered if provision is made for an Indian Economic Service. The structure, functions and powers as well as the technics of policy-implementation to be followed by the contemplated Indian Economic Civil Service will have to be coordinated with those of the I.A.S. The problems of position-classification, hierarchy and span of control, and training have also to be visualised. Other processes like budgeting, manpower survey and resources survey wherein the Economic Civil Service can play an effective role will have to be kept in view.

16. One difficulty in the Secretariat administration today is that sometimes files are started from the top and orders and directions are sent on buff-sheets. Normally the files should start from the secretarial level. If ministers start giving orders and directions on buff-sheets then that is bound to create difficulties. Because of governmental instability in some of the states since 1967, ministers of departments keep on changing and thus sometimes there is no consistent policy. The ministries in coalition-politics are constituted by different component groups which have, sometimes, antithetical, political, economic and social ideologies and programmes. Thus, in the context of ministerial fluctuations, if this system of buff-sheet is to be encouraged, then this will create great difficulties for the administration. One of the cardinal principles of the modern civil service structure is that there should be consistency in the various orders and directions that are passed and except when there are overriding circumstances, the norm of recourse to existing precedents should be followed. Due to governmental instability and the large size of the ministry, it is possible that sometimes young and inexperienced politicians may become the ministerial heads of departments. On the other hand, the

corresponding secretaries in the department may be highly experienced experts in their field. Hence temperamental and other problems are bound to crop up and there may be chances of conflict between the minister and the senior government officers. It has, therefore, to be seen that government officers are not subjected to pressure and demoralisation. There are certain conventions and norms which have to be respected for harmonious mutual relationship between ministers and secretaries. The latter have to act in such a way that they can maintain the dignity of the services. The unseemly controversy between a former Railway Minister K. Hanumanthaia and the Chairman of the Railway Board B. C. Ganguli only illustrated at a dramatic level what might have been done or what might have been going on at the state levels, unpublicised in the newspapers. Hence the old traditions of subservience have to be replaced by considerations of mutual regard. Another evil of secretariat administration is the enormous resort to the system of checks and balance. It was said that for settling some financial problem of one Indian University the file had to move through nine stages to get clearance. In other words, for taking one financial decision regarding an University nine different officers had to see that file and make their noting. This is an extremely complicated process. In these days of expansion and development one cannot afford to waste so much of time and energy on one problem. Sometimes people are subjected to unnecessary harassment to make them conform to certain criteria. It may be suggested that the various forms that have to be filled for different kinds of jobs, assignments and grants may be simplified.[1]

17. An important step in the rational, coordinated decentralization of the power structure is to assign specific responsibility to the officer concerned. The practice of looking up and get

1. It is said that one gentleman in Bihar had taken house-building loan and he had to mortgage his house for that. Even after he had fully repaid the loan he was subjected to harassment for nearly six months because sometimes the department would say that one particular column in the form had not been filled and sometimes it would say that some other column had not been filled. This kind of harassment has to end. The requirement of filling in of unnecessary columns has to be avoided.

sanction from the top officials does involve the higher administrative machinery in the process of decision-making but it also shows that the officers concerned do not want to assume responsibility on their shoulders.

18. A democratic administration does not mean that recalcitrant officers who are guilty of corruption and dereliction of duty should not be punished. The government should have the will and the capability to redeem its pledge to the people by punishing those who transgress the canons of legality and morality.[1]

19. Something positive has to be done about the enormous difficulties created by the Accountant General's Office regarding the payment of the legitimate money of the retired government employees. Heart-rending stories of callousness are often published in papers.[2]

20. Discipline cannot be maintained on the University campus unless the dignity of the teacher is restored and respected. During the emergency the authorities were somewhat trying to imitate the technics of the Moghal Darbar. It had become very difficult to obtain easy access to the Vice-Chancellors. Even urgent telephone calls were not properly responded to on flimsy grounds. In the University, sometimes, matters regarding examinations have to be immediately responded to. Ashoka, the great emperor of ancient India, laid down the maxims for himself that for doing the public job he was available at all times of the day and night. If the high authorities do not perform their assigned duties then there is bound to be an administrative

1. In an editorial entitled "Issues at Election" *The Searchlight* had once stated "... it is idle to expect the State Government to have much credibility with officers when the State Government did not have even the authority to suspend them. The Constitution ought to be amended to do away with the most unjust and uncalled for difficulties placed in the way of governments in taking punitive measures against defaulting officers." *The Searchlight*, Saturday, January 23, 1971, p. 4.

2. Commenting on the hurdles created by the Accountant General, *The Searchlight*, in its editorial entitled "Issues at Election" stated: "Similarly the Accountant General must be made amenable to the wishes of the executive government. Now the situation is such that an existing government servant does not know when he can get his pay and allowances becaues of the peculiar method of accounting." *Ibid.*

collapse. All communications from the Heads of the Departments to the University should be replied to in time. It has been noticed that even D.O. letters are not acknowledged. In such an atmosphere there cannot be the growth of that belongingness-generating attitude which is essential for the effective, efficient and purposeful performance of work. It is extremely regretted that sometimes important files concerning confidential character rolls are missing from the custody of the University office. Those people who are responsible for such criminal activities should be penalised. Decisions should be quickly taken and must be adhered to. If a matter is pending for a long time then there is bound to be frustration and demoralization. Furthermore, Universities should be spared the evils emanating from teacher-politicians. The suggestion that teachers who are elected to legislative bodies should be granted long leave for the period of their membership in the legislature is a sound proposition.

CHAPTER VI

THE SOCIAL PHILOSOPHY OF IDEALIST HUMANISM

A class is a group determined by economic location and solidified by social identification. Throughout history, class has been an *operative* force. Occasionally, it has become a *determining* force but it is a gross exaggeration to say that the entire recorded history of man is a story of struggle among rival and antagonistic classes. History is determined by a multiplicity of forces and factors. The physical environment, forces and methods of production, class location of the different groups, religion, ideas and political factors conjointly determine the progress of human history. History may not be the expressive externalization of the Absolute Real but, certainly, ideas and moral forces have profound impact on the historical structures.

The grouping around tribal sentiments, Gotra, phratry, Jana, Visah etc. has been a dominant factor in history. But, by and large, among the factors responsible for the formation of groups for class crystallization, the economic, is very dominant. This is, certainly, not to deny the role of non-economic factors in social groupings. But the assertion that the class crystallization is governed by common position in the production-process can be borne out by historical data. Class crystallization, however, is not an automatic consequence of the economic location. The identification by the human role-takers of their belonging to a class is also highly significant.

Sometimes the rivalry among different and antithetical

classes foments and promotes sentiments of class polarization. But class polarization is not a permanent factor. There can be occasions also of class collaboration and consequent depolarization.

Philosophical humanism which accepts the profound role of spiritual and moral ideas in the historical process pleads for a consensual approach to the solution of the raging problem of class hostilities, and struggles. But although wedded to mutual accommodation for the solution of class tensions, animosities and struggles, if some class is bent on the forcible exploitation of the weak, humanism, reluctantly, and as a last resort, may tolerate the use of violence, temporarily. Violence has had a role to play in the evolutionary progression of mankind. But at the present juncture of human crisis, one would be loath to sanction any large-scale armed class struggle which is a concept generally associated with communism in its ruthless and militant quest for ascendancy in the political system. Class struggles, whenever they become critically acute, should be solved peacefully and by resort to legal democratic means. Satyagraha may also be sanctioned. For the vindication of justice and equity, as a last expedient, humanism may sanction limited violence by the exploited class, in self-defence. But it must be borne in mind that this is the last device and not the first instrument to be encouraged and deliberately engineered.

The origin of the Varna system which, later on, degenerated into the vulgar display of caste dominance and arrogance is somewhat mysterious. The orthodoxy would ascribe a divine origin to it. Western indologists of the German-American school with the notion of White-Negro struggles at the back of their minds ascribe a racial or ethnic origin to it and find its genesis in the struggles of the Aryans, the pre-Aryans, the non-Aryans, the Scythians etc. On the other hand, research investigators influenced by historical materialism ascribe a functional origin to it in terms of the hardening of a guild structure into the caste. They would regard Varna or caste as an incipient non-crystallised class rooted in economic location, and would corroborate their arguments with reference to the concrete existence of several artisan and industrial castes. I am inclined to consider caste as a status-group clustering around associativeness based on commonality of real or assumed origin and growth. Mythical notions of the transmission of semi-divine charisma and competence were used to support a social system which soon became inegalitarian and thus opposed to the older notions of tribal fraternity. Temporal oppressiveness was sought to be cloaked under the garb of organic interdependence where the head and the feet were equally significant from the standpoint of the working of the physiological system. But whatsoever be the originative constraint around the caste there can be no doubt that the articulation and aggregation of political factors has made it a solid interest group which, in some areas like Tamil Nadu, Maharashtra, and worst of all, Bihar, has plagued the total democratic political system of these states. The dominance of certain feudal castes and their descendants in some parts of India has not only resulted in the oligarchical monopolization of preferments, patronage and privileges by them, with a vast subordinate clientele to buttress their naked display of power but has led to the eruption of violence on a shockingly staggering scale in elections and on other occasions through the competitive mobilisation of force, manipulation and action-sets.

India's most disastrous and corrupting social evil has been the sense of superiority and subordination associated with the caste. Although there might be something to be said for the fourfold Varna order based on the functional differentiation of the intellectual, military, productive and service-rendering jobs and activities, the operative manifestations of caste arrogance and violence have made the Indian society loose, disorganized, divided and lacking in a common community-consciousness For centuries there has been no effective social mobility in the Hindu society and great law-givers have spent the ingenuity of their intellect in devising puerile arguments to substantiate the superiority of the priestly order. Now the old Sanskrit books containing vulgar and abusive epithets against the so-called lower orders of society are in print and have been translated and there may be the counter-production of a large literature emanating from intellectuals of the backward classes who, in retaliation, will heap abuses upon the priests and their ancestors. The dispassionate humanist can only view these developments with alarm. He will favour a classless and casteless society oriented to total egalitarianism where every differentiation will be only functional and not hereditary. It will be a society recognizing merit, quality and excellence in role-performance. There will be no place for scripturally sanctioned privileges nor for any claim to superiority on the basis of physical might or unearned wealth and functionless property.

It is self-evident that an idealist humanist political philosophy can never sanction the mechanism of superiority-subordination nor can it support the old Smrti conception of the divine legitimacy of Varna superordination resulting in the denial of the rule of law to Vaishyas and Sudras. Humanism is fully committed to an open, mobile, dynamic socio-economic order where status is only functional and hence necessarily temporary. A permanent hereditary status-group is totally alien to the humanist orientation. The implementation of legal equality and the continued resort to adult franchise will gradually usher into being an equality of status for citizens. Idealist humanism is also opposed to any kind of perpetuation of class and caste privileges. All privileges have to be related to the pursuit of some function and role-performance. A functionless irrational claim to social dominance is antithetical to the openness and free communicative dialogue that humanism aspires after among human beings.

It is true that in matters of social prescription, Yajnavalkya is more liberal than Manu, and Kautilya's *Arthashastra* is more liberal than either. The Bhagavadgita inculcates greater social tolerance than the Smritis. But Parasara is more dogmatic. The Puranas, possibly due to Buddhist influence, are generally, more liberal than the Vedic literature. But the basic point is that the social philosophy of ancient India as also of Plato and Aristotle is not egalitarian. It is, hence, unable to meet the rising humanist demands and expectations. Humanism accepts the obligatory power of only those social injunctions and ordinances that can meet the challenges of the intimations of the human conscience and of the categories of the steady human intellect. The support of innate superiority on religious grounds to deprive the populace of their rights shows only the cleverness of the unscrupulous apologists of power and their social hypocricy.

In the wake of rationalization and modernization, large and complex organizations are growing in the world. It is an era of gigantic collosality and hence the cry of the small being the beautiful sounds only nostalgic. The governmentalization and forceful coordination of different spheres of life are increasing. It seems difficult, therefore, to make a realistic worthwhile plea for the claims of the healthy moral man of the countryside as made by Rousseau, Ruskin, Gandhi, Madariaga, Fromm and Schumacher. The acute problems of a vast civilization can be solved neither by a reactionary appeal to the serene peace of the primitive days nor by a fantastic utopian chiliasm believing in the advent of an Avatar or prophet. A concrete social realism alone can be the outlook for a humanist commonwealth. However a fight has to be launched for saving the individual from the engulfing attacks of metropolitanism, organisationalism and statism and from that standpoint a humanist sociological manifests can be formulated. A manifesto for Total Social Reform may include the following suggestions and prescriptions:

1. Every human being is to be considered an active, rational and responsible agent whose potentialities should be developed and utilized for building a sane, moral-rational society based on fostering *lokasamgraha* (universal good). Man is a role-taker and an actor and is not the mere cluster of interactions and transactions. He is a spirit in fearless quest of perfection and not the mere aggregate of sensations and impressions. The pathological drives of masochism, sadism and exaggerated narcissism should yield place to Karuna (compassion) and Daya (charity) and Bhadradarshana (seeing good everywhere). The Buddha-Kabir-Tukaram-tradition in Indian social movement has to be stressed. Mere collection and dissemination of information through survey reports, blue books, white papers, brochures and statistical models would not provide the lasting solution of problems. What is needed is an examination of one's conscience. Vivekananda stressed that it was essential to feel one with the masses. If statistical analyses and computed information could solve the problems of mankind it would have been well. But computers are no substitute for the responsible exercise of decision-making. Beyond behavioral research, humanist idealism pleads for the cultivation of wisdom which

signifies the utilization of information for the realisation of the global consciousness for good according to the dictates of the chastened conscience of man.

2. Caste and clan alliance should be replaced by sentiments of solidarity, organic patriotic density, cooperative, national and international fraternity and the realisation of Nara (man) as Narayana (eternal, creative Super-Spirit). Kin groups and associations are to be patronized only to the extent that they foster common interests but any attempt at the utilization of these groups in the game of dominating others is to be foiled. To foster sentiments of nationalistic patriotism is indeed difficult. But the attachment to the concrete symbols of the home and the clan is spontaneous. The cultivation of identity-consciousness with the nation is indeed based on deliberation and will. The development of a feeling of commitment to the interests of the world as a cosmopolis is, indeed, still more difficult. But it has to be developed in the interests of a humanist commonwealth.

3. Caste has been, in a sense, legislated away because there is no recognised legal privilege associated with membership of the so-called higher caste groups but the devil of caste has become a veritable political monster and all the arenas and sectors of our existence are threatened with the rapacity of this formidable deviant force in the political system. At the psychological level, for ending the evils of casteism, it is necessary to foster the recognition of the immanent identity of the Nation as a superior collectively. Furthermore, one has to search his own heart and begin the battle for the eradication of the evils of casteism from oneself.

4. Rigorous penal laws have to be enforced against the practice of social discrimination.

5. Religious books and socio-religious codes which contain sentiments, concepts or indirect allusions against the concept of equality which is not only a cardinal Vedantic principle but is enshrined in the Indian Constitution should be suitably revised and anti-equalitarian notions be expunged therefrom.

6. Intercaste marriages may be encouraged by the state. The discriminatory prohibition of *pratiloma* and the elitist favour for *anuloma* marriages have no place in the humanist

society. A philogenetic (reproductive) approach to marriage has to be replaced by a sociogenetic orientation to it as based on an indissoluble bond. The crude forms of marriages like Paisacha, Rakshasa and Asura have no moral foundation and resort to them should be legally punished. The contractual approach to marriage sounds more congruous with the norms of a rationalist society but is very hard for children. The sanctity of the marriage bond should be reinforced.

7. The ritualistic exclusion of the Vaishyas and Sudras from the Vedic sacrifices should be done away with. Qualified and noble Vaishyas, Sudras and Untouchables should also be appointed as temple priests and the heads of the religious missions. Preconditioned reflexes regarding superiority by birth have to be eliminated through the use of new psychological and sociological devices.

8. Increasingly, the backward sections should be encouraged to throw up leadership from their own classes for their genuine emancipation.

9. Social reformers, innovators, change-promoters and government servants should try to employ Untouchables as domestic assistants.

10. The Arthashastra and Dharmashastra categorization of twelve kinds of sons is not relevant today. Attempts should be made to recognize even illegitimate children.

11. Except in exceptional cases, no person should be allowed to have more than one wife regardless of what may be the pronouncement of his particular legal, or religious code.

12. Women should have place of honour in society. But the sanctity attaching to the position of the mother should not be destroyed in the craze for fighting for rights of women. Values slowly evolve and hence need not be carelessly tampered with. The sacredness associated with the mother and the sister is a unique notion of acient Hindu social philosophy and in the name of female emancipation, feminism, modernity and women's rights this priceless notion should not be interfered with. But while upholding the sanctity of womenfolk, philosophical humanism is not willing to go to the extent of supporting gynarchy or gynaecocracy (rule by women).

13. A uniform civil code for all citizens of this land is an urgent imperative necessity.

14. There is no place in a humanist commonwealth for an oligarchical elite. But a strategic elite based on specialized competence may be tolerated because it is not hereditary. Furthermore, role-differentiation which is the characteristic of an elite should be conjoined with the ethos of social integration.

15. Rural elites create havoc for the depressed sections of society. Their power has to be curtailed through governmental and voluntary agencies and by educational measures which will strengthen the moral and cultural nerve of the people.

16. The selfish manipulation of state subventions and grants by a limited elite amounts to a negation of social reciprocity. Thereby the task-performing capability of the masses is severely curbed. Instead of learning from experience they are exposed to the cruelties of imposed social control and are subjected, sometimes, to crude social sanctions. For building an integrated social polity it is essential to multiply opportunities of goal-gratification for the masses and specially the weaker sections. Only then can their latent capacities be developed and they can genuinely support the polity. Thereby they will feel emotional attachment for the country and its political system and would not experience cynicism, apathy and alienation.

17. The preservation of tribal culture is essential. It will be an anthropological crime to force technology and modernization on the tribes of Assam, Madras, Orissa, Bihar and Madhya Pradesh. But the tribal population cannot exist merely as museum specimens. Adequate measures for their economic growth and political mobilisation are essential. Literacy has to be intensively promoted. Their proselytization by the monetary inducements of foreign missionaries is to be checked by law. They are to be encouraged to participate in the main currents of the nation's social and political life.

18. The twin evils of embourgeoisment and immiserisation of the workers can be met by strengthening the social bonds of a mobile society amongst the Kisans.

19. The political and economic issues facing the electorate should be viewed in their social context. Political sociology

stresses the study of the political processes and phenomena by contextualizing them in the multiple web of social relationships. Comte, Spencer, Ratzenhofer, Giddings, Sumner, MacIver and Parsons have also emphasized the study of the social roots of political institutions and power. Similarly the sociology of law would reveal the hidden social motivations behind the making of law. These disciplines would enable the formulation of a more comprehensive approach to law and politics by revealing the hidden motivational determinants of laws and ordinances.

20. The increase in deviant behaviour-patterns, norm-contraventions, suicide and crime figures indicates social malfunctioning. These have to be checked through measures for social amelioration and correctional technics. Prison reforms are essential and the brutalization of man in the dungeons has to be checked.

21. The rise of the cults of Teutonism, the White Man's burden, and racialism is a threat to world peace. Some leftist elements in India speak of a "multi-racial and multi-national India". Such slogans constitute a threat to the integration of the Indian political and social systems. The rise of Dravidism is also a threat to the national integration of India. According to anthropological researches, the term Dravida has a linguistic significance. According to Sanskrit literary works this term has a geographical connotation. There is no sanction for sponsoring the hypothesis of a Dravidian race.

22. A detailed and intense division of labour destroys the sense of aesthetic satisfaction from job-performance. It is not possible, however, to go back to the days of the medieval gilds. The division of labour is a necessary adjunct of the modern concept of technological rationality. Hence increasing opportunities for sharing in the cultural heritage of the nation should be provided to the workers as an antidote to automatization.

23. Children are the future bearers of the cultural legacy of the nation. Hence an integrated policy of child development is essential. Prenatal care, nutritional facilities, immunization, socialization, and development of the physique, impulses and other latent potentialities of children are essential. The psychological and moral problems arising out of generational

gap can be managed by a revival of the age-old Indian concept of *sthaviravada* (respect for the elders).

24. The moral and spiritual aspirations and potentialities of a person can be manifested only on the basis of a strong physique. Plato recommended gymnastic for the growth of the body of the rulers and soldiers. Kalidasa in his *Raghuvamsa* has depicted the developed physique of Dilipa and Rama. Some teachers have recommended the practice of Pranayama and other Yogic exercises. Others will recommend regular brisk vigorous walking as an antidote against disease. Dayananda, Shraddhananda, Munishwarananda, Satyadeva and Hedgewar were strong advocates of physical exercise. While athleticism may be useful only for a few citizens, general stress has to be put on muscle culture and body growth in the educational curriculum not only in the schools but also in colleges.

25. Education is the process of the rational growth of human capacities. It is far removed from the processes of indoctrination, brainwashing and belief in testimony. Educational opportunities should be equalized to the greatest extent. Public schools need not be abolished but the other educational institutions where free education would be imparted up to the Matriculation standard should be encouraged to improve their standards. Our country and government arc committed to the realization of a democratic and socialist society. Our resources are severely limited. Hence in the name of establishing technological institutes as catalytic agents of social change and modernity, islands of luxury and sophistication must not be built. To some extent foreign money has been pumped in the various Institutes of Technology. But that should not mean that we should create a separate caste of engineers who believe in an alien system of values and foppish living.

26. It is the main function of a university to add to the stock of knowledge. Hence creative adventures for the advancement of learning are essential. But an era of population explosion and mass democracy demands also the pursuit of a pragmatic, instrumental and operational approach to education. Hence the functional and vocational approach to education has also to be pursued. But in age of the acceleration of the processes of knowledge, India cannot afford to lag behind in

the race of adding to the growth of pure and applied knowledge. Humanism however wants to supplement vocational and professional training with a wide growth of cultural and moral catholicity. Educational reforms are essential so that job-oriented competence and skills are fostered in educational institutions.

27. The demand for doing away with the system of degrees like B.A. Honours and M.As or M.Scs. is unrealistic. Our University degrees should be of the highest international comparability.

CHAPTER VII

THE ECONOMICS OF PHILOSOPHICAL HUMANISM

The Capitalist Model of Development

Manufacturing capitalism started with the growth of extensive commodity production carried on the basis of the original accumulation of money as capital in the fifteenth and sixteenth centuries and sponsored by a band of adventurers who, in the early stages, were compelled to live a life of abstinence. The growth and advance of capitalism resulted in large-scale spoliation and exploitation of the working population through extortion of surplus work, the employment of women and children, mechanization resulting in the growth of a technological reserve army, the reckless misuse of the natural resources and crises brought about by overproduction, under-consumption and the disproportionate mobilisation of economic categories resulting in the irrational deployment of inputs. It is true that in the twentieth century some of the evils of nineteenth century capitalism have been sought to be eliminated but even in the name of affluence there are evident, radical disparity, an increasing automatization, an exaltation of the abstract quantitative criterion of mass production, large-scale inflation, the growing threat of unemployment of considerable sections of people and the persistent plague of the diminution of standard of life unless the favourable balance of trade is maintained.[1] Still capitalism

1. According to Hans Gerth, Note in K. Mannheim, *Freedom, Power and Democratic Planning*, p. xi, the characteristics of modern capitalism are :
(i) Dynamic social and economic technology
(ii) Urbanization and mobilisation of uprooted masses
(iii) Steeply graded income pyramids
(iv) Uneven developmental rhythms of economic and national expansion.

has succeeded in Western Europe and the United States because of the initial advantages of these areas in having earlier embarked on the capitalistic enterprise and a fertile colonial and home market.

A capitalist model of economic development is thus contemplated.

1. Purposive Technological Rationalization (based on sophisticated know-how)
2. High Productivity and Enhanced G.N.P.
3. Higher Real Income

4a. Higher Saving 4b. Higher Demand

5. Higher Investment in Home and Foreign Markets
6. Capital Accumulation resulting in growth, development and affluence

But this model is not suited to the Indian context where over fifteen lacs of unemployed people are hankering after jobs. Capital for sufficient utilization for further investment is scarce in the country. Higher savings are not always possible from higher real income. The experience of the middle classes belies this expectation. Hence the urgency of fostering employment-oriented labour intensive industries is great. Philosophical humanism is not opposed to modernization, growth and development. But it holds that the structure, process and norms of the political system can be solidified only if the vast masses are provided food and the basic common amenities. Hence priority has to be given to the generations of conditions and opportunities for full employment and not to mere technological rationalization, through operations research and computerization in some key industries.

The Marxist Model of Development

The socialistic theories of different kinds — utopian, conservative (Proudhon) and petty-bourgeois (Sismondi) — and dialectical communism with its formulas of centralization of means of production, expropriation of expropriators and free association of producers emerged to meet the challenges of industrial capitalism which further intensified its tentacles with the growth of financial capitalism. Among the leftist forces,

Bolshevism alone obtained conspicuous success. St Simon, Owen, Fourier, Lassalle Bernstein, Kautsky and Henry George failed in solidifying any movement of lasting importance. State ownership and management of the total resources of the community is the basic doctrine of the communist economic development. At the theoretical level, the marginalists like Bohm-Bawerk and Ludwig Von Mises challenged the Marxian labour theory of value. MacIver held that the simplicist model of social bipolarity did not apply to the complex and complicated structure of the multi-group western society. While praising the instrumentalist epistemology of Marx and Lenin, Bertrand Russell was opposed to the notion of attaching undue importance to economy and technology as the basic historical determinant. Behind technology is the active human mind. Hence the Marxian categories of technological-economic determinism and social dynamics have to be used with caution and scepticism and it will be unfounded hyperbolism to deem Marx as the Galileo or the Newton or the Darwin of the social sciences. At the level of practice, the conquering career of dialectical revolutionary Marxism has resulted in the neutralisation of humanist values and, in the name of proletarian revolution, has installed dominant regimentation and an unscrupulous negation of freedom. Although historical materialist communism, in action, has fostered the quantum of production, it has not been associated with the release of the qualitative free decision-making potentialities of man as such. The advancing career of communism has been marked by large-scale violence, expropriation, the negation of the right of judicial redressal of grievances, the imposition of the regime of an authoritarian party buttressed by the cruelties of a secret police, the perversities of an allegiant committed bureaucracy and an absence of the creative channels of imaginative expression of the human person. In a sense the operative aspects of communism are thoroughly unpalatable to the free unhindered growth of the human spirit. Hence it is not likely that the communist model of economic growth through the centralization of the economic resources and instrumentalities would have an appeal in the countries professing the humanist and libertarian notions of democratic culture. The centralization of all necessary means of production, transport and credit in the hands of the state marks a phase of accelerated concentration of power before which the individual finds himself powerless, utterly powerless. Total nationalization of the means of production, distribution and exchange may mean the erection of a gigantic state Leviathan which, while avoiding the evils of private capitalism, leads to the enormities of state capitalism with its bureaucratic depersonalization and thus accentuates alienation and moral contradiction. Hence the twin alternatives of capitalism and communism cannot be the ideologies and instruments of providing panacea to the Indian citizen and the national economy.[1] A third alternative has to be sought in *revised Gandhism*.

The Revision of Gandhian Economics

There are numerous grave problems facing the Indian economy. In spite of over 2 crore tons of food-stock reserves there is the persistent problem of food because of mounting population-growth and the lack of purchasing power of a sizable population and chronic unemployment reinforced lately with the lamentable spectacle of several lakhs of educated young men loitering in the streets or crowding in corridors of Government offices and Employment Exchanges. The cry of job-oriented education has proved to be a mere slogan. Since March 1972, there have been devastating inroads upon Indian economy. Today the country is plagued with unemployment, price rise, corruption and recession. The five Five Year Plans have failed to deliver the goods to India's masses. Gandhi's cry of Swarajya for the 6 lakhs of India's villages has proved to be a mere utopia. Numerous students of the Indian economic situation have corroborated the statement that the rich are becoming richer and the poor are becoming poorer. The fashionable and glamorous scenes in the big metropolises do not represent the India of the villagers where there is dire poverty, grim nakedness and terrific frustration. The critic naturally wants to know if Gandhism has a message for the solution of the

1. According to Erich Fromm *The Sane Society*, p. 363, the choice today is between *robotism* (of both the capitalist and the communist variety) Or humanistic communitarian socialism.

economic malady. A critical study does reveal that over the years Gandhism had been radicalising itself. The same Gandhi who had said categorically in 1916 that he was not a socialist began to say in the '40s that he was a socialist for a long time. But as I see it, India's problems cannot be solved by pure unadulterated Gandhian economic technics. For example, we cannot rule out heavy industries and planning. If we would not have concentrated on heavy industry, the fight that was given to Pakistan in 1965 and 1971 would not have been possible. Industrialization and mechanisation are essential for preserving India's Swarajya. At a time when even the small nations of the Middle East are assuming military postures and when Red China is amassing nuclear power, we cannot afford to think in terms only and primarily of cottage industry and Khadi. Nevertheless we cannot neglect the Gandhian realism clearly adumberated in the emphasis on the efficacy of Khadi, cottage industries and bread labour in solving India's problems of poverty and unemployment. We cannot afford to bid good bye to centralized planning, but surely its conception has to be amended and radicalised and made more realistic in terms of integrated planning for yielding quick results for the masses. Heavy industry is economic but on the other hand, the dispersion of some of the industrial units and the setting up of smaller steel plants in various places may have significant effects on the Indian economy. Hoarding, black marketing, profiteering and smuggling have raised their ugly heads during the last decade and specially since 1969, in more devastating forms. Gandhi would not have ruled out Satyagraha against the doers of economic mischiefs and against landlords and capitalists. Both Vinoba and Lohia claimed to be influenced by Gandhi but the latter regarded civil disobedience as Gandhi's fundamental contribution to political technology. Vinoba, on the other hand, has been more conservative than Lohia. J. P.'s concept of total revolution for a participatory communitarian agro-industrial civilization is oriented to radicalise Gandhian economics. The experiences of Punjab point out that even without heavy industry a state can prosper. Small industries and cottage industries in the countryside can go a long way in making the farmers happy. While the protagonists of Sarvodaya have talked of village ownership, Gandhi did not eliminate the concept of the proprietorship of the farmers. If villagers are given or provided a sense of adequate security in their proprietory rights in land and if the high prices of cereals are maintained, then that will accentuate production more than any doctrinaire adherence to the nationalisation of land or villagisation, or cooperative farming etc. Gandhi himself was not a trained economic theoretician but he had a good and firm grasp of the main concepts of economic reconstruction. He had read Ruskin's book *Unto This Last* very thoroughly. During the 1942 movement, while detained in the Poona Palace, he read the first volume of Marx's *Capital.* He was also aware of the doctrines of Adam Smith. He refers to Adam Smith and his notion of economic laws and the disturbing "human factor".[1] Like Smith, he regards work or labour as the true source of wealth. Gandhi had a keen awareness of the problems of poverty, unemployment, exploitation etc. of the country. He showed his realism[2] when he formulated the notion of State regulated trusteeship, pleaded for the realisation of taxes by means of labour, advocated death duty and regarded rationing as leading to several economic evils. He would not have sanctioned India's dependence on foreign aid. He wanted to mobilise the country's own resources. This insight of Gandhi has to be reinforced. The painful sight of the concentration of wealth in limited hands in urban areas and the villages acting as the mere adjuncts and feeders of the towns would have drawn painful shrieks from the Mahatma. Hence our planning philosophy and trade policy as well as legislation regarding farmers, industrial units and workers have to be governed by a sense of realistic concreteness. There has to be a reassessment of the taxation, pricing and subsidy policies which go against the interests of the rural countryside. We need not be opportunists, nor need we be completely sold to any one particular economic ideology. It will be in consonance with the Gandhian spirit if in the succeeding plans more emphasis is given to the

1. *Harijan*, September 21, 1934, p. 25, Mathur & Mathur, *Economic Thought of Mahatma Gandhi*, p. 149.

2. Like Louis Blane, Gandhi also, in his ideal society would recommend equal wages for all persons. But this sounds highly impossible.

accentuation of agricultural production, irrigation facilities, incentive prices for farm goods and decent living wages to workers. No one specific section is responsible for the total economic evils of the country. The CPI locates the root of India's economic evils in the 75 big business houses. Another school may regard smuggling as the main devil. Others would say that the parallel economy created by more than 1100 crores of rupees in the shape of the under-current of black money is the dominant factor responsible for the evil. As objective analysts of India's economic scene, we can only say that economic realism demands that villagers should be provided with a sense of security in land. If adequate irrigation facilities are provided many problems associated with poverty will automatically be solved. But it will be following a policy of escapism if we think that all of India's evils, agonies and contradictions can be solved by the Gandhian economic theory. There is the urgent need today of the progressive radicalisation of Gandhian economic philosophy.

India is an agricultural country and hence top priority has to be assigned to foster intensive agricultural production. But any positing of an antithesis between agriculture and industry is misplaced. Agricultural expansion needs industrial boosting. Without industrial growth, chemical fertilizers connot be procured and an adequate supply of electrical energy is essential for irrigation. Hence in villages also the emphasis should be on agro-industrial development rather than on purely agrarian. Thus while fully endorsing the scheme for increasing investment in the agricultural sector, it is essential to note that for survival in today's world industrial growth is a fundamental imperative. The polarity—agriculture versus industry was conceived in a context when British imperialism was there in the country. Now the situation has to be viewed in the context of the industrial growth of the third world countries. If the neighbouring countries expand their industrial potential and aggressive military capacities, we cannot afford to be apathetic. India has enough potential for the expansion of steel, engineering and chemical industries. Iron, steel, copper, cement, petroleum and power industries are vitally essential for the growth of small-scale industries and rural industrialization. The compulsive need of survival will make essential the development of atomic energy for defense purposes. It is not possible to revive the small-scale caste-oriented agrarian economy contemplated in the works of Kautilya, Manu, Yajnavalkya and Kamandaka. Population has increased, may be, forty times since then and new aspirations have been created. Hence an integrated growth of both agriculture and mini-and-major industries alone can deliver the goods and save the country from the dire catastrophies of poverty. A logico-meaning fully integrated economic philosophy[1] for the nation contemplates the fullest development of agriculture, public, co-operative and private sectors, cottage and small industries and trade for the optimalization of the immanent potential in the country. An integrated pyramid of the different levels of planned growth has to be visualized, where the base will not be crushed by the weight of the top and intermediate layers but will provide sustenance to them. There will be enough channels providing for horizontal and vertical coordination as well as for systemic and sub-systemic linkages in the politico-economic system as a whole. A sense of dedication to national regeneration will be the motivational, normative and valuational determinant of role-performance. A humanist manifesto in economics can be thus laid down :

A Manifesto for Indian Economic Development

1. Overproduction is, often, a factor leading to economic crisis. But penury and indigence hamper the growth of the moral self. Humanism hence, contemplates an economy neither of abundance nor of abstinence but of the "due" satisfaction of physiological and socio-cultural needs. Not only the total quantum of production has to be raised but per capita income growth has also to be accelerated, Hence if conspicuous consumption of luxury goods is limited, then it will be possible to manufacture the basic necessary goods at home. But the dysfunctional mobilisation of inputs and outputs has to be seriously curtailed. Adequate infrastructures in the shape of transport and educational facilities are essential. Administrative

1. Cf. E. Roll, *A History of Economic Thought*, p, 370 : "Classicism, it was said, emphasized production, supply, and cost; modern theory is mainly concerned with consumption, demand and utility. The marginal utility concept was introduced to effect this shift of emphasis ..."

bottlenecks to economic development have to be removed and a program-oriented economic climate has to be built.

2. Philosophical humanism being integral in its approach is opposed to an either-or policy with regard to agriculture and industry. Economic development postulates an integrated or total area approach which fosters agricultural production thorough horizontal expansion by land reclamation and vertical expansion by fertilisers and insecticides and promotes the production of household, cottage and small as well as large-scale industries. Both agriculture and industry are essential for the balanced integral growth of the country. Deindustrialization and technological backwardness cannot be encouraged. That will weaken the bases of agricultural and military growth also. Similarly the attitude which promotes an antithesis between small industry and heavy industry is unrealistic. Household, cottage and small-scale industries cannot, alone, provide full employment. The harnessing of electric power and solar radiation for the generation of heat energy is essential for growth. Solar energy can be utilized for cooking and heating purposes. The decentralized character of solar energy makes its utilization highly congruous with the philosophy of administrative and economic decentralization. There are immense potentialities for the expansion of hydro-electric power in the country. Only heavy industries can supply the necessary technical machines for the production of generators, transformers etc. for electrical power. On the other hand, information transmitted by space satellites can be monitored for purposes of agriculture productivity. A nation of over six hundred million people has numerous and enormous problems of an immeasurably formidable dimension. A sustained growth rate of at least five per cent per annum is essential. Hence all methods and technics which can expand productivity and promote common utility and welfare have to be encouraged in an integrated way.

3. Land may be retained in the private sector but ceiling laws, Bataidari legislation and non-eviction laws should be rigidly enforced. The large-scale fraud perpetrated with the connivance of administrators to deprive all genuine significance to the ceiling laws has to end. The vast gulf between the large farmers and over 20 crores of small and marginal farmers has

to be narrowed down. The cultivation of waste lands, prevention of soil erosion through measures of conservation, scientific and indigenous fertilisers, improved seeds, multi-farming and remunerative prices for agricultural products commensurate with the rising prices of agricultural inputs are some of the means to boost agriculture which is the dominant factor in Indian economy. If agriculture becomes a profitable business, even the educated will be re-drawn to the villages and the evils of metropolitan concentration and unemployment can be reduced to some extent. The abolition of property in land and the setting up of collective farms will be unjust and inequitable and also unpractical from the operative standpoint. But cooperative farming may be taken recourse to in some areas. Attention should be devoted to fostering forestry, dairy-farming, poultry farming, animal husbandry and horticulture as the allied, and even integrated areas of agricultural expansion. Agro-industries corporations can be set up and made financially viable and operative. An integrated and expanded program of agricultural growth demands a restructuring of investment priorities because more finances have to be pooled through budgetary provisions and fiscal technics like the abolition of excise duties on agricultural inputs, for the welfare of the poor farmers and landless agricultural labourers. There are chances of the absorption of labour-power in agricultural sector if there is increasing resort to activities for the acceleration of food production including crop insurance in needed areas and implementation of training programs for rural artisans and cultivators. Tribal and Harijan areas, drought-prone, epidemic-prone and hill areas, marshy areas, rural countryside, forests and command areas have to be carefully provided for. Major, medium and minor irrigation schemes and projects should be fostered. Surface and ground water resources and other latent irrigation potential can be utilized. The buying and setting up of small tubewells can be subsidized by the government. Thus the growth of irrigation potential can be expanded. Irrigations rates should be such that the maintenance charges of the project concerned can be recovered. Agricultural statistical research and technique-improving research need to be promoted. In case there is enhanced agricultural production, land revenue and rent surcharge may be increased proportionately. Rural reconstruction and development needs both institutional and financial support. A program for satisfying the minimum needs of the villagers including provisions for home sites for the needy, electrification and water supply, rural health schemes and rural-oriented primary education has to be finalized and effected. The implementation of an integrated policy on this front does require the mobilisation of the Panchayati Raj bodies and the generation of self-employment potential. Commercial banks should liberally extend credit facilities to farmers to promote the integrated development of the rural countryside. There is no need to set up a corporate structure for it. Rural agro-industrial development needs the curtailment of the vested interests of the Mukhias and the Sarpanches. In case there is enhanced provision for better dwelling houses, clean water, electrification, medical assistance, literacy and road connections, the villages may become genuine "Habitat Villages", and "Cities in fields" may grow as antidotes to mounting urbanization which leads to impersonalisation of relations, slums and growth in criminality. Thus revitalized stabilized villages — the village republics of Gandhi's dream — will be effective antidotes to rising metropolitanism which creates havoc for the safety of a morally healthy civilization.

4. Unemployment, both of the educated and the uneducated unemployed, has to be reduced within a period of fifteen years. By 1985 the number of job-seekers may be to the tune of $5\frac{1}{2}$ crores. The maximization of employment generating potential is essential. But this task has to be done, in hand with the production of low cost mass consumption goods for the poor dwellers of the land. The inclusion of the right to work among fundamental rights would necessarily visualise the compulsive obligation to do some kind of nation-building job.

5. Population explosion at an alarming rate has a dampening effect on economic development. Population control is essential and without resorting to coercion and force all practical psychological and moral methods and technics for checking birth rate should be devised. The population policy of the government should be absolutely uniform with regard to all components of the social system.

6. Decentralization at the administrative level needs to be supplemented with economic decentralization. It requires that units of production be small but not uneconomical. Ten to fifteen villages with a maximum population of 20,000 may form an optimum community for the enhancement of agro-industrial production.

7. Nationalization often culminates in bureaucratization, bitter fights among trade unions and gross corruption. In the absence of adequate countervailing powers of individual free initiative, nationalization leads to state capitalism which breeds totalitarianism. Wheresoever nationalization is taken recourse to it should be supplemented with the growth of the social spirit of sharing in goods, shared legitimacy, shared attitudes and equitable distribution. There should be only limited nationalization of the means of transportation and communication. The press and the newspaper agencies must be free and competitive. It is also possible that production can be left in private hands and the government can only control distribution. But the mismanagement of the public distribution system for some time with reference to wheat and coal in some areas was an eye-opener. Hence the expansion of public distribution mechanism with regard to cereals, cloth, sugar, salt, necessary drugs and medicines etc. has to be carefully planned. Humanism, however, is committed to the equitable distribution of the proceeds of the mobilisation of agricultural and industrial labour-power. All heavy industries need not be nationalized. But those that are not nationalized can be fully regulated by the government by the control of permits, licenses and capital issues. Heavy industries like iron steel and electronics have also to be fully promoted. Their production costs should be reduced and their managerial efficiency promoted and they should become more competitive.

8. Idealistic humanism contemplates a mixed economy. Neither a regimented authoritarian command economy of wholesale planning nor a regime of absolute free enterprise can be the pattern for developing nations. A regimented socialism becomes equivalent to state capitalism with public sector enterprises sometimes running into losses due to managerial inefficiency and the absence of structural channels for enforcing responsibility.

The concept of recovery through inflation with the readjustment of money and credit and managed currency is not practicable in the Indian context. The Sarvodaya scheme of vesting all natural resources in the hands of the community and the total elimination of the profit motive is also unrealistic. The plea for state regulated trusteeship also sounds unpractical. The private sector both in heavy and small industries has to play an important part in national economic development. But there has to be a thorough regulation and control of business through fiscal and legal means. Monopolists and the multinational corporations with their economic tentacles and managerial revolution have, certainly, to be heavily curbed. Genuine trusteeship involving parting with financial power may be encouraged. But fake trusteeship which is illustrated in the division of property among one's own kith and kin is no economic solution to the evils of private capitalism.

9. Price control is essential both for consumer satisfaction and as a motivational agent for production. The serious decline in the purchasing power of the rupee is apalling. Bank credits and consumer loans have to be restricted. The prices of some commodities can be frozen. Loans given to private sector industries by the L.I.C. and the Industrial Finance Corporation may be in the form of equity shares. Due to the increased irrigational facilities, improved seeds and favourable monsoons, the prices of cereals like paddy and wheat are, to an extent, stabilized. But the prices of other commodities have to be brought down. Price courts may be set up to punish the offenders guilty of deliberate price rise. Inflation, stafglation, high interest rates, power shortage, labour troubles, industrial stagnation and the non-utilization of production capacity up to about 35% are responsible for price rise. A direct relationship should be established between the minimum wage structure and the price structure. To check the inflationary impact of foreign exchange reserves (Rs. 2800 crores at the end of March, 1977 and Rs. 4000 crores in 1978) on internal economy, it should be utilized for the purchase of critical raw materials like enriched uranium and heavy water and essential capital goods.

10. Effective measures have to be taken to eliminate corruption in the comprehensive sense of absence of probity and

integrity and the growth of license and dishonesty from economic associations, groups and institutionalized arenas of action. These measures have to be educational, sociological, moral and behavioral. The citizens and employees have to be re-educated in the ethics of integrity, uprightness and rectitude. The atmosphere of the home and the primary groups has to be such as creates a distaste for any resort to questionable technics. The Lokayukta and Lokapal have to be appointed and they should play effective roles in curbing corruption. No guilty person, howsoever big, should be spared. The judiciary and the vigilance police cells can be also effective in this area. The staff of the vigilance cells may be increased for surprise raids on guilty parties. The behaviour-patterns of those in the higher echelons of decision-making has to be such as to set a premium only on the right and correct modes of action and orientation.

11. Labor-intensive industries using *intermediate* technology *appropriate* for the developing world should be fostered in place of capital-intensive industries, so that the enormous manpower may itself operate as a capital-forming agency. The provision for fuller opportunities for absorption in rural jobs should have precedence over the accentuation of capital goods productivity. At the level of democratic public administration, education, rural development, law and order, public works and health are labor-intensive departmental fields and they can be expanded for the promotion of full employment. The overall goal of the economic system has, however, to be the accentuation of the quantum of production and hence recourse must not be had to suboptimization-selecting formulas in industry which will only reduce the size of the gross national product. Hence accurate statistics and a well-knit communication system for monitoring messages and feedback information regarding the economic situation and specially with regard to productions, resources, demand and distribution are essential. Only when correct information is available can there be predictability of economic growth for individual and group security.

12. The production of essential agricultural inputs and the expansion of foodstuff materials is essential but it is also vitally essential as Gandhi said to put more coins in the pockets of the poor consumers so that those articles can be purchased by

them. In place of a metropolitan elitist orientation to development a genuine and comprehensive rural reconstruction program is to be devised. Through prolonged hard work and savings adequate buffer food stocks must be maintained.

13. Money-capital and commodity-capital are needed for economic growth. Non-productive capital like weapons are also needed for the strategic defence of the country. For the formation of capital the restriction of consumption is essential. The borrowing of foreign capital should be avoided unless it is extremely necessary. Foreign borrowing of capital has damaging impact on the nations's political prestige and economic viability. Hence capital formation has to be promoted through internal savings both large and small. Investible surplus has to be generated both in the public and private sectors. But the accumulation of capital through state run lotteries does not seem congruous with humanist ethics although there may be economic reasons to justify it.

14. Appropriate technology suited to Indian socio-cultural conditions has to be devised for capital formation in the rural sector for sustained growth. Mere dependence on the sophisticated skills of outside experts will retard the initiative for growth. The government may buy foreign technology and ask internal experts to make the imported type adaptable to indigenous conditions.

15. Small-scale and rural industries have to be fostered through government subsidization, price-pooling based on a total computation of the available commodities for sale and differential taxation. This may require legislative protection to small-scale and cottage industries. For promoting rural industrialization, some utility goods may be produced from local raw materials and ancillary goods for heavy industries may also be manufactured in the rural areas. Some items in the consumer market may be exclusively reserved for development in the small scale sector to eliminate unequal competition from big industries. Charkha may be plied in every village house. The All-India Khadi and Village Industries Commission may act as an infrastructure for rural industries. For promoting small scale industries, imposition of restraint on establishing new industrial companies near the metropolitan areas like Calcutta, Bombay,

Madras, Ahmedabad, Kanpur etc. is essential. Handloom sector has also to be developed.

16. Futurological long-term perspective planning with reference to the twenty-first century has to be promoted. A ten-year forward-looking perspective plan to render possible financial investment with long gestation projects may be prepared. The annual review of plans is essential for introducing corrections. An ongoing process of plan-information monitoring and their appraisal will make possible feedback corrections according to the plan output shortfalls and will provide a non-variable base level horizon for investment re-structurings. Hence enough mobilisation of energy has to be there for fulfilling the time-bound targets. In place of monolithic centralized planning, integrated planning with emphasis on planning from below has to be encouraged. Sectoral and *indicative* planning are more in consonance with the needs of the country than an imposed total planning.

17. The economic system should generate enough motivational incentive and internal energy and funds to meet foreseen and even unexpected natural and international and internal economic challenges. Furthermore the government may encourage the integrated approach to planning and budgeting (PPES = Planning, Programming and Budgeting System) for the enhancement of the financial capability of the economic system.

18. The private sector should generate internal capital resources of their own and must not depend only on nationalized banks and the government. Private sector units concerned with defence production should engage in researches in collaboration with the public sector and the Defence Department to make indigenization of all necessary defence inputs possible. In industries like shipping, petrochemicals, fertilizers, cement etc. an appropriate ratio of debt-capital and self-acquired equity-capital may be permitted for, say, five years.

19. Political consideration should not be the primary factor in the location of industries. Economic viability and the interests of the nation are to be of the uppermost concern. However only the big metropolises and some states should not devour the slender resources of the nation. In the interests of nation-building, economic imbalance should be avoided.

Development should not be a partisan problem. The ruling party should take the opposition also in full confidence. National consensus may be obtained at least on agrarian schemes of development even if industrial policy pertains to the realm of controversial economics.

20. Exploitation, in any form, whether of the bonded labourer or of children and women, or of the village serf or of the victim of the extortion of surplus has to be ended. The workers should have access to the rich store of knowledge and should be enabled to make a healthy utilization of leisure by providing them a shorter working day. Industry and business have to be imbued with a sense of communitarian responsibility and responsiveness. Harijans, tribals, marginal farmers and landless labourers need special treatment and reservations of opportunities in a humanist commonwealth. For atrocities on Harijans, punitive tax may have to be imposed on the offenders. Agricultural labourers numbering nearly 5 crores of people have a desperately low living standard. They may be encouraged to organize themselves so that rural workers' organizations may take up the cause of the redressal of their long-standing grievances.

21. The recruitment for production-personnel for the "dirty jobs" can no longer be confined to the so-called lower orders of society. It is an era of mass production by all classes and sections of the people The dignity of labour in all its forms has to be recognized and this can be done if all persons devote some part of their working hours to physical labour.

22. The mobilisation of labour-power is not the sole source of the creation of value. Hence there can be no justification of the capture of the state machine and the production mechanism by the armed organisation of the labourers. But certainly the workers deserve a fairer deal and a better position in society. Workers' participation is to be encouraged not only in industry but also in management both in the private and the public sectors and later on in equity. Tripartite management of the administration of firms has to be organized as an anti-dote to industrial sickness, in the private sector. Workers' unions may also send their representatives to the councils of proprietors and directors. The Leninist formula of factories to workers sounds inequitable in a democratic context but industrial democracy has to be promoted.

The idea of an Economic Parliament of Workers, if implemented, may make difficult the coordination of its activities with that of the Parliament of the Indian Union. Industrial discipline is essential. Unjustified strikes as well as illegitimate lockouts have to be curbed. Managerial and allocative decisions for the utilization of a firm's economic resources should be such that their implementation may require minimal coercive sanction.

23. Trade Unions should play a more creative role in modern society. They have to look after the economic, social and moral welfare of the workers and have to be more solicitous about accident and retirement benefits. But humanist idealism is opposed to the technics of sabotage and general strike which disrupt society and economy and almost bring about a state of collapse. Strike is a legitimate technic provided it is for the redressal of economic grievances which cannot be settled by tripartite negotiations. But production-crippling strikes at the behests of parties disbelieving in the canons of democracy cannot be justified. Trade Unions need not become merely the adjuncts of political parties for filling the coffers of the latter and providing them cheap manpower for anti-social disruption.

24. The legal enforcement of limitation upon the enormous profits and dividends of private sector companies and internal and multinational corporations is essential. The total funds under the control of the industrial families are touching the fantastic figure of nearly 10,000,000,000 rupees. This looks incongruous with humanist ideals. Hence ceilings on total shareholdings and intercorporate holdings have to be enforced to check capitalist centralization with its disastrous political, economic and psychological impacts on the total system. The equity participation of multinational firms should be limited to 40%. There is no need of the multinational firms entering the traditional areas of mass consumption goods. The Foreign Exchange Regulation Act (FERA) has to be rigorously enforced with reference to foreign companies operating in India.

25. Public sector undertakings in the fields of steel, coal, petroleum, chemical fertilisers and cloth should make profit on the sale of their products which can be used in investment for common good. But humanism is opposed to public sector undertakings in the field of medicine making any profit. The

public sector has a significant, if not commanding role to play in the national economy as the producer of basic and strategic goods and for acting as a stabilising force for the supply of some essential consumer goods and as a trail-blazer in risk-ridden areas where the private sector is afraid of venturing. But the government need not enter into the area of manufacturing soft consumer goods. The Railway as the biggest public sector undertaking need not run only on no profit no loss basis. Some profits may be charged for investment in other sectors. The unit cost of production in the public sector has to be lessened.

26. Social services constitute a significant infrastructure for growth. Extensive expansion of social security and health schemes, hence, has to be implemented. Rural workers may also be covered under these schemes. Pensions to all persons beyond the age of 70 who have no other source of maintenance and may be on the verge of starvation should be provided.

27. Buffer stocks of essential commodities other than food are also essential in the interest of security. No economist can, however, propose the feasibility of autarchy which, *inter alia* also smacks of authoritarianism. A self-sufficient economy oriented to the satisfaction of human needs as near home as possible can only be an economy of stability and not of dynamic growth. But although autarchy is impossible of realization in the complex industrial world of today, technological independence fostered through indigenous research in applied science has to be the aim of developing nations so that they may be spared the dependence upon foreign developed nations and foster their own indigenization of economic outputs.

28. Taxation cannot be structured on the basis of proportion. Not the quantum of benefit derived but the ability to pay should be the criterion of fixing taxation rates. A progressive and graduated tax-structure has to be devised. But taxation should not be so exorbitant as to become inhibitive for production. For promoting agrarian reconstruction tax relief may be granted to enterprising businessmen.

29. The State Trading Corporation should concern itself with those enterprises where private business has failed to meet public expectations.

30. There should be no bonus system in government departments and undertakings even if bonus is considered to be deferred wages and not as profit-sharing. Private sector may pay bonus to accelerate productivity. It may also be encouraged to pay bonus in the form of equity shares to promote workers' participation in management.

31. Cooperative Societies and banks are essential for boosting the mobilisation of labour-power, expansion of rural credit and for acting as a check on the evils of state absolutism. Russian Narodniks like Herzen, Mikhailovsky and Lavrov have also stressed the importance of individual initiative and the cooperative building of society. Rural cooperatives for facilitating maternity and child welfare, managing clinics and dispensaries, drinking water schemes, SFDAs and MFALs are to be encouraged.

32. Voluntary agencies should promote the feelings of patriotic solidarity. The communes of the Chinese and the Kibbutz of Israel may provide some model for rekindling community spirit in India.[1] The Association of Voluntary Agencies for Rural Development (AVARD started in Delhi in 1958) has to be activized. An optimal community with improved housing, schooling, employment and recreation facilities can, however, be built by the mobilisation of citizenship initiative through the efforts of dedicated workers and not simply by setting up a department of community development. The cap:talist model of community development based on competitive bargaining and negotiation for conflict management is not suited to the poverty-stricken Indian countryside.

33. An idealist humanist economic organization will take special care of the retarded children, and of the physically disabled, abnormal, subnormal, extremely old and diseased persons. Alcoholism, juvenile delinquency and rising criminality have to be curbed.

34. Strict standards and specifications should be maintained regarding quality control. Necessary equipments for quality

1. Charles Fourier's scheme of Phalansteres or small villages with a population of 400 families or 1600 persons occupying and cultivating 400 acres of land is too utopian in the present context.

control of raw materials and finished goods even by small-scale units are to be provided. Quality control and reliability are highly essential in real estate construction.

35. The economic problems of developing countries have been made enormously difficult by the abundance of labour-force, inadequate opportunities for the absorption of labour-power in gainful employment and the low rate of saving resulting in the paucity of accumulated capital surplus. The help of the United Nations Industrial Development Organisation (UNIDO) may be sought for boosting industrial growth. The gap between North and South has to be narrowed down. The countries of the Third World have to impress upon the World Bank, the International Development Association (a wing of the World Bank disbursing soft loans, the International Monetary Fund, the Gatt (GATT), the OECD, the Club of Ten and the Bank for International Settlements to follow a more liberal policy towards their investment priorities. India herself has, wisely, helped the economic development of some Asian and African countries through offering them expert technical and medical services and training opportunities.

Thus an integrated rather than a narrow departmentalized model of economic development is relevant to the contemporary situation. Instead of waging a battle against mechanization and industrialization, the integrated model would plead for a balanced growth of industry, agriculture, public health, education, arts and science and manual and atomic energy. The integrated model also stresses the simultaneous pursuit of the advancements of household, cottage, small-scale and large-scale industries. Similarly the integrated approach would plead for the advancement of the means of production both through sophisticated technology and the growth of appropriate and intermediate technology. In place of mere nationalization, the integrated approach would also plead for the pursuit of thè other two technics of municipalization and cooperation. Cooperative associations have to play an increasing role in the growth of the economy. Similarly the rampant and glaring antithesis between the urban and rural sectors will be sought to be reconciled through the development of educational, health and recreational facilities and amenities in the countryside. Thus the trend towards urban concentration can be checked. Thus development instead of being solely directed by the centre should be result of the total utilization of the administrative energy of decision-makers at the state, district, block and village levels. Administrative collaboration at the five levels of decision-making will be a needed antidote to the slogans of committed bureaucracy and democratic centralism.

CHAPTER VIII

GENERALIZED CONCLUSIONS, REFLECTIONS AND SUGGESTIONS

Humanism in modern Indian thought has three sources. First, the revival of the positivistic and world-affirming gospel of the Upanishadic Vedantism, the Bhagavadgita and Buddhism. The dynamic and inspiring teachings of the Bhagavadgita that man should bring about his transformation by his own efforts and that one is one's own friend and one's own enemy, and of Buddhism that one should be a light (*atma-dipa*) and refuge unto oneself (*atma-sharana*) can be interpreted as supporting humanism because they neutralize the view that faith in or surrender to an incarnation or a prophet or a teacher will bring about one's redemption. Furthermore, the concepts of *samadarshana*, *sarvabhutahita* and *samya* which propound universal compassion can be the ideological foundation of a humanist democracy. The Gita inculcates *samadarsana* not merely with reference to human beings but also with regard to the animal world and thus propounds the noble transmutation of humanism into a profound universalism. The conception of man as enunciated by idealist humanism is inspired by an acceptance of the immanence of a spiritual Absolute or a personal God. Man is significant but he derives his significance from being a part of God or an appearance of the infinite spiritual Consciousness or as a mode of the transcendent—cosmic Reality. The concept of Swaraj founded on natural right based on a spiritual world-view and oriented to the realization of the total equality of the sweeper and the lawyer in the matter of the receipt of remuneration has been nurtured by ancient Indian idealism. The neo-Vedantism of Vivekananda, Gurudatta Vidyarthi, Aurobindo, Rama Tirtha, Satyadeva, Radhakrishnan and D.M. Datta, the concept of Swaraj of Dayananda, Tilak, Gandhi and Aurobindo and the integral humanism of Deendayal have their roots in the ancient Indian tradition.

The second source of modern Indian humanism is the exposure of the ancient and medieval Indian soul to the western scientific methods and criteria of enquiry and a quest for the rational enlightenment of the spirit. The advance of modernity in India has been fostered by the adoption of large-scale western methods of growth, developmental planning and technological rationalization. The rise of Indian nationalism partly accelerated by scientific communication has been a terrific blow to the continuing vestiges of feudalism. The printing press made unpractical the realisation of the priestly claim that the Vedic literature was to be kept immune from being studied by the non-Dvijas. The large-scale printing of the old literature and their study by modern intellectuals revealed the ugliness, pettiness and crudeness of the claims to caste superiority sponsored in the Smritis and the Puranas. Furthermore the Lockean gospel of liberty, the Rousseauic slogan of equality, the Marxian call for the socialization of the means of production and the ideologies of individualistic liberalism and empirical collectivism have provided the intellectual roots for the programme of the conquest of alienation, pain and destitution. The modern means of transportation and communication have made possible the growth of a dynamic intellectual atmosphere and the consequential acceptance of an intersubjective mode of enquiry and verification. Thus western rationalism, scientific cosmology, critical modes of investigation and sociological philosophies of history have been the second major source for the release of humanist trends in modern thinking. Humanism has been oriented to reason in place of orthodoxy, dogmatism and superstition and has supported individual rights and freedom as antidotes against the violent or corrupt aberrations of power. The humanistic elements in the thinking of Ram Mohan, B.N. Seal, Ramavatara Sharma, M.N. Roy, Jawaharlal, Beni Prasad, J.P. and Lohia have their roots in Western thought patterns. M.N. Roy was a pronounced votary of materialistic cosmology and mechanistic methodology.

The third source of contemporary Indian humanism is a revival of the poetic spirit of the romantics. Tagore in his earlier days was inspired by the Western romantics. His emphasis on the significance of the non-repeatable individual seems to be western-inspired because a commitment to the Hindu philosophy of transmigration will make the advocacy of the notions of non-repeatability and uniqueness of the human being somewhat incongruous. Tagore's *The Religion of Man* can be said to be influenced by the poetry of Kabira, the songs of the Bauls and the Upanishadic concept of the Bhuma (the mighty all-comprehensive Being) but the poetic lyricism that pervades Tagore's philosophied writings has much in common with the western romantices like Schlegel, Goethe and Wordsworth.[1] Jayshankara's *Kamayani* with its gospel of the synthesis of intellectual and intuition based on spiritual faith (*shraddha*) has its roots in the Upanishadic concept of *ananda* (bliss) and in Shaivism but has also been inspired by the prevailing currents of western romanticism.

Although the anthropocentric humanism of Protagoras, Eramus and Leonardo was conceived in the framework of a non-theistic cosmodicy, it is possible to link up humanism with a spiritual orientation to life and the cosmos. The humanism of Tagore, Gurudatta, Gandhi and Aurobindo is linked up with a spiritual outlook on life.[2] They adhere to the metaphysical notions associated with *Ekamsat*, *Tad Ekam*, Purushottama, Hiranyagarbha, Parameshwara, Sahasrashirsa Purusha, Virat, Mukhyatmā, Antaryamin and Vaisvanara. Deendayal's integral humanism also adheres to the spiritual ontology. The spiritual idealists sponsor humanism because they consider the human body and the embodied human self as manifesting an immanent

1. F.C.S. Schiller, *Studies in Humanism*, p. 19, says : "Humanism in addition may point to the personality of whatever cosmic principle we can postulate as ultimate and to its kinship and sympathy with man." Tagore's method resembles Schiller's.

2. A.J. Balfour, *Theism and Humanism* also adheres to a theistic humanism.

trans-mechanical teleology They regard man as the vehicle for the realisation of God as a super-temporal being.

Both Tagore and Gandhi were spiritual humanists. They cherished man and his ideals and aspirations because man is a replica of the Divine spirit. While the *Gitanjali* breathes a devout spirit of submission to the monotheistic Godhead, the *Atma-katha* and the *Anasakti-Yoga* inculcate the superiority of a belief in moral absolutism and in Truth as an ontological category. Ravindranath delighted in aesthetic contemplation and worshipped God as the resplendence of "Surplus" energy, but Gandhi, the puritan, equated God and his impersonal laws of providential governance. Deendayal's spirit has more kinship with that of Gandhi than that of Tagore. Gandhi delighted in worshipping God in the form of the naked, starved and sweating humanity. Tagore's spirit was influenced by the Upanishadic concepts of Bhuma and the Vaishvanara Atman and delighted in romantic exuberance, sentimental effusions and aesthetic delight. But Deendayal, like Gandhi, was a lover of simplicity, abstinence and self-abnegation.

Both Aurobindo and Deendayal were integralists. Aurobindo stressed the supramental transformation of man into the gnostic divinized superman through psychicization, integration and the deep cognitive awareness of the triple powers of the Supermind, — the comprehending, the apprehending and the projecting. Deendayal also would not be satisfied with only the social, economic and political development of the empirical man. He was a Vedantist of the monistic Samkarite school but was also deeply moved by the gospel of Bhakti. Like Tilak, he accepted the gospel of Karmayoga or disinterested actionism.

The integral humanism of Deendayal, thus, is opposed to the materialistic new humanism of M. N. Roy and the agnostic humanism of Jawaharlal. Roy and Jawaharlal were eulogistic of human aspirations and volitions because man was regarded by the exponents of scientific humanism as the climax of the evolutionary process that started with the phyla protozoa and coelenterata and evolved through the mollusca and chordata and the classes pisces, amphibia, reptilia, aves and mammalia and has reached the highest point in the form of the *homo sapiens* in the

Quaternary era.[1] But the metaphysical idealists like Aurobindo and Deendayal exalt the immortal human spirit and the salvationist and soteriological aims of man to attain higher cognitive splendours. While M.N.Roy was committed to materialistic cosmology, Deendayal was rooted in the cognitive-noetic aspects of Indian culture. Although, later on, Roy renounced the triplicity of the dialectical method, he passionately clung to the materialistic ontology.[2] Roy would regard the metaphysical, exiological and spiritual aspects of the ancient Hindu culture with the jaundiced eye of the materialist worshipping at the shrine of Democritus, Epicurus, Lucretius, Hobbes, Helvetius, Diderot, Haeckel, Marx and Lenin. But Deendayal wanted to reincorporate the spiritual *elan* of the old Hindu culture into the fabric of contemporary civilization. While Nehru was an agnostic and had neither the aptitude nor the time and training for spiritual and ontological quests, Deendayal can be regarded as an avowed exponent of the sanctity and superiority of Dharma, Rita, Vrata, Diksha, Shila, Yama and Niyam, Samvara and Atmanigraha. He would accept the Upanishadic thesis that without self-restraint even the cognitive splendours of the intellect cannot be revealed. While M. N. Roy and Nehru, between them, drew inspirations from Marx, Lenin, Bertrand Russell, Robert Frost (1874-1963), Bernard Shaw and Napoleon, Deendayal, in the traditions of Shivaji, Dayananda, Tilak and Vivekananda, wanted to advance through the conservation of whatever was good in Indian culture. He was neither a blind worshipper of the past nor a sentimental admirer of the Occident. It is essential to build a comprehensive system of idealist humanist philosophy and sociology based both on the natural and the behavioural sciences. Earlier also, Leibnitz, Hegel and Whitehead were interested in the meaningful correlation between philosophy and science. Researches in the field of Marxism have further deepened interest in the

1. According to the Chandogya Upanishad, the human body is the city of Brahman (*brahmapura*) wherein the purusha resides (*purusha purishaya*).

2. M.N. Roy's "New Humanism" bears : terminological resemblance to the American publication, *The New Humanist : a Bi-monthly Journal of Religion and Culture* (Dayton, Ohio, 1928).

epistemology of the sciences and it is essential to formulate a criticism of the dialectical methodology based on the insights of the various physical and biological sciences. Empirical political science is also becoming interested in the epistemology of the social and behavioral sciences. Such problems as the meaning of analytical explanation, the role of understanding in political science analysis, and the impact of the acceptance of meaningful humanistic dimensions on concrete social research, need further clarification. Some of the sociological concepts and methods that have been used by Ernst Troeltseh, Max Weber and Mannheim have not been sufficiently commented upon in the Indian universities. Whether political knowledge is idiographic or nomothetic also demands clarification. If political knowledge is purely idiographic, then the demand for causal explanation which postulates the existence of uniformity and recognisable regularity in the political system may not be met with. The meaning of analysis is also another significant area of political epistemology. Schumpeter's major book is titled *History of Economic Analysis*. The word analysis is used here to include the explanations offered in regard to the dominant questions of the economic system, by the major thinkers of the past and present. On the other hand, when we talk of statistical analysis, we use this term analysis in a different sense. The statistical classification and analysis of the data gathered from the use of the questionnaires, the schedules etc. is not of the same type as the method for economic analysis used by Schumpeter. It is also to be pointed out that the methods of political analysis that have been formulated by the exponents of the systems analysis approach are different from the synthetic historical-philosophical approach as expounded in this book. The philosophy of science has to be re-formulated for assessing the extent to which it can substantiate the concept of man as a spiritual and moral subject. The humanistic quest of the Western Renaissance indirectly spurred the growth of the physical sciences. But the latter should not end in the frenzy for the dry and dull quest of cold quantitativism. Scientific knowledge has to be used for promoting the good of all living beings and not the thermo-nuclear annihilation of mankind.

The reconstruction of humanist political philosophy also

requires the study of the history of Indian political philosophy from the Vedas and Buddhism to Tilak, Gandhi, Aurobindo, M. N Roy, Beni Prasad, J. P., Lohia and Deendayal. The studies in the idealistic, humanist and collectivity-stressing aspects of Hindu political thought and its metaphysical foundations at an elaborate critical level are essential. The historical method should be followed in the arrangement of the topics and the method of qualitative and philosophical appreciation should be used in evaluating the concepts. Modern Indian political thought should be intensively taught in the universities.

Ancient Indian political philosophy specially as propounded by the Vedanta and Buddhism has taught the vital importance of a spiritually-oriented moral code of injunctions for the development of human life. The sermons, the postulates and the concepts of an ethical code of life that have been corroborated with moral intuitionism in some of the Hindu Dharmasastras, the Ramayana and the Mahabharata constitute a great contribution to world culture. Several thinkers have maintained that a man who follows the dictates of his moral and spiritual conscience can challenge the arrogant excursions of the political structure. This theme has been elaborately worked out in the Mahabharata. The epic asserts that if the king fails to provide protection then he is to be shunned like a broken canoe in the sea. It also contains the story of the killing of Vena who transgressed the moral code. It (the Mahabharata) lays down that the unjust and unrighteous ruler is to be killed like a dog. Such statements support the theme of tyrannicide, and they constitute a theoretical negation of the pretentions of oligarchs and potentates who want to amass illegitimate power. The philosophical tradition of politics as accepted by integral idealist humanism stresses the evolution of evaluative criteria for judging political action because moral and spiritual individualism has been regarded as the foundation and the support of democracy. The concept of resistance to the aberrations and perversions of coercive power that has been formulated in the Mahabharata has only a few parallels. No such sentiment may be discovered in Confucius, Lao-Tse, Homer, Augustine, Ibu Khaldun, Averroes or Milton. Only John of Salisbury, Hotman and the *Vindicea Contra Tyrannos* approach the Mahabharatan spirit.

Gandhi was one of the greatest exponents of the creed of challenging the political rulers in the name of the *antaratman* or the human conscience. Compared to the Gandhian Satyagraha, sentiments of protest supported by Green and Laski appear very dull. Green supported the concept of disobedience and resistance in non-democratic politics but he circumscribed his affirmative statements with so many reservations that the chance that some sensitive individual or some group would really fight against illegitimate laws or unjustified codes was almost reduced to a minimum. Similarly Laski also watered down his concept of contingent anarchy which he had formulated in *A Grammar of Politics.* That concept he never repeated in his later works and even his concept of contingent anarchy was only a conditional technic for very occasional use. Laski's sentiments of protest in the name of conscience as formulated in his *A Grammar of Politics*, later, gave way to the support for socialist ideologies. Green and Laski have not been as eloquent as Mahatma Gandhi in glorifying the sentiment of protest against the established political structure in the name of conscience. The Gandhian legacy which can also be supported by sentiments of tyrannicide inculcated in the Mahabharata constitutes a notable contribution to the advance of human civilization. A political philosophy cannot afford to ignore such important testifications to the sanctity of the human conscience at a time when gigantic structure in all departments of organised human activity are invading human society and are gradually minimising the importance of the monadic individual as an empirical embodied entity. Gandhi's philosophy of Satyagraha which can be carried on even by a single truthful individual is a humanist contribution to political technology because it vindicates the autonomy of man against organized authoritarianism. The Gandhian theory of resistance to the ravages of legislative and executive centres of authority as enshrined in the philosophy of Satyagraha relevance to the politics of protest. The philosophy of resistance nurtured on the foundations of moral and spiritual individualism is a contribution to democratic political philosophy. It is a support to the notion of democratic right of dissent. If this inalienable right is sought to be disturbed, this will lead to the triumph of the quantitative colossality of the omnipotent state or the authoritarian monolithic party or the armed crusading ecclesiastical religious groups or the large business corporations. Humanism, therefore, based on the philosophy of protest is a vindication of the moral spontaneity of man.

A philosophy of freedom for man as a moral and spiritual subject can alone be the antidote to the excesses of nationalistic chauvinism, ethnocentric imperialism, totalitarian materialism and the fascist cult of racialism, controlled economy and power politics. The Vedic and Vedantic tradition inculcates the supremacy of a primordial archetypal spiritual Reality which is simultaneously transcendent, cosmic and individual. Buddhism enunciates the sanctity of the ternal law recognising the superiority of right, justice and forgiveness. The most significant and permanent contribution of Buddha to human ennoblement is the concept of Dhamma — the eternal primordial, categorically imperative moral law in operation. A large number of people are subjected to the devastating onslaughts of frustration, maladjustment, *anomie*, despair and disquiet. To a humanity full of anxiety and the unhappy consciousness due to the triumph of social atomism and naturalistic positivism Buddhism preaches the noble way — the Aryan eightfold way, Vaishnavism had tried to democratize the spiritual teachings by preaching them among the masses of suppressed humanity. Tilak asserted that there are higher powers moving the destiny of things. Lajpat Rai stated that his conscience constituted his court. Gandhi claimed to listen to the inner voice. Philosophical humanism is based on these traditions. But it also claims to incorporate in its formulated propositions the tradition of political individualism associated with Hotman, Locke, Mill and Spencer. It is scientific in the sense that it pleads for a revision of its cosmological bases in the light of the advances in physics, chemistry, geology, physiology and genetics. It is trenchant and uncompromising in its quest for freedom, equality and justice. An economic and social realism also is one of its major dimensions and it clamours for the inalienable natural right of all human beings to a life of dignity, capability-facilitation and total fearlessness (*abhayam*). Thus a humanism deriving sustenance from the spiritual and moral traditions of the sanctity of Satya as formulated in Indian culture and corroborated by the conclusions of contemporary natural and behavioral sciences can provide an alternative to bourgeois capitalism and coercive communist totalitarianism.

An ethical and spiritual humanism is the integral, democratic response to the challenges of the times. The democratic heritage of Swaraj and freedom is precious and it has to be preserved against external and totalitarian encroachments. The stress on social realism manifested in the quest for justice for the suppressed proletariat is timely. But the method for the emancipation of the wage earners, the agricultural labourers and the other suppressed and backward sections can be only peaceful. Legislation and Satyagraha are sufficient for solving the problems of poverty at the instrumental level. Violent class struggle may appeal to certain sections but a humanist is opposed to blood bath even for the liberation of the oppressed and backward sections. To endorse lightly the idea of violent class struggle in a country of over six hundred million people is an irresponsible exercise in political opportunism. The valuational dimensions of life and politics need to be re-asserted. In a growingly mechanistic and atheistical civilization, men are tending to become unscrupulous and hypocritical for egoistic gratifications. Hence a humanist appeal in the name of spiritual and moral values is still more and relevant to the contemporary civilization.

INDEX

Abel and Cain 119
Abhayam 9, 10
—as component of humanism 197
Absolute Real, The 16, 60
Adler 29
Administration, Public 142-55
—Civil service 147
—Decision-making 151
—Organisation and Method 151
—Problem of discipline 154
—Rural administration 146
Administrative goal-gratification, impediments to 143-44
Ahimsa 111, 129
Ahriman and Ormuzd 119
Akbar 56
Alexander, Samuel 25, 36
Almond G. 87, 123
Alienation 101
Aquinas, Thomas 1
Antarātman 103
Areopagitica, (of Milton) 1
Aristotle 7, 23, 37, 79, 82, 87, 89, 92, 123, 159
Arnold, Mathew 6
Aryabhata 34
Ashtāngika Mārga, Aryan 108
Atharvaveda 36
Augustine, St 1, 39, 195
Aurobindo, Sri 5, 11, 29, 30, 36, 46, 57, 121, 190, 191, 192, 195
—and Deendayal on idealist (=philosophical) humanism 192
Austin 115, 149
Ayamātmā brahma and monistic idealism 5

Bacon, (*Novum Organon*) 1
Baker, R. H. 12
Balfour, A. J. (*Theism and Humanism*) 191
Barker, 2, 101, 104
Barth, Karl 113
Behavioralism 100
—and philosophical humanism 45-50
Bentham 149
Berdyaev 40, 44, 120
—and Aurobindo 48
Bergson, H. 7, 38
Bernhardi 114
Bernstein, Eduard 29, 169
Besant, A. and M. Blavatski 3
Bhagavadgita, The 3, 77, 159, 189
Bhaskara 34
Bhave, Vinoba 171
Bhishma 12
Bismarck 112, 114
Blackstone 115, 149
Blavatski 3
Boccaccio 5
Bodin 115
Bosanquet 101
Bradley, F. H. 7, 14, 16, 17, 26, 29, 45
Brahman 14
Buddha, Gautama 3, 6, 9, 34, 51, 65, 75, 100, 106, 111, 134, 141, 196
Buddhism 4, 48, 63, 77, 189, 195
—as basis of idealist humanism 195
Burgess 84
Burke 89

Carlyle 52, 93
Case Study Method, The, and multidisciplinary humanism 83
Catlin, George 38
Christ, Jesus 1, 34, 43
Christianity 59, 63, 100
Churchill 112
Clarke 73
Clausewitz 114
Cohen, Hermann 29
Cole 2, 101
Comte, Auguste 29
Condorcet 6
Confucius 75, 195
Cudworth 73
Culture, The Indian and the roots of philosophical or spiritual humanism 120

Dampier 11
Dandaniti 93
Dante and divine humanism 8
Darwin 2, 82, 169
Dasaratha 9
Dayananda, Swami 3, 5, 8, 64, 121
Decision-making and behavioral politics 151
Deendayal 191-93, 195
—more Gandhian than Tagorean 192
—and Samkara and Tilak, 192
Democritus 2
Deussen, Paul 3, 58
Deutsch, K. 87

Development,
—The Capitalist Model of, 167-68
—A Humanist Manifesto for Indian Economic 174-88
—The Marxist Model of 168-70
Dharma (religion) 30
Diderot 2, 8, 193
Disarmament 116
Disraeli 112
Dravidian, no racial connotation 164
Drona 12
Duryodhana 93

Eddington and the Indeterminacy concept in physics 25
Einstein 1, 34, 52
Eliot, T. S. 113
Emerson 3, 57
Engels, Fr. 38
Epicurus 2, 193
Explosion, Population and Indian Economics 177

Feuerbach L., 2
Fichte 2, 118
Figgis 104
Finer 87
Florensky (Sophiology) 32n
Follet 104
Fourier 169, 186
Frederick, L. W. (*Astronomy*) 12n
Fromm, Erich 68, 160
Frost, Robert 193

Galileo 34, 169
Ganguli, B. C. 153
Gandhari 6, 28
Gandhi, Mahatma 3, 5, 30, 51, 56, 78, 106, 111, 160, 169, 172, 180, 190-92, 195-96
—as idealist humanist 195
Gandhian Economics,
—The Revision of 170-74
Gautama 7, 64
George, Henry 169
Gerth, Hans 167
Glaucon 37
Goethe 28, 191
Goodsell, Willystine 15n
Gosala, Makkhali 7
Green, T. H. 79, 196

Haeckel 193
Haldane, Viscount 6
Hartmann 73
Heavy industries 159
Hedgewar and Indian Renaissance 5
Hegel 2, 10, 23, 39-43, 89, 92, 114, 123, 193
Heidegger 3, 40
Helvetius 193
Hemacandra 8
Hess, Moses 2
Hewart 149
History of Science 11n
Hobbes 10, 29,75,82,102,115,127,193
Holland 149
Homer 64, 195
Hotman 195, 197
Hugo de Vries 36
Humanism, Spiritual (=Idealist philosophical) 1
—and the Behavioral Sciences 45-48
—and Conservatism 112
—and the Critique of T. S. Eliot 113
—and Dialectic 37
—and Evolution 35
—and Existentialism 40
—and Indian Political System 120-41
—and Monotheism 27
—and Non-Violence 78
—and Ontology 12
—and Political Obligation and Satyagraha 102
—and Public Administration 142-55
—and Religion 29
—and Science and History 33
—and Sovereignty and Natural Right 104
—Theoretical foundations 1-61
Humanism, Philosophical (=idealist spiritualism) 207
—And Theory of Punishment 110
—And Time, Space and Causality 25
—And Values 75
—As a Critique of the Marxian Economic Determinism 55
—As a Philosophy of Life 49
—As Ontopolitics 57
—The Economics of Humanism 167-88
—Epistemological Problem of Humanism 18
—for India 3
—meaning of Humanism 6-12
—The Social Philosophy of Humanism 156-66
—The Sources of Humanism 71
—The Methodology and Concept of humanism 81-119
Humanist Values, 63
—and Decision-making 65
—and Ethical Absolutism 63
—and Political Science 68
Humboldt 3

Individualism 127
Individualism, Ontological 9
Indra 29

Jaimini 100
Jainism 59
Janaka 51
Jaspers and Heidegger 2, 40
Jatātu 6
Jefferson 98, 127
Jehova 1, 29
Juridical, approach to political science 149
Justice 109, 110

Kabir 8, 191
Kalidasa 34, 51
Kamalākara 8
Kāmandaka 174
Kant 2, 3, 7, 23, 39, 43, 61, 63, 75, 79, 91
Kantianism 59
Kapila 23, 75, 100
Karmayoga 50, 70
Kashmir 130
Kautilya 51, 75, 123, 159
Kelvin 82
Keysen, C. J. 15
Khaldun, Ibn 195
Kierkegaard 2, 40-44
Krishna, Lord 12, 51
Kshemendra 8
Kumarila 100

Lagrange 1
Lao-Tse 195
Laski, H. 2, 10, 44, 45, 86, 99, 101, 106, 112, 113, 196
Lassalle 169
Lasswell, Harold 123
Lavosier 1
Leibnitz 193
Lenin 38, 98, 169, 193
Leninism 2, 112
Leonardo 1
Leviathan 10
Locke 1, 79, 98, 127, 197
Lohia, R. M. 171, 190, 195
Lokapal and corruption curtailment 180
Lokayukta 180
Lucretius 193
Luther 1, 41
Luxemburg, Rosa 98

Machiavelli 93, 114
MacIver 2, 84, 101, 121
Mackenzie, J. S. 6
Magna Carta, The 1
Mahābhārata, The 4, 52, 95, 96, 195, 196
Mahavira 3, 7, 34, 51, 134
Malaviya 5
Manetti, G. 8n
Mannheim, Karl 21, 84, 90, 101, 167, 194
Manu 64, 103, 123, 159, 174
Maoism 2, 101
Marduk 29
Marshall 82
Marxism 2, 29, 86, 97, 98, 169, 193
Marx, Karl 38-40, 82, 89, 98, 121, 123, 169, 193
Materialism, Historical 97
Maurya, Chandragupta 51, 56
Mendel 36
Merriam 2
Mill, J. S. 2, 10, 81, 98, 127, 197
Milton 1, 34, 127, 195
'*Mind and Society*' (Pareto) 16
Mirandola, G. 8
Modern Indian political thought as a challenge to Americanization or Russianization 195
Moksha and freedom 100
Montaigue 5
Montesquieu 89, 123
Morgan Lloyd 6
Morgenthau, H., as humanist democrat 2
Moses 2, 56
Müller, Max 3, 58
Munro 87
Mussolini 112
Myrdal, G. 124

Nagarjuna 8
Nahusha 93
Nanak 8
Napoleon 193
Narodniks (Herzen and Lavrov) 186
Narayan, J. P. 171, 190, 195
Nation-state and humanism 114
Nehru, Jawaharlal 68, 190, 192, 193
Nero 93
Newton 1, 16, 25, 34, 52, 169
Niebuhr 113
Nietzsche 52, 73, 114

Ogburn 84
Ogg 87
Ontology 12
Ontological Individualism and Humanism 122
Ontopolitics 57-62
—and Empirical Political Analysis 91
—and Historical Materialism 97
Owen, R. 169

Paine, T. 127
Panini 52

Paracelsus 5
Parãsara 8, 159
Pareto 16, 55
Park 84
Parkinson's law 148
Parsons, T. 84, 87, 123
Patanjali 3, 8, 141
Patel, Vallabhbhai 130
Paul 1
Pearl, Raymond 82
Peter, St 43
Petition of Right, The 1
Petrarch 5
Philosophy of Ontological Spiritualism 191
Planck, Max 1
Planning 182
Plato 10, 23, 38, 63, 79
Plekhanov 98
Political System, Indian 123
—Democracy 132
—Development of system 125
Politicalization and Politicization 141
Polybius 89
Polylogism and humanism 97
Pope, A. 28, 116
Prabhãkara 100
Prasad, Beni 190, 195
Prasad, Jayshankara 191
Prasad, Rajendra 130
Pratap, Rana 56
Protagoras 5, 37, 127, 191
Proudhon 168
Punishment, Theory of, and humanism 111
Purana, Bhagavata 3

Radhakrishnan, S. 19, 47, 65, 191
Raghunandana 8
Rai, Lajpat 197
Ramakrishna 8, 106
Rama 6, 9, 12, 51
Ramanuja 3, 23
Ramatirtha 3, 191
Ramayana, The 52, 95, 96
Ranke, Leopold von 121
Ravana 92
Recall of a legislator 105
Reform, Social
—Indian Context 160-66
Republic, The 10
Ricardo 2, 127
Rigveda, The 3
Rita 106
Roll, E. 174
Rousseau 2, 160
Roy, M. N. 68, 190-93, 195
—and Deendayal Upadhyaya 193
Roy, Ram Mohan 8, 28, 191
Rumi 16
Ruskin 160
Russell, B. 11, 13, 169, 193

Samavãya 100, 119
Samkara 3, 23, 34, 51, 131
Samkhya 48, 100
Sartre, J. P. 40
Satyagraha 102
Savarkara 5
Schiller, F. C. S. 6, 191
Schlegel, Frederick 3, 57, 191
Schopenhauer 3, 57
Schumacher and the revision of Marxism 160
Schumpeter 194
Seal, B. N. 190
Shakespeare 34, 64
Sharma, Ramavatara 190
Shaw, Bernard 193
Shivaji 51, 56, 193
Shraddhananda 5, 8
Simon, St 169
Sismondi 168
Smith, Adam 172
Socialism, Guild 86
Sociological Method, The 84
Socrates 37, 101, 106
Somnath and Indian Culture 130
Sorokin 11, 16, 31, 84, 101
Spencer 11, 82, 197
Spengler 16, 52, 89
Stoicism 59
Structural-functional approach 87
Suez-Canal-Crisis 114
Suradãsa 16
Swami, Narayana 8
Swaraj 141

Tagore, Rabindranath 28, 32, 190-92
—and Gandhi Mahatma 192
Teresa 65
Thoreau 3, 57
Thrasymachus 37
Tibet 136
Tilak, B. G. 5, 51, 56, 64, 108, 121, 190, 195
Tirtha, Rama 8, 28, 32, 121
Tolstoy 64
Total Social Reform, manifesto of 160
Toynbee, A. 16, 31, 89
Troeltseh, Ernst 194
Tulasi 51

Unemployment 177
United Nations, The 114
University administration, reform in 154
Upanishad, Chãndogya 193
Upanishads 3, 7

Vaideha, Karala 93
Vaishnavism 197
—and humanist democra y 141
Values 63
—Humanist 63-80
Vasistha 9
Vasubandhu 30
Vātsyāyana 7
Vedāntism 189
Vico 89
Vidya 15
—*apara* 15, 20
—*para* 15, 20
Vidyarthi, Gurudatta 190
Vivekananda 3, 8, 29, 51, 121, 160, 190
Voltaire 8
Vyasa 3, 23

Ward, Lester 39
Weber, Max 64, 67, 87, 121, 194
Whitehead 193
Wiese, Leopold von 11
Wollaston 73
Wordsworth, W. 191

Yajnavalkya 51, 64, 174
—more liberal than Manu 159
Yajurveda, The 4
Yoga-Sutra 3

Zink 87
Zoroaster 34

CORRECTIONS

Page	*Line*	*For*	*Read*
1	Last line	Becun	Bacon
3	4	Herdegger	Heidegger
,,	10	Indealistic	Idealistic
,,	2 from bottom	Beauatski	Blavatsky
5	11	Montaigue	Montaigne
39	fn. 1.	synorgy	synergy
40	15	Satre	Sartre
56	9 from bottom	satisfactionis	satisfactions
62	5	Lokayatta	Lokayatra
73	12 from bottom	action (*nivrti*) and renunciation (*pravrti*)	action (*pravritti*) and renunciation (*nivritti*)
77	22	intesification	intensification
	7 from bottom	searing	swearing
119	5	Ornuzd	Ormuzd
143	15	portion	partisan
177	3	needs	need
198	2 from bottom	more	valid